*Good Relationships Are
Good Medicine*

GOOD RELATIONSHIPS ARE GOOD MEDICINE

by
Barbara Powell, Ph.D.

Rodale Press, Emmaus, Pa.

Copyright © 1987 by Barbara Powell, Ph.D.

All rights reserved. No part of this publication may be reproduced or transmitted in any form or by any means, electronic or mechanical, including photocopy, recording, or any information storage and retrieval system, without the written permission of the publisher.

Printed in the United States of America on recycled paper containing a high percentage of de-inked fiber.

Library of Congress Cataloging in Publication Data

Powell, Barbara, 1929–
    Good relationships are good medicine.

    Includes index.
    1. Stress (Psychology) 2. Interpersonal relations. 3. Health. I. Title.
BF575.S75P68   1987   155.9'2   86-29808
ISBN 0-87857-655-X   hardcover

2 4 6 8 10 9 7 5 3 1   hardcover

For those with whom I have
the closest relationships:

David, Rich, Sue, Jenny, and Julie

Contents

Preface **xi**

PART 1
Generally Speaking

1. *People, Stress, and Other People* **3**
2. *Relationships Can Keep You Healthy* **5**
3. *Happy Marriages Are Good for You* **8**
4. *It All Adds Up* **10**

PART 2
To Be More Specific

1. *Can Your Family Drive You Crazy?* **15**
2. *Or Drive You to Drink?* **19**
3. *It's a Weighty Problem* **22**
4. *"You Make Me Sick!"* **26**
5. *Your Emotions and Your Heart* **28**
6. *"I Give Up!"* **31**
7. *"You're a Pain in the Neck"* **34**
8. *What's in It for You?* **36**

PART 3
Sizing Up Your Situation

1. *Tune In Your Feelings*   **41**
2. *Recognizing Symptoms*   **46**
3. *Identifying Problem Behavior Patterns*   **52**
4. *Spotting Nervous Habits*   **57**
5. *Charting Your Course*   **60**
6. *Is Your Network Working?*   **69**
7. *Is Your Closeness a Comfort?*   **77**
8. *How to Know When It's Hopeless*   **88**
9. *Breaking Broken Records*   **98**

PART 4
First Aids

1. *Becoming Yourself*   **109**
2. *Relax and Live Longer*   **111**
3. *Exercise and Feel Better*   **115**
4. *Eliminating Nervous Habits*   **119**
5. *Interrupting Problem Behavior Patterns*   **123**
6. *Changing Someone Else's Behavior by Changing Your Own*   **126**

PART 5
Be Nice and Be Healthy

1. *The Affectionate Touch*   **131**
2. *The Power of Positives*   **134**
3. *Laughter Can Save Your Life*   **141**
4. *To Tell the Truth*   **146**
5. *"You Must Have a Guilty Conscience"*   **149**
6. *"Do Unto Others"*   **151**
7. *Listening Is Therapeutic*   **154**
8. *Keep in Touch*   **156**
9. *Hold that Temper*   **158**

PART 6
Speak Up for Your Health's Sake

1. *Get It Off Your Chest* **167**
2. *Healthy Speech* **172**
3. *Happy Talk* **174**
4. *Assert Yourself* **178**
5. *Say What You Really Mean* **183**
6. *Expressing Your Needs* **186**
7. *Learn to Say "No"* **191**
8. *Necessary Negatives* **196**
9. *Assertiveness at Work* **199**
10. *Improving Communication with Children* **206**
11. *Sexually Speaking* **210**

PART 7
If You Become Ill

1. *Who Are the Survivors?* **217**
2. *You and Your Doctor* **221**
3. *How to Find Psychological Help* **227**
4. *How to Find Help within Yourself* **232**

Index **235**

Preface

Stress is a fact of life. There is no escaping from stress, but there are means of coping with it. Some people cope better than others, and so they experience fewer stress-related symptoms and illnesses. They are healthier in general, both physically and emotionally, than those who cope less effectively with stress, since virtually every illness is somehow involved with stress.

The sources of stress are many.

But there is one primary source that has attracted relatively little attention either from the medical profession or the general public: the stress resulting from interpersonal relationships.

The chances are that you have at least one relationship in your life right now that is a major source of stress: your interactions with your husband or wife, with a child or parent, with an employer or an employee. You may experience frequent stress as a result of encounters with salesclerks, taxi drivers, and others who have relatively little importance in your overall scheme of things. But if you are like the majority of my patients, it is your interactions with the significant people in your life, those with whom you have ongoing involvements, that are most likely to cause you stress and distress.

Perhaps the signals of your discomfort are obvious. You may be like Linda, a young woman in her twenties who develops a headache every time she speaks with her lover; or Tammy, a woman in her thirties who has to "psych herself up" before every conversation with the boss's wife because she knows she will have an upset stomach after listening to her put-downs; or Elise, one in her forties who, after her frequent shouting matches with her husband, feels so physically depleted that she literally has to take to her bed.

You may feel trapped in a relationship that is literally making you ill, like the engineer whose demanding, irate supervisor was giving him stomach ulcers and migraine headaches, or the phobic woman whose domineering mate would not allow her to leave the house without his permission or to have a checking account of her own.

Or it could be that you have not connected the symptoms of your distress to your personal relationships, like the explosive housewife who did not realize that her angry outbursts at her husband and children were driving her blood pressure sky-high, or the middle-aged woman who understood only after leaving her husband that her colitis and chronic insomnia were the results of their stormy relationship.

Of course, I do not mean to imply that *all* symptoms, even those that are clearly psychosomatic, can be traced to problem relationships. Some are due to unreasonable schedules, noise, pollution, or failing to live up to your own or your parents' expectations.

Yet, in my own professional experience as a clinical psychologist, whatever a patient's initial complaint—insomnia, a phobia, depression, generalized anxiety, or a lack of life direction—the discussion usually gets around to a stressful relationship or the stress of *not* having a relationship. There's just no denying that people are important to people.

And so it is certainly possible, as our familiar folklore expressions imply, that someone in your life—or, more specifically, the way you interact with that someone—is making you sick, driving you crazy, breaking your heart, or turning your stomach.

If you suspect that this is the case, or you find yourself constantly swallowing your pride, choking back your tears, or boiling with rage after a conversation with someone who is important to you, you can—and you should!—do something about it.

You can improve your health by improving the way you deal with others, because there's absolutely no doubt that good relationships are good medicine.

PART 1
Generally Speaking

1
People, Stress, and Other People

Think back to the last time you felt upset, uptight, frustrated, depressed, or angry.

Any one of those emotions *could* have occurred because you were stuck in traffic, dissatisfied with your living conditions, or faced an impossible deadline at work. But based on my experience as a clinical psychologist, talking daily with patients about the things that distress them most, I'd venture a guess that when you recall a strong negative emotion you relate it to some other person—spouse, parent, child, or employer.

And you may well have expressed it in terms such as these:
"He's driving me crazy."
"She's making me sick."
"You're breaking my heart."
"You're a pain in the neck."

As these familiar expressions imply, your relationships with other people can literally make you sick—or they can make you well.

Hans Selye, a leading authority on stress, declares in *Stress without Distress* (New York: Harper & Row, 1974) that our feelings toward others, both negative and positive, directly affect our health. But Selye was not the first to state the idea that psychological factors can cause illness. Socrates told his compatriots that the body could not be cured without concern for the mind; Hippocrates emphasized the influence of the environment on health and disease, and stressed the relationship between physician and patient.

In the 1960s, Thomas H. Holmes and Richard H. Rahe of the University of Washington School of Medicine definitively established a correlation between stressful life events and disease. This included infectious diseases and traumatic injuries as well as so-called psychosomatic disorders.

Based on research with more than 5,000 patients, Holmes and Rahe devised a Social Readjustment Rating Scale, which assigned numerical values to such stressful life events as death of a spouse (100), divorce (73), separation (65), and death of close family member (63). The higher an individual's total score for events occurring during the past year, the greater the probability of serious illness.

Stressful events included on the scale were not limited to those usually considered "upsetting"—marriage ranked high, as did outstanding personal achievement and pregnancy. The researchers found that any change, whether for better or for worse, produced stress. In the area of relationships, not only marital problems but "trouble with in-laws" and "trouble with boss" made the list.

Holmes' and Rahe's Rating Scale reinforced Selye's view of stress as the body's response to any demand for change, whether the change is pleasant or unpleasant.

Stress is unavoidable, since we are under constant pressure to adapt to change. But stress that is too damaging or unpleasant, or continues for too long, becomes distress.

The body's reaction to stress has been called the General Adaptation Syndrome (GAS). The first stage of the GAS, the *alarm reaction*, occurs whenever a real or perceived threat triggers an emergency discharge of adrenaline and sets off other physiological mechanisms the body needs to stay in control. The muscles tense, the heart beats faster, the rate of respiration increases, the stomach may clench. We all know the feeling.

Generally, the most acute signs of the stress reaction pass quickly and a normal level of functioning is restored when the threat subsides. But if it continues, the body enters the stage of *resistance;* now efforts to adapt are intensified or maintained. The body is weakened and open to illness.

If there is still no relief, a third stage, *exhaustion*, follows due to fatigue and irreversible damage to the body. Signs of the alarm reaction reappear, and the individual dies.

Stress does not *cause* disease but, by exhausting the body's natural defenses against infection, sets the stage for it. That is how your interpersonal relationships, like other stressors in your life, can predispose you to illness. Still, many people are able to withstand the inevitable stresses created by interacting with others without developing serious illness.

By improving your own interpersonal relationships, you can lessen the likelihood that stress will become distress.

2
Relationships Can Keep You Healthy

Despite the potential for stress in close personal relationships, it's becoming increasingly clear that healthy, long lives depend on strengthening our bonds with others. A full and rewarding social life can nourish the mind, the emotions, and the spirit, and good physical health depends as much on these aspects of ourselves as it does on a strong and well-functioning body.

When these social supports are lost, we feel it. A young mother who moved to Connecticut from California four years ago recently complained to me of social isolation.

"I had five or six close friends in California and a job I loved," she said. "When my husband was transferred here, we didn't need my income any more and I had just become pregnant anyway. He travels constantly—he did even when we lived in California—and I have no one to turn to except my 75-year-old mother who comes in once a week to stay with the children. I should be helping *her*. But I'm so overwhelmed with the demands of parenting that I have no strength left. I don't even have anybody to talk to. In one move I lost my job, my friends, and my entire support system. Bob's life stayed almost the same."

For Mildred, a single woman in her mid-thirties, loneliness was a chronic problem. She describes the abrupt development of asthma in her life at age 14, shortly after her mother, a teacher, gave up full-time homemaking and returned to work.

"I found myself completely alone," she said. "I saw my mother's working as abandonment, a total lack of caring. We hadn't been close before, but suddenly she wasn't even there. My father was a doctor, but he wasn't successful financially; I guess my mother felt she *had* to work. None of my friends' mothers had careers or even jobs."

Today, more than 20 years later, this young woman still feels abandoned, and is still wasting her energies blaming her unsuccessful father and her uncaring mother for her difficulties.

"I'm sick," she said, coughing into a Kleenex. "I've been sick since I was 14. I changed from a healthy, athletic kid who had never been sick to a chronic patient.

"I'm totally alone except for my brother, Josy," she declared. "And he lives a thousand miles away. I'd like to have a relationship, but how can I? I cough constantly."

Mildred is so caught up in her asthma, her loneliness, and her abandonment by her mother that she cannot get on with her life and form rewarding connections with others.

In a 1974 study conducted by Lisa Berkman, Ph.D., of 7,000 people in Alameda County, California, it was found that those who had extensive social ties had death rates two to three times lower than those who were isolated. And a ten-year University of Michigan study of 2,754 adults in Tecumseh, Michigan, echoed these findings: people with the greatest number of social contacts had one-half to one-fourth the mortality rate of those without supportive social networks.

On the wider canvas of a national society, Japanese culture emphasizes social ties and social support systems, and the people benefit both in health and morale, according to Leonard Syme, a professor of epidemiology in the School of Public Health at the University of California at Berkeley.

The Japanese, he points out, often have the same friends throughout their lifetime. They may attend school together, play together, and work together. Employers respect these social values and seldom transfer one employee alone. If necessary, they will transfer an entire work group.

In Japan, people also cling to the concept of their native place, a place where you not only grew up but to which you will retire in your later years. Even if they leave Japan, the social-supportive lifestyle of the Japanese is protective of their health.

Among Japanese who move to California, those who adopt Western customs develop disease patterns like those of Americans, while those who adhere to their Japanese ways remain healthier, almost as if they were still in Japan. In a study of 12,000 Japanese immigrants, those who became Westernized exhibited coronary heart disease rates five times as great as those who kept their community ties.

Just what accounts for the protective value of social supports?

According to recent research, such psychosocial factors as loneliness can adversely affect the human immune system, and thus make us more susceptible to illness.

It seems likely that when stress levels are low, social support may have relatively little effect on health outcome, but that during periods of high stress the presence of adequate social supports can significantly affect your physical well-being.

In other words, if things are going well in all areas of your life, you may not need much in the way of social support. But if you lose your job or your husband leaves you, close relationships with others can help you withstand the stress.

3
Happy Marriages Are Good for You

While living alone can be a positive experience, there's little doubt that the strongest buffer against illness is a happy marriage.

Studies consistently find that the married are in better mental and physical health than the unmarried. On the whole, married people live longer than the unmarried, and they make fewer demands on health care services.

This isn't necessarily true of women who have never married. Many studies find them to be equally healthy as, or even healthier than, the married. However, the termination of marriage, whether through death or divorce, significantly affects both men and women in terms of health.

One woman told me today, "I've been physically sick ever since my husband told me he wanted a divorce three months ago. I can't sleep at night without a sleeping pill. My diverticulitis has become so bad that I'm afraid to eat anything—I've lost 15 pounds. I've had a skin cancer removed from my forehead, and my rosacea, which is embarrassing because it's so obvious, almost never goes away." She pointed to a reddish spot, about the size of a quarter, on the bridge of her nose.

"Somehow I have to keep functioning, but every day is a struggle," she continued. "I live with a kind of dread, not only of the end of my marriage, but of getting even sicker than I already am."

The Hardy Will Survive

Yet most people survive.

What do the surprising number of people who manage to endure stressful events without becoming ill have going for them? In the view of some experts it is simple "hardiness." A hardy person thinks about, and reacts to, stressful events in a way that counteracts the negative impact.

According to Milton Viederman, M.D., professor of clinical psychiatry at Cornell Medical College, hardiness involves *commitment*, which means valuing your own actions; a sense of *control* over your own behavior and its effects; and *challenge*, which views change as a chance for learning and growth. Since women generally cope better than men after the death of a spouse, Dr. Viederman believes that women may have a natural edge in terms of hardiness.

While the relationship between marriage and health is generally positive, statistics show that it is *happiness* in marriage, not just marriage itself, that is conducive to emotional and physical well-being.

In a survey of marriage and mental health conducted by researchers at Vanderbilt University, respondents who rated themselves "not too happy" or "not at all happy" with their marriages were in poorer mental health than the unmarried. Another study involving 5,373 individuals produced similar results concerning mental health, and physical health as well.

The healthful effect of "marital helping," that is the understanding, support, and assistance that "marital partners" provide to one another in times of stress, has been studied in some detail by Ronald Burke and Tamara Weir of Canada's York University. They found that "the marital helping relationship acted as a moderator between the stress experience by the individuals and their resultant well-being."

Burke and Weir surveyed 189 professional-level husband-wife pairs in terms of job stress, life stress, mental and physical well-being, and satisfaction with the helping provided by the spouse. Husbands and wives were asked to complete separate questionnaires independently.

The results showed that an individual who was satisfied with the spouse's help was also happier with his or her job, life, and marriage, and had fewer psychosomatic complaints. This held true with or without stress in the picture. However, the impact of marital helping was more pronounced under conditions of high stress. In other words, the more helpful and supportive you are to your mate, and vice versa, the better off you both will be.

4
It All Adds Up

You are the sum of your roles.

And, according to some recent sociological evidence, the more roles you have—up to a point—the healthier you are.

A study by Dr. Denise Kandel, a sociologist in the department of public health at Columbia University, suggests that women who play multiple roles—wives, mothers, providers, students, members or leaders of religious, social, or civic organizations—function better than those who have fewer roles. Why? One possible explanation, says Dr. Kandel, is that these additional obligations allow an individual to get away from the stress she experiences in one situation by going to another. "If someone has trouble with her marriage, for example, the added job may help."

Research by Dr. Peggy Thoits of Princeton bears this out. In her study, women who had up to five roles were better off than those with fewer roles. However, those who had more than five "suffered from overload."

Dr. Thoits also found that one combination of three roles—wife, mother, and provider—produced significantly higher levels of anxiety.

It isn't too surprising that these particular three roles in combination are an exception to the rule that more roles lead to better functioning. When women try to be superwomen, they naturally feel stress from the conflicting roles they must play. According to Dr. Thoits, it isn't yet clear whether work serves a protective function for women with young children or leads to increased stress.

Research at the Wellesley Center for Research on Women suggests that psychological well-being, at least in women of the higher socioeconomic groups, is improved by career involvement and that the most stressful experiences occur not on the job but at home.

While it had been predicted that women would have coronaries at the same rate as men as a result of increased career involvement, that didn't occur, says Wellesley's Dr. Grace Baruch. She feels the explanation is that women's lives at home were already stressful. When they joined the work force, those stresses didn't increase; instead, they may have decreased.

In Dr. Baruch's view, an interesting occupation provides gratification to many women which may shield them against pressures at home; between the ages of 25 and 55, she says, women find being a mother and homemaker more stressful than working.

Why does increased role involvement lead to enhanced psychological well-being?

Your roles give direction to your life. They lend a feeling of meaningfulness and purpose. In addition, there is the obvious point that more roles mean more relationships.

Those who hold few social identities—the unmarried, the unemployed, the retired, housewives, those who live alone—have a greater risk of developing psychological disturbance than do those who are more involved with life and with other people.

You'll be healthiest if you create several different roles for yourself. But not *too* many.

PART 2
To Be More Specific

1
Can Your Family Drive You Crazy?

The answer to that question is yes.

If you think your spouse or some other member of your family, or all of them together, are driving you crazy, you could be right. It is becoming increasingly clear that disturbed marriages and family relationships can be—and often are—at the root of psychiatric problems.

Freud and his followers and practitioners of a wide variety of other individual therapies believed neurotic conflicts to be the result of pathological family influences in childhood. But they chose to isolate their psychoanalytic patients from their families, usually refusing to communicate even with a marital partner about the patient's progress.

Eventually, however, the effect of family interactions on psychiatric problems became apparent.

During the 1950s, several different mental health professionals including Gregory Bateson and Jay Haley began seeing schizophrenic patients with their families to observe their patterns of communication.

And psychiatrist Nathan Ackerman, often considered the founder of family therapy, entered the field from a different route. He shifted his focus from individual therapy to sessions that included not only the immediate family but everyone living under the same roof. His goal was to enhance family functioning and individual happiness as well as to resolve symptoms and protect family members against future stresses.

Despite the rapid and continuing growth of family therapy, most patients today in treatment for psychological problems are still being seen individually.

"A Shock Theory of Marriage"

While marriage is protective of mental health in general, it has been known for decades that married women are more dissatisfied, and have more psychological problems, than do married men.

In a recent study of people 17 to 69 years old, Dr. Robert Sternberg, a psychologist at Yale University, found major differences in the way men and women evaluated their marriages. Men rated almost every aspect of their relationships more favorably than did their wives. They were more satisfied with love-making, finances, ties with parents, and communication with each other, and were more tolerant of flaws in their mates.

According to sociologist Jesse Bernard, wives complain more about marriage than their husbands because marriage is harder for them. It is her belief that marriage is much more costly psychologically for wives than for husbands.

Back in 1942, Dr. Bernard proposed what she called "a shock theory of marriage." The idea was suggested to her by a study by Raymond R. Willoughby of 1,400 urban men and women of upper socioeconomic status which found that married women had far more fears, phobias, and anxieties than did those who had never married.

A Sex-Role Problem?

When and if psychological symptoms develop in married people, the lack of a supportive, intimate marital relationship is a major factor. The sex-role stereotyped attitudes in some husbands make it difficult for emotional intimacy to develop.

In a 1983 study based on 16 prominent, successful men (attorneys, corporation presidents, etc.), all suffered acute psychiatric crisis following a change in their relationships with their wives.

The wives of these men, without exception, had been entirely devoted to husbands and families until they withdrew from their subservient marital relationships and began to take part in personally gratifying activities. Subsequently, the husbands collapsed emotionally.

Often women with a poorly defined sense of personal identity unconsciously choose sex-role stereotyped men to protect and support them.

But, if they later mature and seek greater independence, the husband resists the change and tries to reinforce dependence. The resulting internal conflict may bring about the development of psychological symptoms.

Competitive women, those who do not accept the traditional feminine sex-role stereotype, have particular problems adjusting to a domestic role after marriage. They may envy and resent their husbands for the freedom and fulfillment they obtain from their work, and their desire for personal gratification may create a profound conflict between preserving their full-time domestic roles and returning to the work force. Sometimes the conflict is so intense that severe anxiety symptoms, including panic attacks, occur.

"I'll Starve Myself"

The role of family interaction in anorexia nervosa, which usually afflicts teenage girls and is potentially life-threatening, is well known.

Since the development of anorexia is closely related to abnormal patterns of interaction between the patient and her family, successful treatment must involve resolution of the underlying family problems, according to Dr. Hilde Bruch, a leading authority on anorexia and bulimia.

Usually the problem is one of overly involved and overly close family relationships that have prevented the emergence of a healthy sense of independence.

Anorectics and their families frequently deny family problems initially. If anything, things may seem too perfect; the anorectic was usually a model child. But as a teenager she comes to feel, at least subconsciously, that her diet and her body weight are the only aspects of her life over which she alone has control.

Obviously the symptom itself must be addressed at the beginning of treatment and the patient must sometimes be hospitalized to prevent starvation. However, without successful family intervention, the problem will only recur after discharge.

"In anorectic families, the boundaries that keep family members overinvolved with each other and separated from the world are well defined and strong," says Salvador Minuchin, a leading family therapist. "The boundaries within the family, however, are diffuse and weak." Often one or both spouses remain strongly attached to their parents, interfering with the marriage relationship. Anorectic families generally focus on bodily functions, with many members presenting somatic complaints, and the entire family is often preoccupied with eating, table manners, diets, and food fads.

A "New" Eating Disorder

Some authorities view bulimia, the "new" eating disorder, as closely related to anorexia, but Dr. Bruch is one who disagrees. Bulimics, she points out, make an exhibitionistic display of their lack of control over food intake, while the true anorectic maintains rigid control over her eating behavior.

Those who suffer from bulimia alternately gorge and purge, usually by self-induced vomiting. Many bulimics blame others for their problem, often those who taught them to counteract an eating binge by vomiting.

Most bulimics are of normal weight; many appear, superficially, to be well adjusted; but underneath they experience deep feelings of shame for a behavior they are deeply ambivalent about giving up, since they will have to learn to eat responsibly or get fat—a prospect they contemplate with horror.

While it is seldom life-threatening, the physical complications of bulimia are many: depletion of potassium, chloride, and sodium; cardiac irregularities; kidney dysfunction; swollen salivary glands; gastrointestinal disturbances; menstrual irregularities; and dental deterioration.

Like anorectics, most bulimics are highly enmeshed in their families, which tend to be overprotective and to attach a great deal of significance to eating and to appearance. Many bulimics had an overweight sibling who was nagged at for being fat; the bulimic became preoccupied with remaining thin and attractive to keep parental approval.

Like anorectics and compulsive eaters who do not purge, bulimics have trouble expressing emotions directly. They tend to value themselves solely in terms of physical attractiveness. By gaining self-confidence and by finding new sources of gratification in their lives and by becoming able to confront and express emotions, bulimics can gradually relinquish the binge-purge syndrome—provided they really want to do so.

Since a bulimic's dealings with the family are almost always centered around food, other family problems are usually buried. But generally the bulimic cannot recover until she gains control over her life and her relationships.

In conclusion: many—if not most—psychiatric illnesses are, in fact, family problems.

2
Or Drive You to Drink?

It can't be as simple as "you drive me to drink." If alcoholism is strictly a *behavior* pattern, then everyone must assume responsibility for his or her own. If it is a *disease* then presumably no one is responsible. Contemporary opinion, supported by the widely accepted philosophy of Alcoholics Anonymous (AA), regards alcoholism as a disease—conveniently absolving the victim as well as the family of all responsibility for causing it.

Yet it seems reasonable to assume that if stress, including that resulting from unsatisfactory relationships, is a factor in precipitating other diseases, it might also be a factor in precipitating alcoholism.

There is no doubt that alcoholism tends to run in families and that both genetic predisposition and environmental influences are involved. But this is also true of schizophrenia, manic-depressive illness, agoraphobia, diabetes, cancer, and coronary heart disease—to name only a few of the more obvious examples.

No one questions the fact that certain individuals are genetically predisposed to the development of certain illnesses. Yet some individuals in high risk groups do not develop the illness.

Considerable attention has been devoted to the role of the family in maintaining alcoholic behavior, and the changes in family patterns produced by living with an alcoholic. There has been, however, little or no investigation of the marital relationship as a *causative* factor in the development of alcoholism.

It isn't a question of shifting the blame for alcoholic behavior to someone else, as much as many alcoholics would like to do so. But unresolved marital difficulties may trigger the mechanism of drinking to escape. What leads up to the condition, except in terms of frequent early exposure to alcoholism, is generally overlooked.

We often hear that alcoholics can overcome their disease—or, in AA terminology, "arrest" it, since the organization claims there is no cure—*if they want to*, and that they can do so through an ongoing process of group support and involvement. There is no doubt that this process works.

On the other hand, no one claims that diseases such as cancer, heart disease, or arthritis can be controlled without medical intervention, even though emotional stresses are among the acknowledged causes. This seems a curious paradox.

How can a disease be a disease if its primary symptom is behavior rather than organic impairment, and if it can be treated successfully by psychological methods alone?

Alcoholism and Marital Cohesion

It seems probable that there are two types of alcoholic marriages. In the first type, both partners have sociopathic characteristics. Both come from families where at least one parent was alcoholic, and one or both partners were already alcoholics when they married.

In such a case it makes no sense to blame the alcoholism on the marriage, since it was there before the marriage. When the alcoholic selects a mate who is also alcoholic or deviant in other respects, the stage is set for the behavior to continue conveniently.

In the other type of alcoholic marriage, the alcoholism develops *after* the marriage. While there may have been alcoholism in the family history of one or both partners, it is likely to have been of a different character, without the crime, violence, or other drug abuse of the first type. If the marriage remains intact, the partners can recall a "problem-free" period early in the marriage, before the alcoholism developed.

"The Controlling Wife"

The dependent, immature alcoholic or alcoholic-to-be often selects a mate who will take charge and assume the role of caretaker. In fact, it seems that the "well spouse" is attracted to, and therefore contributes to, the continuation of the deviant partner's deviance. Sometimes the caretaking function is assumed by a woman, often a nurse, who had an alcoholic parent and took on the responsible, parental role early in life. In others, the role of the well spouse may provide an outlet for expressing distrustful, hostile, and resentful feelings toward the opposite sex in general.

"If Joe marries Mary because he was attracted by her warm maternal quality, as many alcoholics do, he is asking to be the dependent one," according to *The Dilemma of the Alcoholic Marriage* (New York: Al-Anon Family Group Headquarters, 1971).

By her protective care she makes it easy for him to avoid getting sober. Until she learns what she is doing to encourage his behavior and how to change herself so he will be forced to take responsibility for his own actions, the situation isn't likely to get any better.

Similarly, a man who marries a shy, submissive woman who will allow him to dominate will not necessarily be dissatisfied if alcoholism makes her more dependent. He, too, will cover up her drinking, protect her from public disgrace, and assume all the responsibilities that should be hers.

Poor communication, whether a cause or an effect of alcoholism, is always a factor in the alcoholic marriage. At Al-Anon and Alateen meetings, family members learn to confront the alcoholic by expressing their feelings honestly and insisting that he or she face the consequences of his or her own actions.

Clearly stress is a factor in the development and worsening of some, if not all, cases of alcoholism. It is equally clear that family interactions play a part in maintaining the problem as well as in successfully treating it.

3
It's a Weighty Problem

For every anorectic who tries to demonstrate independence from her family by refusing to eat, there are several people who eat to defy someone in their families.

In counseling hundreds of patients with weight problems, I have become convinced that relationship issues, as well as early experiences relating to food, metabolic factors, and a family history of obesity, are almost always involved.

Carole, 17, weighed 180 pounds. Her father sarcastically referred to her as "the cow," both at home and in public, and offered her various bribes if she would lose 50 pounds. He viewed her as an embarrassment to the family. When he saw her binging in the kitchen—which she did openly—he berated and ridiculed her.

"I *hate* my father!" she declared. "I want to lose weight, but I don't want to give him the satisfaction of giving in to his nagging." When she went away to college, Carole was able to lose 50 pounds and keep it off.

Estelle, a 200-pound nurse, had two people in her life who drove her to episodes of overeating: her supervisor and her husband.

"You ought to write a book about the ridiculous reasons why people eat," she told me one day. "You won't believe this one. While she was complaining about something I'd done, my supervisor *stepped on my foot!* I couldn't believe she was doing it. Maybe she noticed she did it—maybe she didn't. I didn't say a thing. Instead, I went down to the cafeteria and ate two sandwiches.

"Yesterday it was my husband," she continued. "I was cooking dinner and he came in and exploded because I hadn't left a glass of water in the microwave oven. He has this idea that you have to keep a glass of water in it, and he looks in there every time he comes in to see if it's there. It wasn't, so he started yelling at me about it. Did I yell back?

No. I stood there and listened to him, and then I sat down and ate a whole Hershey bar. A *big* one."

Noelle, a bright, talented, and successful editor, had been angry at her mother all her life. Her mother wanted to control all aspects of her behavior, including her weight. As a child, Noelle had been made to feel that love and acceptance were conditional on maintaining an acceptable weight. If she gained too much she was hauled off to the doctor and put on a stringent diet. She resented these attempts to impose controls on her behavior, and retaliated by eating when no one was around.

Although as an adult she lived a continent away from her mother, she had never resolved her angry feelings. Thinking about her mother frequently provoked eating binges; and when she visited her mother in California, her mother's disapproval of her weight—and that of her chubby daughter—prompted more anger and more eating.

When it is the spouse who is attempting to monitor a partner's food intake, weight may become a focal point for the couple's problems.

"Everything would be all right if only my wife would lose 50 pounds" is often the viewpoint of the husband of a fat woman, but the matter is seldom that simple. She may have gained the weight to avoid an unsatisfactory sexual relationship or because she is disappointed in the marriage.

It is rare, though not unheard of, to find an obese person who is well adjusted beneath the smiling facade that is often presented. Frequently the eating behavior serves as an outlet for negative emotions that cannot be stated verbally.

Most eating binges are directly preceded by some event that is frustrating, annoying, depressing, or anxiety provoking, though these connections are not necessarily made by the binger. Somehow—most often through early conditioning—the individual has learned to respond to emotions by eating rather than by direct confrontation.

When an obese person is married, the weight is usually an important issue in the marital relationship. And the spouse's attitude and behavior may be the factor that determines whether or not a patient will succeed in losing weight.

There are several reasons why the spouse plays an important role in obesity.

A wife or husband may be in control of food that enters the house, or may openly or more subtly encourage or discourage the patient to lose weight. The marital relationship or the sexual relationship may change as the obese person loses weight.

A Saga of Sabotage

Sabotage from the spouses of dieters is familiar to all who deal with the problem. As the dieter becomes more attractive physically the spouse may fear that the person will leave or will become a target of sexual advances from others.

And increased self-confidence may motivate the dieter to become more active socially, to seek a job, make a career change, or become more assertive.

Some men and women are sexually attracted to fat people and find their mates less appealing physically as they lose weight. Others—especially those who are overweight themselves—are threatened by the spouse's success in taking control over eating behavior.

Naturally, the sabotage is not straightforward; it involves increasing invitations to dine out, urging the consumption of fattening desserts, bringing home candy or other special treats, eating more snacks than usual in front of the dieter, or making it impossible for the dieter to keep appointments for therapy or weight control sessions.

Sometimes obesity stems from the *lack* of a relationship: being suddenly alone after a death or divorce, going away to college, or being transferred to a distant city. Or it may result from insufficient nurturing in childhood.

I saw a pronounced case of this just recently in a 19-year-old "mother's helper" from the Midwest. She had gained 30 pounds since leaving home a few months before, and was not happy with her new "family." But she had not been happy with her old family either; her parents divorced when she was 5, and she had lived with her abusive mother though she preferred her father.

"We didn't get along," she said sadly, tears streaming down her cheeks. "I don't think she loved either me or my sister."

All day long, while doing housework and child care, Gina ate. Cookies, candy, sandwiches, potato chips, bagels—whatever was available. And she drank—water, soda, and iced tea, but fortunately for her, not alcohol. She knew she wasn't hungry, but felt compelled to fill the vast emptiness within her with enormous quantities of food she didn't need.

Others eat to avoid relationships, especially sexual relationships. Calvin was losing weight successfully until he reached 190 pounds—his goal was 180. Suddenly progress ceased. When I questioned him about his associations with the weight of 180, he at first declared he didn't have any. Then he recalled that he had had an extramarital relationship, the only one in a 20-year marriage, the last time he weighed 180.

"It was too much emotional conflict," he declared. "The relationship was very exciting to me, but I couldn't possibly subject myself to that kind of strain again." His subconscious mind had been protecting him; it wouldn't let him reach the weight he associated with marital infidelity.

Niki, a 23-year-old girl, weighed almost 250 pounds. She had never had a boyfriend and didn't want one. As a child she had been involved in an ongoing incestuous relationship with her stepfather. She protected herself from sexual involvement by remaining grotesquely overweight.

The widespread failure of dieting alone to bring about lasting weight loss is a well-known and discouraging aspect of the field of weight control.

And it is seldom sufficient to attack bad eating habits from a behavioral point of view. Most seriously overweight people must successfully address the emotional issues in their lives, which almost always involve relationships with others, in order to produce permanent change.

4
"You Make Me Sick!"

"I'm fed up with you!"

"You make me sick!"

"You make me want to vomit!"

Utter disgust is so frequently expressed in terms of the functions of the stomach that it is not surprising that the gastrointestinal tract is peculiarly responsive to emotional upsets.

As part of the alarm or "flight or fight" reaction, the stomach releases hydrochloric acid, which normally helps in the digestion of food. If it is released when the stomach is empty, hydrochloric acid can burn the lining of the stomach and intestines. This reaction, if repeated over a period of time, can—and does—lead to the development of ulcers.

Ulcers are widely regarded as the result of tension in both sexes; this view is especially well substantiated for women.

Often the onset or aggravation of symptoms occurs in conjunction with the death of, or rejection by, a husband or fiance. While the family history of ulcer patients generally indicates a genetic predisposition to the disorder, an emotional loss or conflict usually precipitates the attack.

Ulcerative colitis, too, is often clearly evoked by a relationship problem.

One 18-year-old male with moderately severe colitis, as reported by John F. O'Connor, lived in a household where his parents fought constantly, and the boy was frequently the target of his father's anger and the butt of his jokes. When he graduated from high school and went off to a college well removed from home, he soon became symptom-free.

We probably all have experienced, at one stressful time or another, a bout of gastrointestinal difficulty.

"You Get under My Skin"

The skin, like the stomach, is highly reactive to emotional stimuli. "Just thinking about the things my family did to me makes me break out in hives," one patient declared. "It makes me feel like I was taking a beating."

"Whenever I feel frustrated or embarrassed, my skin begins to itch," said another who suffered from eczema. When emotionally upsetting topics were discussed during interviews, this patient began to itch.

"You're Choking Me!"

Frustration has also been identified as the predominant emotion in psychosomatic attacks of asthma. (In many cases, allergic factors are clearly present as well.)

"I wanted to shout at my mother when she humiliated me," an asthmatic patient said, "but I couldn't allow myself to let go like that. I wanted to run away, but I couldn't do that either. I just stayed and made the best of it—and started wheezing."

The feeling of "oppression" or irritation experienced by asthmatics produces the same type of breathing as if there had been an actual compression of the chest or an irritation of the upper air passages.

While psychotherapy has been relatively ineffective in treating asthmatics, good results are usually obtained if patients, especially children, are removed from the family home to a different environment. When they are in the hospital, many patients are completely free from attacks of asthma.

However, in most cases the attacks recur, often immediately, when the patient returns home.

For some patients family therapy has proved helpful, and in others psychotherapy for the *mother*—and not the child—has improved the child's symptoms.

5
Your Emotions and Your Heart

Your heart knows when you're upset—even if you don't. Emotional stress produces measurable changes in pulse rate, cardiac output, and arterial blood pressure.

In one early study, reported in *Psychosomatic Medicine* in 1953, of 25 patients admitted to a hospital for congestive heart failure, severe emotional stresses were clearly identified in 19 of the cases. These patients had been deserted or rejected or had lost a spouse or child through illness or accident.

The increased incidence of heart attack during bereavement (sometimes immediately following a spouse's death) has been noted by several investigators. Stressful life experiences have also been found to correlate with elevated levels of cholesterol.

In addition, disruptive social relationships are a major factor in the Type A personality found by Drs. Meyer Friedman and Ray Rosenman to be far more subject to coronary attack than individuals without the characteristic traits of aggression, hostility, and "hurry sickness."

They describe the Type A personality as aggressively involved in an ongoing struggle to achieve more and more in less and less time. Though most patients studied were married, Drs. Friedman and Rosenman found that the Type A's life style guaranteed that they would have little time for socializing with their families or anyone else. Many were so busy with work that they grossly neglected their families; the shared times they did have were often notably unpleasant.

"We have frequently had a widow of a Type A man tell us that though she is sorry her husband died, she nevertheless felt relieved to be spared the tensions of living with such a man," writes Dr. Friedman in the book *Treating Type A Behavior and Your Heart* (New York: Alfred A. Knopf, 1984), which he co-authored with Diane Olmer, R.N., M.S. That meant no more having to think and act precisely as their husbands demanded, no worrying about frequent and unpredictable outbursts of anger, and no more duty as "umpire" between yelling husbands and children.

Dr. James Lynch of the University of Maryland Medical School declares that the link is clear between marital discord and the development of heart disease and premature death.

In *The Broken Heart: The Medical Consequences of Loneliness* (New York: Basic Books, 1979) he writes, "In a surprising number of cases of *premature* coronary heart disease and *premature* death, interpersonal unhappiness, the lack of love, and human loneliness seem to appear as root causes of the physical problems."

How to Talk Yourself into Trouble

To interact with other people you obviously have to talk to people. And just talking raises your blood pressure. But the pressure of hypertensive patients goes up more than that of any other group, sometimes surging as much as 50 percent above baseline levels as soon as they begin to speak.

Researchers speculate that hypertensive patients are trapped inside their own bodies, damned if they withdraw from their fellow human beings and damned if they try to relate to them. It seems likely that hypertensives unconsciously avoid emotional encounters that could prove damaging or even fatal, protecting their health by withdrawing from others.

"The response of our hearts, blood vessels, and muscles when we communicate with spouse, children, friends, colleagues, and the larger community has as much to do with our cardiovascular health as do factors such as exercise or diet," Dr. Lynch writes in his book *The Language of the Heart: The Body's Response to Human Dialogue* (New York: Basic Books, 1985). "We can understand and cope with illness only when we are able to view ourselves as part of a complex world beyond the confines of our own individual skin."

The typical hypertensive personality has been characterized as experiencing lifelong conflicts over the expression of hostility, aggression, dependency, and ambition. And what these patients talk about, the way they speak, the way they breathe or fail to breathe, and the way they manage to hide their feelings from themselves and others, all contribute to the dangerously high increases in blood pressure that occur while talking.

In other words, it isn't just the emotional content of what one says that is significant, but the way those emotions are expressed or not expressed.

The typically loud, rapid, and explosive communication style of the Type A personality sends blood pressure soaring. Every time.

"It Goes to My Head"

Typically, migraine patients—like hypertensives—are unwilling or unable to discuss their feelings. If questioned directly, they answer indirectly. They don't realize when their hearts are racing, when blood pressure is rising or falling, or when their hands are freezing cold (a common feature of the condition).

The link between emotional stress and some migraines has been repeatedly observed, but patients commonly fail to see the connection because the migraine, a throbbing headache, does not occur during stress. It follows a period of relaxation (often a sufferer wakes from a full night's sleep with a migraine), which was preceded by an acute or prolonged episode of stress. The hands and feet are cold during stress because blood flow to the extremities becomes severely restricted; when circulation is restored to these areas, cranial arteries swell and the headache appears.

The typical migraine patient is generally seen as obsessive, perfectionistic, and resentful. But Dr. Oliver Sacks, a leading authority, doesn't believe there is a typical sufferer. However, he views one type of headache—the frequent, severe, and unremitting migraine—as a reaction to chronically difficult and intolerable life circumstances. He believes migraines are often "expressions of chronic, and usually repressed, emotional needs."

6
"I Give Up!"

Don't despair.

It's normal to feel depressed and to experience deep feelings of grief when you lose someone you love. But despair—which goes beyond depression into an attitude of barren hopelessness—has been found to correlate with the development of cancer.

According to Lawrence LeShan, Ph.D., the despairing person feels hopeless about ever achieving any meaning, zest, or validity in life. He or she regards relationships as inevitably leading to disappointment and pain, and expects no improvement in the future.

Dr. LeShan observed the factor of despair in 16 of 18 cancer patients seen in intensive psychotherapy, compared to 1 in 15 in a group of 15 noncancer patients. It had existed before any signs of the tumor appeared. These people had gone on with their everyday existences with no hope for satisfaction in their lives. Most of them accepted this as their lot in life.

Typically, Dr. LeShan's patients saw their illness as just one more example of the hopelessness of life. The cancer was solving the problem of their unbearable existence in a final, irrevocable way.

In an analysis of the personality and emotional life histories of over 300 cancer patients, Dr. LeShan observed a particular life pattern in over 60 percent, compared to 10 percent of a control group.

Early in life, these patients learned to perceive relationships as dangerous, to be invested in only at the risk of much pain and rejection. To protect themselves, they kept relationships with others on a superficial basis. They held back emotionally and felt isolated and different from others, though they appeared to be functioning well.

Then, usually in adolescence or early adulthood, a relationship came along that seemed relatively safe. Slowly this new relationship became the central focus of life.

Then for one reason or another, the loved one was lost. A spouse died, children grew up and moved away, or a divorce occurred. Cancer developed following the loss.

"Nothing Good Can Happen"

Often the cancer patients in Dr. LeShan's study seemed to be saying: "I was right to be so pessimistic. This proves it. Nothing really good can happen to me, and if I allow myself to hope, it just leaves me open to more disappointment and anguish."

O. Carl Simonton, M.D., whose revolutionary and controversial approach to cancer treatment has attracted widespread attention, also believes that "cancer is often an indication of problems elsewhere in an individual's life, problems aggravated and compounded by a series of stresses six to eighteen months prior to the onset of cancer.

"The cancer patient has typically responded to these problems and stresses with a deep sense of hopelessness, or 'giving up,'" he writes in the book *Getting Well Again* (Los Angeles: J. P. Tarcher, 1978), which he co-authored with Stephanie Matthews-Simonton and James L. Creighton. "This emotional response, we believe, in turn triggers a set of physiological responses that suppress the body's natural defenses and make it susceptible to producing abnormal cells."

While he acknowledges that external agents, radiation, genetics, and diet may all enter into cancer causation, Dr. Simonton feels that none of these factors explain fully why particular individuals, at particular points in their lives, develop cancer.

One clue is the fact that lymphocyte function, a critical measure of the body's immune system, is significantly depressed in those who have lost a wife or husband. Chronic stress suppresses the immune system which is responsible for destroying abnormal cells, leaving the body vulnerable to the growth of cancer.

Dr. Simonton reports that, during therapy, cancer patients often recall an earlier time when they wished they were dead or felt hopeless and thought death was the only way out. Frequently these feelings occurred because of an apparently unresolvable conflict.

"For many of our patients," states Dr. Simonton, "the conflict occurs when they discover their spouses have had affairs, particularly if they will not consider marriage counseling or if their religious beliefs prevent them from accepting the idea of divorce, but they nevertheless feel unwilling to stay in the marriage.

"Edith Jones faced this problem in the extreme when she discovered that her husband, the father of their six children, was having extramarital affairs. She did not believe she could tolerate the situation but she also did not believe in divorce. There appeared to be no alternatives and so she felt trapped. She contracted cancer and soon died. For Edith, death represented a solution. Other women might have found a basis for continuing the relationship, and still others might have given themselves 'permission' to obtain a divorce."

Another case Dr. Simonton cites is that of a successful entrepreneur who took a relative into the business in a major supervisory role. When the relative proved incompetent and business began to deteriorate, the businessman felt he was faced with an intolerable problem for which there was no solution. After developing cancer a year or so later, he entered therapy and learned to confront his difficulties more directly.

Such stresses and conflicts do not *cause* cancer, but they lead to feelings of helplessness or hopelessness that permit cancer to develop.

While we cannot control everything that happens to us, we—consciously or unconsciously—choose our reactions. And by assuming the stance of the victim we increase our body's vulnerability to disease.

If you recognize aspects of your own personality, your life experience, or your response to conflict in the histories of these patients, it does not mean that you will develop cancer. But, as Dr. Simonton says, "If you can see yourself in this psychological process . . . recognize it as a call to action and make changes in your life."

7
"You're a Pain in the Neck"

Like the typical cancer patient, a person who develops rheumatoid arthritis tends to appear calm, composed, and optimistic, rarely expressing or even consciously feeling anger. However, one expert, after reviewing data involving over 5,000 patients, found that in a high percentage of cases the patients suffered from worry, work pressures, marital disharmony, and concerns about relatives immediately prior to the onset of disease. Another researcher expressed his growing conviction that the arthritic process is not merely frequently, but always, the expression of a personality conflict.

On the rare occasions when arthritics directly express the rage they feel, they are frequently overcome by guilt, remorse, and a need for self-punishment.

In one study of 16 female patients and their healthy sisters, significant differences were found between the patients and their siblings. The patients described themselves as nervous, tense, worried, struggling, depressed, moody, highly strung, and easily upset, while their sisters said they liked people, were active and constantly busy, easy to get acquainted with, productive workers, and enjoyed life in general.

The sisters were much freer to express criticism, and nearly all said their marriages were reasonably happy. Patients characterized their husbands in one of two extreme ways: "so good to me, it's pathetic"; "marvelous, very easy going, calm and relaxed"; or "irresponsible, alcoholic, completely unundersanding"; "mean, used to torture me." Yet, 13 of the 16 patients—even those who had asserted they had very poor marriages—claimed they never argued with their husbands. They were martyrlike and masochistic, often putting up with considerable abuse.

"Patients will endure stressful situations longer than their siblings," the researchers concluded. "The arthritic patients' inability to express anger may make some situations more stressful to them than these same situations would be to other people."

People with multiple sclerosis also seem to have an excessive need for love and affection that was not gratified in childhood. They feel angry, but repress these feelings for fear of experiencing further rejection.

Instead, repression of feelings may lead to the development of autoimmune disease.

8
What's in It for You?

Whether we like to acknowledge it or not, most illness has a certain payoff in terms of what psychologists call "secondary gain."

Chicken soup, breakfast in bed, a backrub, flowers, and telephone calls, not to mention loving expressions of concern from other members of the family, are among the reinforcements we receive for being sick. If we enjoy them too much, we may be tempted to be a little sicker than we really are—or to be sick more often.

Nowhere is this more evident than in the case of chronic pain—pain for which no physical cause can be found, or that is disproportionate to the physical cause—and hypochondria.

Chronic pain syndrome is a recognized medical entity that causes changes in a patient's mood and behavior. Depression is common, the search for successful treatment becomes an all-encompassing activity, and complaints about pain dominate the patient's conversations with all who will allow it.

Some pain teaches us to avoid injury or signals us that something is wrong that requires medical attention. Chronic pain, however, serves no biologically useful purpose.

The fact that chronic pain may be *real*—phantom limb pain, for example, is a well-known phenomenon—does not alter the fact that the secondary gains associated with the pain may be powerful factors in maintaining it.

While chronic pain behaviors usually start as a result of uncomfortable bodily sensations, they soon take on a secondary value—special attention or escape from unwanted activity such as going to work, performing an arduous task, or a spouse's demand for sexual intercourse, for example.

Many patients who suffer from pain do not really wish to relinquish it because they gain desirable benefits from their discomfort. Subconsciously, or consciously, they decide that the attention and sympathy they attract make the pain something they prefer to keep.

Edith, 65, had organized her life around her pain—an ongoing case of abdominal distress for which no physical cause could be detected. She made a constant round of hospitals demanding exhaustive tests and surgery, and had worn out the attentions of several internists. She complained volubly to her husband, her friends, and her daughter, all of whom responded sympathetically.

Her husband, a busy attorney with a need to nurture others, began every day by asking Edith how she felt and bringing her coffee in bed. He patiently listened to her complaints and encouraged her unremitting efforts to find a better doctor. She outlived him by several years.

"I Must Have a Terrible Disease"

Hypochondria is much like the chronic pain pattern, but the preoccupation with disease is more general, and symptoms often travel from one part of the body to another.

Chronic pain patients' complaints are usually triggered by an actual illness or injury, but hypochondriacs simply misinterpret physical signs or sensations as abnormal, and refuse to accept medical assurances that they are not ill.

The hypochondriac, like the chronic pain patient, may use physical complaints to control relationships with family and friends. There is generally a family history of hypochondria, and often an early exposure to illness and hospitalization led to a focus on physical concerns.

If you frequently complain of pain or illness, what are you getting out of it—and what would you lose if you gave up your symptoms?

O. Carl Simonton lists five areas that patients most frequently cite as providing benefits from their illnesses:

> "1. Receiving permission to get out of dealing with a troublesome problem or situation.
> 2. Getting attention, care, nurturing from people around them.
> 3. Having an opportunity to regroup their psychological energy to deal with a problem or to gain a new perspective.
> 4. Gaining an incentive for personal growth or for modifying undesirable habits.
> 5. Not having to meet their own or others' high expectations."

Do any of these motivations apply to you?

Remember that there are other ways to satisfy these needs. It is not necessary to do so by becoming ill.

PART 3
Sizing Up Your Situation

1
Tune In Your Feelings

So far I've been speaking about the relationship of general health and specific illnesses to the emotions—and to the way people interact with other people.

Now I'd like to suggest ways in which you can more directly evaluate your own situation in terms of your health and your relationships. First let's consider your awareness of your bodily sensations, because you cannot possibly judge how your relationships are affecting your health unless you are finely attuned to these inner feelings. I still remember what a surprise it was to me the first time I realized, during an intense argument, that my stomach had literally tied itself into a knot.

Many people, especially those suffering from psychosomatic disorders such as ulcers, migraines, colitis, and hypertension, literally do not know how they feel at any given time. In 1972 Dr. Peter Sifneos, a Harvard psychiatrist, labeled the problem "alexithymia," which literally means "without words for feelings."

When asked to describe their feelings, such patients, who have been called "emotional illiterates," relate events in the outside world rather than responding in terms of their stomach churning or their blood pressure boiling. Their lives are remarkably devoid of fantasy.

While alexithymic patients can use emotional terms, they cannot apply them accurately to their own sensations—an intense surge of bodily feeling might be construed as sadness, anger, or love.

Whether or not you suffer from alexithymia, you will profit from an increased awareness of your inner feelings. A technique hypnotists call "the bridge" can help you develop the right hemispheric capacities for emotional awareness. This is not an exercise in talking or analyzing, but simply in feeling.

The shift to emotional awareness is facilitated by first relaxing your mind and body. You may be able to do this simply by focusing on your own breathing for five or six minutes, or it may help you to follow the relaxation procedure I describe in Part 4, Chapter 2.

When you feel thoroughly relaxed, tune in to your own body by focusing your awareness on some part of it—any part. Then let the awareness of that part of your body give rise to its own associations.

Sometimes a symbolic representation of the sensation you associate with that part of the body will spontaneously arise: "a silvery bolt," "a flash of white light," "a heavy black cloud enveloping my entire body."

Sonia visualized her own breath as "a visitor entering my body." She could enter a state of inner awareness easily by "following the path of the in-breath" and literally saw herself as a visitor entering her own body on her breath. She thought of her breath as bringing relaxation, peace, and health to any parts of her body that were undergoing stress or tension, and experienced an enhanced sense of peace and tranquility as a result.

Whenever you feel aware of tiredness, a pain, or a headache, allow it to become the focus of concentration and let it develop its own memories and psychological connections.

"Somebody Has His Foot on My Chest"

"I'm beginning to feel so limited," a 35-year-old woman with many phobic complaints told me recently. "I can't go on a vacation because I can't get on an airplane, and I'm terrified I'll have to go to New York on business, and have an anxiety attack on the train. If I go to the movies I have to sit on the outside aisle to avoid feeling trapped."

"What do you feel in these situations?" I asked.

"Panic!" she exclaimed.

"How does the panic feel?" I asked.

"Like I have to get up and leave."

She continued to describe her experience and her behavior intellectually, until I asked her to close her eyes, take a few deep breaths and visualize herself in one of the actual phobic situations. "I feel like I can't breathe," she said. "Like somebody has his foot on my chest."

She had initially stated that her problem started only one year before. But focusing on the sensation itself, rather than her intellectual knowledge of it, brought her the recollection of the same sensation at age 21 following an automobile accident.

"I kept calling up my doctor complaining that I couldn't breathe," she said. "He told me I should see a psychiatrist, but I never did. After a few weeks, I felt all right again."

Josh, a rigidly defensive, socially isolated, overintellectualized engineer whose early self-esteem depended totally on his academic talents, described his anxiety in conversational encounters (which he avoided determinedly) as "uncomfortable."

When I asked him to explain further, he said, "You tend to think people are looking at you and thinking you will say something stupid."

"Not people in general, Josh," I said. "I'm only asking about *you*. I want you to tell me how you feel. Close your eyes for a moment and imagine yourself in one of the situations you find most anxiety-provoking—a dance."

Josh had told me previously that his "discomfort" approached panic levels when he was in close physical proximity to a woman, even though he spent much of his time fantasizing about just such an event—to the detriment of his work and his past academic pursuits.

With his eyes closed, breathing deeply, Josh reported that his stomach was tightly knotted and that this was the sensation he felt at dances and on the rare occasions when he subjected himself to normal social interactions.

"I feel very uncomfortable right now," he added. "Just thinking about it is giving me the sensation again."

I used the bridge technique recently with a young married woman whose complaint was that "I'm so angry in the mornings my husband is beginning to avoid me." She described her rage as "a high powered bomb about to explode inside me."

Most recently, she had pounded her fists on the window of her car when her husband refused to go home and get the watch she had forgotten (they were on their way to work, and were already late). On another morning she screamed at him when he suggested she go out and buy bagels for breakfast.

Although Eleanor admitted she could control her outbursts at work, she insisted she was powerless to do so at home.

When she "let herself go" with the pounding sensation in her chest, an image of her father spontaneously developed.

"I see him kicking me down the stairs after an argument," she related. "We were always at odds. My two sisters were meek and obeyed him, but I rebelled against his domineering control. I tried to fight back and got physical abuse as a result. He still makes me furious. Not long ago I drove five hours to Cape Cod, where my parents have a house. As soon as I got there, I had a terrific fight with my father. I turned right around and drove home."

You can also begin to develop a greater awareness by beginning with a specific memory rather than a specific part of the body or a bodily sensation. For example, recall a very sad experience. Visualize it in as much detail as you can, and then notice your body's response. Repeat the experience with a happy memory and again observe what happens internally.

When I asked Catherine, a 45-year-old woman who came for help with her depression, to let herself go back to the day of her daughter's death ten years before, she was reluctant to do so. She had tried to shut off her feelings at the time, and had refused to talk about the drowning with anyone in the family. By beginning with visualization rather than discussion, she was finally able to face her feelings and complete the mourning process.

You will probably discover, as so many people do, that you can tune in your own feelings much more easily and directly by mental imagery than through intellectual analysis. Reorienting yourself to this approach takes practice, but you'll find it very helpful.

How Aware Are You?

To help you evaluate your awareness of your own feelings, circle the number that most closely describes your reaction to each of the following statements.

	Definitely True	Somewhat (Sometimes) True	Not True
1. I am aware of my feelings.	3	2	1
2. I can readily put my feelings into words.	3	2	1
3. I encourage those close to me to express their feelings.	3	2	1
4. I often awaken remembering a vivid dream.	3	2	1
5. When I feel a tightness in my chest or stomach, I know exactly what has caused it.	3	2	1

(continued)

How Aware Are You?—*continued*

	Definitely True	Somewhat (Sometimes) True	Not True
6. If a friend tells me how upset he (or she) is, I often feel tears come into my own eyes.	3	2	1
7. I cry when watching a sad movie.	3	2	1
8. If I think about a very sad experience in the past, I feel sad all over again.	3	2	1
9. If I relax and visualize myself at the beach or some other beautiful place, I can almost feel that I'm there.	3	2	1
10. I am very excitable.	3	2	1
11. I fall in love easily.	3	2	1
12. Even if I try, I can't conceal my feelings very well.	3	2	1
13. My friends consider me a sensitive person.	3	2	1
14. I enjoy reading poetry.	3	2	1
15. Beautiful music can evoke a strong emotional response in me.	3	2	1

If you are highly attuned to your own feelings, you probably scored between 40 and 45. If your score was under 30, you are quite out of touch and need to work on tuning in.

2
Recognizing Symptoms

Generally, if you have a symptom you know it.

You may not be aware of the underlying feelings, but you know you have a headache or a stomachache *at the time you have it.* However, you may never have stopped to consider how often you have the symptom, or what it may be telling you about your life and your relationships.

Everybody has a headache or a stomachache once in a while. And an aching back following severe back strain is not indicative of personal problems. It's when a symptom is recurrent that it may represent something more than a passing physical problem.

Among the most frequent bodily symptoms of stress are flushing, chest pain, headache, backache, stomach problems, fatigue, and insomnia. Feelings of panic, irritability, and unusual forgetfulness may also be indicative of stress. There are many others as well.

Whatever the symptom or pattern of symptoms, these reactions mean that your body is sending you a message. It is up to you to receive and interpret that message.

With a few obvious exceptions, such as insomnia and worry, your search for relief for these symptoms rarely begins at the psychological level. Your first stop—often the first of several similar stops—is your family doctor's office where you seek to combat your distress medically.

Many patients seen by physicians are actually suffering from problems that are psychogenic in origin. But the patients don't know that—nor, usually, do they want to. It's much more acceptable to have a *physical* problem than one that originates "in the head." And anyway, most of these problems clearly *are* physical.

Only after medical interventions have failed is your physician likely to recommend that you seek psychological or psychiatric help. And even then he or she may not; that depends on your physician's attitudes and beliefs.

Back in 1929, Walter Cannon presented convincing scientific evidence that the autonomic nervous system and the neuroendocrine systems affect the cardiovascular system in his book, *Bodily Changes in Pain, Hunger, Fear and Rage* (New York: Appleton-Century-Crofts, 1929). But the medical profession as a whole has been—as he predicted—reluctant to integrate this concept into medical practice.

As Cannon commented, "Although physicians have not infrequent occasions to observe instances of functional disturbance due to emotional causes, there is an inclination to minimize or to slight that influence, or even to deny that it is part of a physician's service to his patient to concern himself with such troubles."

Over 50 years and thousands of research studies later, the debate rages on. A June, 1985, editorial in the *New England Journal of Medicine* by Marcia Angell declared that "our belief in disease as a direct reflection of mental state is largely folklore."

"I'm not saying that there's no point in pursuing this research," Dr. Angell said in a follow-up interview. "But I'm saying the conclusions don't follow from the findings. I'm still waiting for proof that the way we think has a major clinical impact on the immune system. The studies so far are inadequate."

Dr. Angell's editorial generated an avalanche of mail, most of it critical. "The editorial was just bad science," said Barry Flint, director of the New York-based Institute for the Advancement of Health, a clearinghouse for research on the relationship between the mind and disease. "It ignores the thousands of studies showing connections between mental factors and disease."

Norman Cousins, whose bestselling books on the mind-disease link have popularized the idea that positive attitudes can restore health, and Barrie Cassileth, the University of Pennsylvania sociologist whose study of advanced cancer patients triggered the editorial, issued a joint statement declaring: "Few things are more important in the case of seriously ill patients than their mental state. . . . Even so, patients should not be encouraged to believe that positive attitudes are a substitute for competent medical attention."

Jerome L. Singer, a Yale professor and one of several psychologists issuing an American Psychological Association resolution denouncing Dr. Angell's article, said, "No one argues that you can get cancer just because you're feeling depressed, or hypertension just by being hostile. . . . But emotions clearly contribute to the onset and course of the disease; it's dead wrong to call it folklore."

If the medical profession itself is so uncertain, is it any wonder that so many other people are confused? It's hard to know *what* to believe. So, often when a recommendation for psychiatric help is made, the patient refuses to act on it.

"My doctor told me two years ago I should see a psychologist to get some help with my ulcers," a patient told me earlier this week. "But I didn't."

If someone other than your physician suggests you get help for a psychosomatic symptom (from a psychologist), you may be even more resistant. It isn't easy to hear that a friend or family member thinks you have a psychiatric problem. Even the most tactful suggestion is likely to come across as an insult.

Why are we so reluctant to believe that our physical ailments may be related to our emotions and to our interactions with others?

Many of us are willing to accept that connection where *other* people are concerned. It is important for you to realize that this concept applies to you as well if you are to understand your own symptoms and overcome them.

The particular symptom you exhibit most often may have a genetic component; most things do. If your mother had tension headaches or migraine headaches and you also have them, this does not mean that psychological factors are not involved. The development of almost any symptom or illness is a complex issue entailing genetic factors, environmental factors, viral factors, and emotional factors.

For the moment, let's zero in on your particular symptom. Ask yourself when you first experienced it and what associations it has for you. The bridge technique described in the preceding chapter may be helpful. Let your symptom lead you spontaneously to its own associations.

Sometimes your unconscious mind will provide you with a language association: "He's a pain in the neck"; "She makes me sick at my stomach"; "He's giving me the cold shoulder"; "I can't swallow my pride any longer"; "He goes for the jugular." If such an association comes to you, follow it, and you may discover who or what is making your blood boil or your spirits sink.

Brainstorming is one technique for evaluating your reaction to stress. This simply means listing or recording (on a tape recorder) all the signs of stress you can recall during the past week, and write or record everything you associate with each experience. Let the words and thoughts come freely—don't worry about editing.

When brainstorming, set a timer for 15 or 20 minutes and begin writing or talking. Don't stop until the timer tells you to. Your initial associations will lead you on to further ideas that may suggest a pattern to your reactions.

What Else Was Happening in Your Life?

Think back to your last major illness, whatever its nature, or the last time you had a bad cold or a worse-than-usual backache.

What else was happening in your life at about that time? I find that patients are often surprised by that question, yet it is remarkable how often they report that a major emotional trauma occurred within weeks or months of the illness.

Elaine, a woman in her fifties with a history of severe anxiety and high blood pressure, recently told me about a weekend trip with her husband to their vacation home. They owned several houses in the same town, a resort where Tom had spent his summers as a child, and to oversee this rental property he stopped by frequently when traveling on business.

"I had often felt angry and hurt because Tom talked so much about how good looking and talented Jeannine, the tenant, was and how much she had accomplished." On this particular trip, Elaine overheard Tom and Jeannine talking shortly after their arrival at 10 P.M. on a Friday night, and deduced from their conversation that the two were having an affair.

She reacted with shock and disbelief. In 25 years of marriage, she had never doubted Tom's faithfulness and had assumed they would live out their lives together.

"I became so sick I couldn't function," she recalls. "I felt so dizzy I could barely stand up; it was as if I was literally surrounded by a fog. It was all I could do to concentrate on the simplest conversation. I'd planned to drive to Pennsylvania the next day to see our daughter, but it was out of the question. I knew I'd have an accident."

Within two weeks, Elaine developed an acute stomach problem that was diagnosed as diverticulitis and continued to disturb her for the next several months, during which time her husband announced his intention to get a divorce.

Leah, 25, had suffered for seven years from ventricular tachycardia: "I woke up one morning when I was 18. My face was black and blue, I was nauseated and felt I couldn't breathe. I called my mother and said I wanted to go to the hospital. An hour later, eight doctors were standing around me. They told my mother I had less than two years to live."

Less than two months before this episode—which was followed by nine months of hospitalization—Leah had been told by her high school that she could not graduate with her class. At about the same time, the boy with whom she'd gone steady for three years had broken off with her. "He was my first love," she said. "I still think of him every day."

Episodes of chronic illness, as well as onset, are also frequently related to stressful life events. Myra was diagnosed as having rheumatoid arthritis during her sophomore year in high school, but after several years of treatment the illness went into remission. It became worse again when she obtained a major new client for her advertising agency, which would put her earnings into six figures.

"Suddenly I felt very uneasy," she said. "I was asking myself what I'd done to deserve all this success, and couldn't come up with the answer. I felt I should move into an apartment of my own and was afraid to do it—I was comfortable living with my family. Within two weeks of getting the new client, I began to experience a lot of pain again. My last flare-up occurred following the breakup of a long-term relationship. On both occasions I felt very alone."

Ginny, a bulimic, had learned to control her episodes of binging and vomiting for months at a time. She consulted me when this problem once again had assumed frightening proportions.

"Almost everything else in my life is going well," she said. "I've received another big promotion and have enough money saved up to buy a condominium. The problem is that I frequently work at home now, instead of going into the office. Things start off all right, but if I'm feeling the least bit lonely or down I find I'm right back into my old habit of binging and vomiting."

A few years previously, Ginny was divorced after a brief and unhappy marriage, and her bulimia had been bad in the first months immediately following the divorce. Now it was back again.

"I broke up with that doctor I told you about the last time I was here," she said. "He was so inconsiderate I couldn't put up with him any longer. I was the one who broke things off. But the next day I stayed home to work and felt miserable. I went out and bought food for the express purpose of binging, and then I had to make myself sick to get rid of it. That was two weeks ago and I've been doing it almost every day. I want to stop."

Your symptom may not take the form of a physical symptom at all. Perhaps it is just a sense of being "down" or feeling tense or anxious. While these emotions may sometimes result from internal causes, especially in women (due to hormonal changes associated with the menstrual cycle, pregnancy, or the menopause), most often they are related to some stressful event.

Patients often tell me they don't know *why* they feel depressed. Nothing special has happened, they say—initially. Almost always, though, a thoughtful discussion will unearth some trigger: a dispute with a friend, a critical remark from a spouse, failure to defend one's self-esteem.

Feelings of anxiety are perhaps even more common. We all know about the anxiety we feel before an important examination, before a public speech or performance, before a job interview, or before getting married.

These anxieties are normal, up to a point.

But what about the anxiety you feel before your mother-in-law comes over for dinner, when you confront your boss about a long-overdue raise, or tell your best friend you don't want to answer a question he or she has just asked you? Should you continue to feel these anxieties, or is there something you can do about them?

Yes, there *is* something you can do. But before you can do anything, you must identify the problem. On the list below, check any symptom or symptoms that you often experience.

Excessive worry	Diarrhea
Feeling "blue"	Abdominal cramps
Concentration difficulties	Constipation
Unusual memory problems	Headache
Feelings of panic	Backache
Obsessions about illness or death	Excessive perspiration
	Blushing
Fatigue	Dry mouth
Irritability	Shakiness
Difficulty falling asleep	Breathlessness
Early or frequent waking	Dizziness or faintness
Loss of appetite	Chest pain
Vomiting	Heart palpitations

Start now to observe that symptom or symptoms more closely to determine exactly when it or they occur. I'll be giving more detailed suggestions for your self-observation in Chapter 4.

3
Identifying Problem Behavior Patterns

Sometimes the indication that something is wrong in your life or in an important relationship isn't a symptom or an illness, or even an emotional state such as depression or anxiety. Perhaps it is an unhealthy or undesirable behavior pattern that you (or someone else) recognize as unhealthy or undesirable.

"That's just the way I am," a patient may say in describing a problem behavior. "And there doesn't seem to be anything I can do about it."

But there is. I always ask such patients to reframe their thinking about the behavior. Saying "I haven't been able to control it in the past" or "until now I haven't found any way of stopping it" sets the stage for change by allowing the possibility that the future can be different from the past.

If you *want* to change a behavior pattern, you can do so.

Jessie's problem was her temper outbursts. She justified them by saying that she came from a family of yellers. Her mother, whom Jessie admittedly didn't like very well, had been a lifelong model for the kind of behavior Jessie was displaying. Her father, a physician, absented himself from home much of the time and turned a deaf ear when circumstances forced him to be in his wife's company for extended periods of time.

But Jessie's husband didn't want that kind of marriage. Frank loved Jessie but declared that unless she stopped screaming at him he would divorce her. Jessie couldn't understand why he felt so upset and hurt after one of her attacks.

"When it's over I forget it," she declared. "I don't know why Frank can't do the same."

Jessie became enraged when Frank was slow getting organized in the morning, and screamed at their daughter when she didn't get ready for school on time.

"You're a loser! No wonder you're not earning more money!" she might say to her husband, or "You must have been sent here just to make my life miserable!" to her daughter. Later she'd say that, of course, she hadn't meant it—she'd just lost her temper.

Interestingly enough, Jessie had never lost control at work or with any of her friends, which proved to me that she *could* remain in charge of her behavior when necessary. When it became apparent that her husband no longer would put up with her the way she was, Jessie came for help in changing her behavior. And she did change it.

Clarissa drank too much. It wasn't an everyday occurrence, but she would escape into alcohol if she wanted to blot out an argument with her husband or mother, or assuage her conviction that she "couldn't cope" with her children. For years she had complained that her mother was an alcoholic, but until she smashed up her car in an accident she refused to admit her own problem.

Clarissa preferred to think of her drinking as a "disease" and questioned me carefully on her first visit to make sure that I agreed with her. She had already left several therapists who had attempted to get her to take responsibility for her drinking; it was more convenient for her to maintain the "disease" concept. "Even if the tendency to drink is a disease," I said, "do you really believe it is impossible to alter the way you act upon that tendency?"

Eventually she did alter it. But first she had to accept the concept that her behavior could be changed and that she herself would have to do it—with help.

Charley's response to stress was to smoke even more heavily than usual. A pack-a-day smoker most of the time, he could smoke over two packs when things weren't going well with his wife. That only increased his marital problems since the smoke bothered his wife so much.

Periodically Charley stopped smoking, but only for a few days. Not smoking made him cranky, his wife would complain about his bad mood, and after a confrontation with her he would rush out to the corner store for a pack of cigarettes.

Two heart attacks and stern warnings from his doctor had not been enough to convince Charley to quit smoking, and the more his wife nagged him about it, the less motivated he was to stop. It seemed clear to me that Charley did not want to stop smoking, but was using tobacco as a way—perhaps a slow one—out of a difficult marriage and an increasingly precarious financial situation.

At his wife's insistence, Charley came to me for hypnosis to stop smoking. But he did not want to stop, so he was not successful.

Betty did stop after only one session of hypnosis, as most of my motivated (and hypnotizable) patients do. She succeeded because stopping was her own decision.

When she came she listed all the reasons why she wanted to stop, which I ask all nonsmoking candidates to do:

"I don't have the energy I'd like to have, and I feel the effects of cigarettes in my chest. Smoking is interfering with my ability to exercise. I'd like to be able to run again. When I do aerobics, I get out of breath very quickly. In the morning I wake up feeling congested. Smoking wastes a lot of time when I could be doing something better. And I don't *like* the habit of smoking any more. I want to be free of it. Most of all, I hate lying about it. My husband thinks I stopped five years ago—but the minute he walks out the door, I light a cigarette."

Mel's reasons were different—but they were *his* reasons, and he also was successful in stopping.

"These things are killing me," he said. "I know what they're doing to me. I'm wheezing and I'm nervous and jittery. I feel lousy. I have such bad pains in my chest that I've been to the doctor about it. I feel better if I avoid smoking even for six to eight hours. Even my sense of smell and taste has been affected. At times I have difficulty speaking clearly, and I'm convinced that even that is a result of my smoking. With all this, wouldn't you think I'd be able to quit on my own? It's just crazy to continue a habit that makes you feel so rotten. But every time I feel the least bit nervous, I light up—even though I know that in the end smoking will make me more jittery. These things are controlling my life, and I'm sick of it."

Wilma's response to stress was to escape into sleep. When pressures mounted, so did her need for sleep. She would even fall asleep in exams if she felt unable to perform up to her level of expectations. "I don't want to be here," she would say to herself, and promptly fall asleep.

The same thing happened when she was studying. Hours later she'd awaken feeling guilty, knowing that once again she would arrive unprepared for class. She slept in response to personal problems as well.

"I've had a terrible week with Ivan," she said one day. "We were together over the weekend and fought a lot. After he went back to school, I slept all day, missing my classes. I wasn't that tired. I just didn't want to face up to the fact that this relationship isn't going well."

George tuned out too, but not all the way. Closing his eyes, he would enter easily into a hypnotic state that observers (and even George at first) mistook for sleep. He could awaken easily if challenged, and frequently did so. His professors, and later his legal colleagues and clients, were astounded by his ability to open his eyes and respond to a question in such a way that it was obvious he'd been listening intently.

Since George had such a keen mind, his peculiar habit didn't get him into trouble as far as his work was concerned. Personally, it was another matter. His wife was infuriated by his passive, sleepy countenance and by the fact that he could tune her in and out at will.

Since Amanda's mother had been a poor housekeeper, it wasn't surprising that Amanda was too. She was simply keeping house the way she thought everyone did. Her housekeeping habits became a problem when she married Jed, who came from a background where everything was scrupulously neat. Cat hairs, dirty dishes, dust, and general clutter drove him crazy.

For a while he tried to cope with the problem by straightening up himself. He didn't mind doing his part, but eventually he grew to resent doing what he saw as Amanda's share.

For Amanda's part, she found Jed's constant complaints irritating, but as time went on she also became critical of herself. She recognized the fact that, trivial as it had seemed at first, their divergent attitudes toward housekeeping could easily wreck the relationship if she could not tighten up her casual approach to housekeeping.

When Dotty was in high school, she and her best friend Toni had developed the habit of talking a kind of silly baby talk to each other. It was harmless, but other people found it irritating. For Dotty and Toni, it was a unique form of communication that they both enjoyed.

Later, though, after graduating from college and beginning a career in banking, Dotty discovered to her horror that occasionally, without realizing it, she lapsed back into this juvenile habit. She knew that she had to eliminate it and immediately set about doing so.

Dale was consistently late for appointments. The product of an overly punctual family who arrived at the airport hours before flight time, he had originally used lateness as a form of rebellion. But eventually, like most problem behaviors, his tardiness became self-perpetuating.

Like Dotty, Dale discovered when he began a career in business that his old habit was getting in his way. He knew it was time to put it behind him, but it had become so deeply ingrained that he needed help in overcoming it.

Problem Habits Checklist

Do you, too, have problem habits you'd like to eliminate? Use the following checklist to help you take stock.

Yes   No

1. I often regret expressing my temper the way I do.
2. I'm known as bad-tempered.
3. I drink more than I should.
4. I smoke too much.
5. Sometimes I go on eating binges.
6. I use sleep as an escape.
7. I'm consistently late.
8. People I live with often complain about my messiness.
9. I procrastinate a lot.
10. I do more than my share of complaining.
11. Other _____

4
Spotting Nervous Habits

Sometimes tension is manifested by nervous habits such as nail biting, hair pulling, stuttering, or nervous tics. These mannerisms usually arise initially as a response to stress, but soon become habitual. However, most people who have them find that they are more pronounced during periods of increased tension.

Billy, 15, was brought to me by his parents for treatment of his nervous tics, which variously had taken the form of foot tapping, blinking, and now head jerking. Characteristically, the parents were much more concerned about the problem than Billy. They had already tried family therapy with a counselor who concluded that there was no family problem, and referred Billy for hypnosis.

Yet it soon became apparent that Billy's tics occurred most often when he was alone in a room with his father, a perfectionist who demanded excellence from Billy and viewed his tics as a glaring imperfection and an embarrassment to the family. Understandably, Billy was afraid to display the tics in his father's presence—and consequently he almost always did.

Jud, a 70-year-old physician, presented an unusual behavioral complaint: he continually "sharpened his tongue" (his wife called it "wiggling your mouth") by rolling it around in his mouth. He described the behavior as symbolically sharpening his words before speaking.

"I'm exhausted from the mental effort of doing it and at the same time trying not to do it," he declared. "Somehow I seem to need my tongue to push my thoughts."

When I asked him to describe the behavior more exactly, he said, "I begin by moving my tongue slightly as if exploring the inside of my mouth. Then I begin to move it more actively until I am pushing and twisting it against the roof of my mouth just as you might sharpen a pencil by rubbing the side of the lead against a piece of paper."

On further consideration, he remembered being aware of "a tingling feeling in my fingers when I begin to get irritated. I usually touch my belt with that finger and about the same time I begin sharpening my tongue."

"Relaxing puts a mental pressure on me," he added, explaining that he now wanted to gradually give up his practice and travel more. "I have to put brakes on my mind and that makes me nervous."

He described his wife as exceptionally pleasant and congenial, but a "boring talker." He categorized his entire family, including his children, as "not very stimulating. They all discuss trivial matters endlessly," he said. "It's so tiresome to listen to that I either fall asleep or go off on my own thoughts and start sharpening my tongue. My wife doesn't like either habit and I don't know what to do about it."

Although he professed strong love for his wife, her empty conversation annoyed him constantly. He often found himself polishing (with his tongue, but silently, of course) the comments he would make to her if he didn't mind hurting her feelings.

"At times I feel considerable thought pressure in my head," he said, "as if the thoughts are lined up in a row someplace. Pressing my tongue against that row of thoughts seems to help me in my search for a more perfect expression. But, of course, as far as my wife is concerned, I never say what is on my mind."

"I Just Have to Pull My Hair"

"I have three habits I'd like to get rid of," a college girl told me recently. "I smoke too much, I bite my nails, and I pull my hair out. Right now I've decided that the one I just can't live with any longer is pulling my hair out. I've been laughed at and teased because of it; I go to any extent to conceal it; and yet I keep doing it. You can't tell how bad it is, because I never go out of the house without using an eyebrow pencil. If I forget, I have to stop myself and go back. A few weeks ago I was completely eyelash-less.

"If my eyebrows are uneven, I have to pluck them to even them out," she continued. "And when I have a little stubby eyelash growing in, I just *have* to pull it out. Of course, if I didn't put my hand up there in the first place, I wouldn't know I had a little stubby hair."

Rona had been plucking hair—eyelashes, eyebrows, and sometimes a spot on her scalp—for almost as long as she could remember.

"My father looked at me one day when I was in the sixth grade and noticed I didn't have any eyelashes," she commented. "I've already been the shrink route, but it didn't help, at least not with my eyelashes. I hate myself for doing this, and yet I can't seem to stop."

Like most hair pullers and nail biters, Rona indulged most in her habit when she was nervous or bored. "If I'm reading a book or if I'm watching TV I'm almost sure to do it," she said. "I've learned how to hold my hand over my eye in a certain way so I can do it even if I'm watching TV with other people, and they don't notice. Or at least I tell myself they don't.

"One place I never do it is in class, though," she said. "Once in math class I heard a guy behind me describing how he'd seen somebody else do it. And I thought 'Yuk!' What if he'd seen *me*? I never do it when I'm with my boyfriend—and I don't think he knows about it. Some of my friends do, and try to help me by telling me to stop. Others pretend they don't notice. I'm so sick of this habit that I've just *got* to stop. I want to feel like I'm in control of myself."

Almost everyone who suffers from a nervous habit like hair pulling or nail biting finds it a source of embarrassment. They may avoid situations where it is difficult to conceal the habit and avoid people who might be likely to point it out.

The first step in overcoming a nervous habit is to develop a keen awareness of the exact pattern in which it occurs, and discover what sets it in motion. If you have a nervous habit, begin now to think about how you would describe it to someone who had never met you. I'll be giving more detailed suggestions for doing so in the following chapter.

5
Charting Your Course

The first thing you must do to overcome a symptom or a problem behavior is to recognize the fact that you have it.

The next is to chart its course. You must become aware of the exact context, interpersonal or otherwise, in which the symptom or behavior occurs. Only then can you eliminate it or change it into an acceptable form.

Often it is instructive simply to *describe* the symptom. If the symptom is a hay fever attack, for example, what is the very first indication to you that it is on the way? Usually you don't go from apparent good health to a violent sneezing attack; there is some preliminary signal of which you may not even be aware until you begin to tune it in.

Perhaps it is an itchy sensation in your nose, a dry feeling in your throat, or an anticipatory cough. Or it may be a thought that says apprehensively, "What if I get another attack of hay fever?" In some cases it is actually the thought that brings on the attack. Or it may be your entrance into a particular room or building where you have experienced hay fever attacks in the past—a Pavlovian conditioned response.

If you happen to suffer from classical migraine headaches, you are no doubt aware of the aura you experience in advance of the actual attack. While the constellation of symptoms, and the intensity and duration of the attack itself, may vary dramatically in an individual's experience, the visual hallucinatory experiences that signify the onset tend to be relatively constant.

Richly detailed accounts of migraine auras have been recorded by many sufferers, partly because the migraine aura provides material for the kind of dramatic detail that may be lacking in the onset of other disturbances. But the more detailed and careful your observations of your inner state as well as of your physical behavior, the more accurate an account you can produce—and the more helpful it will be to you.

"I Might Have a Panic Attack!"

A panic attack, characteristic of those experienced by most agoraphobic patients, was identified by one sufferer as beginning "the moment I think that I *might* have a panic attack.

"I could be feeling perfectly fine," she said, "not being upset about anything emotionally, being in excellent physical health and actually enjoying what I am doing, when suddenly, for no reason, the thought comes into my mind, 'What if I should have a panic attack?' "

This particular patient was prone to have panic attacks whenever she was more than half an hour from home by herself. Her first move would be to telephone her attorney husband and ask him to come and get her, which he invariably did.

"The very thought that I *might* have a panic attack is enough to drive me into a frenzy," she continued. "I begin to think to myself, 'my heart is beating faster already.' I don't know whether it is or not at that point, but I know that I am afraid it will. Then I say, 'and my hands are beginning to feel very cold.' I try to stiffen up and fight it off, but the more I fight, the stronger my symptoms become. Soon I feel dizzy and lightheaded, as if I might faint, my heart is pounding, and I feel I can't catch my breath. I feel that something terrible is about to happen—I don't know what.

"Simultaneously I want to ask someone for help and at the same time I don't want anybody to know that something is wrong with me. If I am standing up, I have to hold onto a wall or a table to keep from falling down. My knees feel as if they are shaking and by this time I am gasping for breath. I feel sure I'm going to make a fool of myself in some way—I don't know exactly how. I'm desperately trying to look as if everything is all right, yet I'm inwardly terrified. I feel rooted to the ground, but somehow I always make it to a telephone to call Jim. As soon as he promises to come and get me I begin to feel better, and when he finally gets there I am fine."

"What if I Blush?"

Francesca, whose problem was excessive blushing, described the onset in much the same way—as a mental process that triggered off the actual event of blushing.

"It's happened to me so many times when I am talking to a woman who is about my mother's age, or one who reminds me of my mother in some way, even if I only observe that she has especially good taste or that she wears a similar kind of glasses. I think to myself, 'What if I blush?'

"It doesn't *always* happen. In a brief conversational encounter I may feel perfectly fine, and the idea of blushing may not occur to me. It's when the other person is especially friendly or nice, or has initiated the conversation, that I am most likely to get into trouble. As soon as I feel that someone likes me and is beginning to accept me, it's as if I mistrust their motives. I think, 'they can't really like me,' and the next thought I get, irrationally I know, is 'if I blush they'll know how silly I am and they won't want to have anything to do with me.' And before you know it I feel myself blushing."

When I first asked Jan to describe the habit of hair pulling for which she sought help, she initially said that she simply pulled out hairs when she felt nervous, but was becoming concerned because she was developing a bald spot that she had to hide by combing her hair in a certain way. She was obviously embarrassed by talking about her problem—not surprising, since she had never revealed it to anyone before. Even her parents didn't know. She refused to show me the spot, declaring, "Oh, I *couldn't*."

Eventually, with some thought, she was able to relate her habit pattern in detail. It occurred only when she was alone or felt certain she was not being observed, but it frequently followed a stressful interaction with her mother or her boyfriend.

She would begin by pushing a stray hair back into place, sometimes deliberately shaking her head forward so there would be a need to push the hair back. Then she would smooth it with the palm of her left hand before grasping several hairs together and twisting them in her left hand. Slowly she would extract a single hair while focusing her awareness on the pain—which she experienced as pleasant. Finally she would put the hair in her mouth and keep it there until replacing it with another and repeating the sequence from the beginning.

Flora's complaint was nail biting, a habit she had had for over 20 years when she consulted me. Like most nail biters, Flora led up to the actual event by moving her hand up to touch her face and gradually letting it "meander" toward her mouth. She then rubbed her lips with her hand and softly stroked her teeth with the end of a finger, perhaps pausing to bite a roughened cuticle before biting the nail itself.

"Mirror, Mirror on the Wall"

Often these preliminary movements are so completely automatic—like riding a bicycle or driving a car—that you may not be aware of the sequence. If your symptom is a motor activity like eye blinking, tongue rolling, nail biting, hair pulling, or some variety of nervous tic, one method you can use to heighten your awareness is to watch yourself in the mirror while you deliberately perform the activity.

Observe carefully exactly what you do, and as you watch describe your actions aloud in detail: "First I let my hand wander up to my face, then to my hair. I pull the hair back with my left hand. Then I take a small clump of hair and roll it around between my fingers. I choose one and slowly pull it out. Then I put it in my mouth and chew it while I start again with the wandering hand. I don't like the way this looks. It's disgusting!"

Try viewing your sequence in terms of a Woody Allen movie such as *Annie Hall*. You may remember that in this film the characters were acting and talking to one another while simultaneously thinking other thoughts that appeared as captions on the screen. If you haven't been a careful observer of your own mental processes, you may not realize that it's not unusual to be saying one thing and thinking something else—possibly the opposite. In your visualization, try to recapture the unspoken thoughts as well as the words.

Writing the Script

Now write the scenario, with the goal of making your description of the action so vivid and so detailed that the reader can visualize it exactly as it occurs. Include such details as the time of day, the length of time involved in the sequence, and the presence or absence of supporting actors. If sound effects are relevant, describe them as well. And, parenthetically, include the unspoken thoughts.

Be very specific, photographically so, in your description. Include everything you can remember even if you don't consider it important. If the problem was an eating binge, list the items eaten and the order. State whether they were eaten sitting down or standing up, how many trips to the refrigerator or cabinet were involved, and what thoughts, feelings, or actions (your own or anyone else's) preceded, accompanied, and followed the actual event.

An overweight but underassertive young attorney told me, "I ate two doughnuts yesterday because my boss spoke to me in a nasty way. He came into my office and literally exploded about something he felt I hadn't done exactly right. While he was talking to me, he wasn't even looking me in the eye. I felt he was looking at me like I had dandruff all over my jacket. I couldn't believe he was making me feel so crummy.

And do you know, I didn't say a word? But I thought to myself, 'I'd like to kill him.' Instead, I went out to a bakery and ate two doughnuts."

Only by putting a symptom or behavior into context can it be looked at, understood, and overcome.

Often it is not until I've asked many specific questions that I get an accurate picture of a patient's complaint. In describing your own behavior, you must ask yourself just as many—or more.

An adequate description is a beginning, but only a beginning. The next step is to determine exactly when the symptom or behavior occurs so it can be related to its cause. If you have been able to recapture your thoughts as well as your actions in reexperiencing an episode of your symptom, you may have made these connections already. But often they are not that apparent.

Frame It in Time

Put the problem into a time frame. Is there any time of day when the problem is certain *not* to occur, or any time of day when it *always* occurs?

A hairdresser complaining of shaking hands told me that her symptom never bothers her if she is at home alone with her husband, but that she begins to be aware of it when she is dressing for work in the morning, and that it is a problem (in varying degrees) every day while she is at work.

"And," she added, "if my boss comes in and watches me work, forget it!"

Walt, who weighed 265 pounds when he came for hypnotherapy, said he was never tempted to overeat during the day, that he ate a normal breakfast and a normal lunch, but always ate seconds at dinner and continued to eat steadily until bedtime, while watching television.

Lou never smoked at home—in fact, he did not even keep cigarettes at home—but lit one up as soon as he arrived at the automobile showroom where he worked as a salesman, and smoked steadily all day.

Ellie's displays of temper occurred only at home, most frequently around 11:00 P.M. Her husband, an overbearing and critical person, was equally annoying in the morning, but she never lost control of herself before 10:30 P.M. I had listened to several of her accounts before I discovered the trigger.

"I blew up at Ed again last night, " she announced. "It just makes me furious when he puts on such a superficial display of his religion! A truly religious person doesn't abuse his wife emotionally like he does and then act so pious. The sight of him down on his knees praying absolutely drives me wild!"

Keep a Stress Record

Keeping an accurate record of your stress reactions for several weeks will help to define the problem. When I ask patients to do this they often resist initially, whether the task is to keep a food intake record, to chart their daily feelings of anxiety, or to complete a "sleep log" every morning when they wake up.

Keeping records is time-consuming, but illuminating. Insomniacs, for example, may find that they are sleeping much more than they thought, or that their insomnia occurs only on Sunday nights when they are suffering the pangs of reentry into school or office.

Once the idea of recordkeeping is accepted, it becomes an interesting exercise in self-discovery. You may enjoy acting as a careful observer of the most important person in your life—yourself. At least once a day I hear a patient say, "I've been thinking a lot since our last conversation, and I've discovered that. . . ."

I provide my patients with prepared record forms for some of the more common problems, which are reproduced at the end of this chapter. You can modify one of these forms for your own use, or simply carry a pocket-sized notebook and use a page for each entry. Your notations should include:

- Date and time.
- Events prior to symptom.
- Symptom or behavior.
- Duration.
- Circumstances (where, who was present, what else you or person with you was doing).
- Events immediately following symptom or behavior.

If the problem you are charting is a frequently or constantly occurring habit, such as a nervous tic, you should keep your record in the form of a tally indicating the number and/or duration of occurrences. For this type of record I recommend the "Week at a Glance" type of pocket appointment calendar, which has 15-minute intervals indicated for each day. Simply make a vertical slash for each occurrence, connecting each four lines with a diagonal as the fifth, to make your tally easier.

When there is a noticeable rise in occurrences, be sure to note where you were, what you were doing, whom you were with, and what preceded and followed the increase. It may be necessary to enter these descriptions in a separate notebook, or you can devise a single daily form large enough to accommodate your entries.

After keeping your record for a few days or weeks, you may spontaneously see a pattern of cause and effect. It may be as simple as noting that every time you talk to your Aunt Agatha on the telephone, you develop a splitting headache. Or you may discover that your back acts up when your husband comes in from a business trip.

Or you may still feel that there is no rhyme or reason to your complaint.

I assure you, however, that there is. If you persist with your observations, your free associations, and your recordkeeping, you will find those connections. And I'm willing to bet that when you do, you'll find that a relationship with someone else is involved—or possibly the lack of one—and that it may very well be the principal factor in your distress.

Sample Daily Headache Record

NOTE: Rate intensity on a scale of 1 to 10, 10 being the most intense.

Day of week ———————   Date————————

Time		Inten-sity	Medica-tion Taken	Loca-tion of Pain	Events Pre-ceding	Events During	Events Follow-ing
Start	*End*						

Sample Daily Sleep Log
(for Insomnia)

Night of week _____ Date _____ Total hours of sleep _____

Activity before Retiring	Time of Retiring	Minutes to Fall Asleep	Awakenings	Medication	Time of Arising	Scheduled Events for Next Day

Sample Daily Anxiety Log

Day of week _____ Date _____

Rate your level of anxiety on a scale of 0 to 100, 100 being the highest, for each hour of your waking day, and graph by connecting points at end of the day. Note events preceding, during, and immediately following peak anxiety.

6A.M. 7 8 9 10 11 12 1P.M. 2 3 4 5 6 7 8 9 10 11 12-6A.M.

100
90
80
70
60
50
40
30
20
10
0

Sample Daily Food Record

Regard this record as your "license to eat" and carry it with you at all times. Enter each item immediately after eating it. For "M," enter first letter of your mood. For "H," rate hunger on a scale of 0 to 5, 5 being hungriest. When binge eating occurs, describe events before, during, and after.

Day of week _____   Date_____

	Time Start	Time End	Place	Physical Position	Alone or with whom	Associated Activity	Food and Calories Amount	M./H.
6–11 A.M.								
11 A.M.–4 P.M.								
4–9 P.M.								
9 P.M.–6 A.M.								

Binge behavior: Events preceding_____

During_____

Following_____

6
Is Your Network Working?

You know you need friends.

But it isn't enough to surround yourself with a group of acquaintances who may or may not be there when a crisis occurs. You need people you can really count on. As we all know, "fair weather friends" won't stick around when the going gets rough.

The loss of friends following a divorce is a shock to almost everyone who experiences it, yet this is understandable in terms of divided loyalties and the implied threat often felt to one's own intact marriage when close friends separate. It's less understandable when friends fail to stand by a widow or widower, or someone who has been stricken with a serious illness or family tragedy—but it happens. And it happens more often than most of us would like to think.

"My friends were there for a few weeks after Tim's death," a patient told me, "and then they conveniently disappeared. It was as if they'd forgotten I existed. Maybe they just didn't know what to say. Maybe they couldn't adjust to me as only half of what used to be a couple—not the better half, apparently.

"I don't think the couples' world has any place for singles," this woman continued. "I had to find a whole new support system of single friends. It wasn't easy. The experience of losing my friends was almost as devastating as losing my husband. We'd had an active social life for years—and suddenly everything was gone all at once. One of those women we used to see became a widow recently—that's when I heard from her again. I tried to be helpful, but I can't help remembering that she wasn't there when I needed her."

Perhaps one moral to be learned from the story is that your support system should include some single people, even if you are happily—and, you hope, permanently—married. You should actively pursue some interests of your own with compatible friends no matter how happy you are with your spouse. If your activities are all couples' activities, you may find yourself suddenly left out of events you've always taken for granted if you become only half a couple.

"Over ten years ago Tim and I initiated a Fourth of July picnic for our group of friends," this patient recalled. "It was such a success that it was repeated annually, at different homes. This year—you guessed it—I wasn't invited. I was shocked. It seemed so rude and so unfeeling. The following day I encountered an old acquaintance—I'll no longer call her a friend—at the supermarket and she had the nerve to tell me all about the party."

A formerly single person who marries, even one who has already been through the experience of losing married friends by becoming single, is just as likely to drop her single friends as the married are to withdraw from the newly divorced or widowed.

A divorced patient who has been working hard to establish a social network complained bitterly to me recently about a friend who was "no longer available. She has this man in her life now," Sally explained. "They're a twosome, so she has no time for me. She used to call me often and want to get together, and we had some good times. For a while after she met Edgar I tried to stay in touch with her, but I'm very hurt by her behavior. I feel there's nothing we have in common any more anyway—all she talks about is her relationship with Edgar. Maybe we *never* had anything in common.

"Occasionally she calls and wants to see me on a weeknight, when Edgar is working. But that's not convenient for me. I have to get a babysitter and rush back home, because I have to get up early for my teaching job in the morning. I need friends to do things with on weekends, but she's with Edgar then. The friendship just isn't working any more, if it ever was working.

"Before all this happened I'd offered her a rug she liked which I didn't want any more. Now that she and Edgar are moving into a new apartment together, she wants the rug. She called me up last week and asked me about it. I hesitated, but I really didn't feel like giving it to her at this point. And that's what I told her, though it wasn't easy for me to express my feelings so directly. She didn't give up gracefully. 'The friendship isn't working?' she asked. 'You mean I can't have the rug?'

"This experience has been very painful for me," Sally added emphatically. "I feel that if I ever do become part of a couple again, I won't drop my single friends. It's just so difficult and exhausting to change all your friends when you go from being a couple to a single. I don't like throwing out friends like old clothes and going out for a whole new wardrobe. But maybe that's the way it is."

Some connections, if they are strong enough, do survive. But most do not. "When I was divorced with a young child, living far away from my family, I found myself with no support system," Phyllis Diamond, a social worker, told me. "The married friends I'd had just weren't what I needed any more. They were all busy being couples—and I was busy trying to learn how to be a single again. I knew I had to find others who were in the same situation, so I asked around and located a few other single parents with children. I put an ad in the paper too. Twenty single parents showed up for the first meeting at my house, and we have become a very strong mutual support system. A few dropped out, of course, but others heard about us and wanted to join. My closest friends now are all single parents with children. On weekends we do things together, and we include the children."

Phyllis called her group "Kindred Spirits." Soon she found herself invited to appear on television and radio shows—she had struck a chord with wide appeal.

She now has groups in several cities, the membership is growing rapidly, and Phyllis is occupied full-time in administering the program. But the organization's goal remains the same: to provide a mutual support network for single parents and their children.

When illness, rather than divorce or death, strikes, friendships may also founder. Cancer patients, like the divorced or widowed, often find that friends and family retreat from them following the diagnosis and that they feel stigmatized and ostracized as a result.

Psychologist Camille Wortman of the University of Michigan stresses the need for cancer patients to develop friendships with similar patients in order to be able to learn first hand what they will experience: "They have a need to associate with people who not only have empathy with their situation, but can explain to them what may happen, to provide social comparison, and to assure them that their condition is not unique—others know and appreciate what is happening...; support, in order to be effective, must also be appropriately contingent on what patients say or do, rather than be unrelievedly buoyant."

Organizations such as Alcoholics Anonymous, Overeaters Anonymous, Candlelight (for parents of children with leukemia), Widowed Persons' Services, and groups for families of Alzheimer's patients all provide support from others in similar situations.

But some people, like Ilona, a cancer patient, manage to find ongoing support among their already established circles of friends. A highly gregarious person who loves to entertain, Ilona had been surrounded by friends for years and they continued to be there during her struggle with cancer. She had given generously of herself to many of these same friends in the past.

Her friends were not *all* supportive, though. "Doris isn't my friend any more," she declared emphatically the last time I saw her. "I have no desire ever to see her again. When her husband had a heart attack and she desperately needed emotional support as well as practical help for months, I was always there to provide it. But when I told her about my cancer she couldn't be bothered. She told me how her father had died of cancer—*that* was a big help—and then she vanished. I understand it was upsetting for her, and my illness reminded her of her father. But what about me? We'd been friends for 20 years."

Ilona was not ashamed to discuss her condition, but she recoiled from the idea of seeking out other cancer patients. Fortunately she didn't need to.

Many cancer patients lack close friends with whom they can discuss their illness. Yet they hesitate to publicly identify themselves as cancer patients by joining a cancer-specific group.

Psychologist Lillian Rubin, comparing the experience of two families when their children were stricken with a life-threatening illness, commented that one was abandoned by their friends while the other was surrounded by "a circle of support and nurturance that has been the mainstay of their lives in this nightmare." The more fortunate family had, prior to their tragedy, led "a life of commitment to the public welfare.

"In the process," Dr. Rubin writes, "they have gathered around them a community of friends . . . linked together by friendships that are rooted in a shared set of social, political, and personal values—deeply held beliefs out of which their commitments to others have grown."

The point is that the strongest friendships must go deeper than having a good time, participating in shared social activities, or perhaps even the exchange of mutual confidences. They must encompass lasting beliefs and values and a demonstrated willingness to give as well as to receive.

One powerful aspect of strong social supports is the feeling of being loved, cared for, and valued. When something happens to threaten self-esteem or make one feel unloved (such as rejection by a spouse or loss of a job), the reassurance of loving friends appears to be a major factor in maintaining equilibrium.

As Jerome Singer and Diana Lord put it in *Handbook of Psychology and Health* (Hillsdale, New Jersey: Lawrence Erlbaum Associates, 1984), "It rains on both the loved and the unloved. At least that is what conventional wisdom among the folk teaches us. Among the folk who work in health care, there is a corollary truism that although both the loved and the unloved are rained upon, it is the unloved who get sick from it."

Not All Support Is Positive

Sometimes the emotional support offered by family and friends is not positive. "The irony is that sometimes we are least able to help the people we care about most," according to James Coyne, a psychologist at the University of Michigan.

In a study of people whose spouses or children had died in traffic accidents, presented at the 1985 meeting of the American Psychological Association, many reported being upset or angry as a result of things said to them by well-intentioned friends and family members. They resented comments that dismissed the bereaved's true feelings or implied they shouldn't feel as bad as they did. In the unwelcome advice department, one woman mentioned a neighbor who suggested she take down the pictures of her dead son. Very pious or philosophical attitudes frequently annoyed and angered the recipients.

The most effective support, researchers found, came from simply listening and encouraging the expressions of feelings without advice or judgment.

People who are overly invested in a person's well-being, Dr. Coyne said, are especially susceptible to pitfalls that can make their effort to help a source of stress. For example, he reported, studies of couples in which the husband had experienced a heart attack found many wives' overprotectiveness to be a problem. Attempts to restrict the husband's activities were viewed as punitive and were deeply resented.

Well-meaning efforts to encourage stroke victims with a "you can do it" attitude may end up resulting in failures, and subsequent depression, if the tasks are beyond the patients' capacities, another study reported.

A commonly recurring problem among families and friends of seriously ill patients is that they repress their own frustrations and anger. But helpers have to take care of themselves too. That often means airing grievances and resentments to clear the air. Or it can mean getting some support for themselves.

Nathan Azrin and Gregory Nunn, authors of *Habit Control in a Day* (New York: Pocket Books, 1977), also point out that social support has its dark side.

They believe that one important reason a nervous habit may have persisted is that your friends and family have accepted it as beyond your control and have acted as though it didn't exist.

One facet of their habit control program is enlisting the support of friends and family by asking them to help you become aware of the problem through some prearranged signal. The ability to use social supports in this way obviously requires a willingness to discuss the problem openly and trust in friends' sincere desire to help.

I have found that some patients with habit problems are quite unwilling to take this step. Often they are fully convinced that no one has noticed their habit—even if it is perfectly obvious to the casual observer.

Twenty Questions

Perhaps you already have a good idea of how your own social network is working—and would work in times of crisis. If not, the following 20 questions may help. Circle the number of names (aside from spouse or lover) that come to mind in response to each question.

Social

1. Whom do I see, on a one-to-one basis, in an average month?　　0　1　2　3　4　5　5+

2. Whom do I have a personal telephone conversation with in an average month (over five minutes)?　　0　1　2　3　4　5　5+

3. Whom could I telephone if I felt lonely and wanted to go out for dinner or a movie?　　0　1　2　3　4　5　5+

4. Whom could I comfortably call just to talk?　　0　1　2　3　4　5　5+

5. Who would be likely to invite me to do something on a one-to-one basis?　　0　1　2　3　4　5　5+

(continued)

Twenty Questions—*continued*

Practical

6. If I suddenly became ill, whom could I call to take me to the hospital?   0   1   2   3   4   5   5+

7. If I needed a loan of $100 or more, whom could I ask?   0   1   2   3   4   5   5+

8. Whom could I count on to help me find a job if I suddenly lost mine?   0   1   2   3   4   5   5+

9. Who would lend me a car if I really needed it?   0   1   2   3   4   5   5+

10. If I desperately needed a place to stay, who would take me in?   0   1   2   3   4   5   5+

Emotional

11. If I were alone on a holiday, who would welcome me into their home?   0   1   2   3   4   5   5+

12. If my circumstances changed (married-single or the reverse), whom could I count on?   0   1   2   3   4   5   5+

13. If there were a death in my family, who would be there emotionally after the first few weeks had passed?   0   1   2   3   4   5   5+

14. If I were in the hospital for a serious illness, who would keep in close touch with me?   0   1   2   3   4   5   5+

15. If something awful happened to me—I was raped or arrested, for example—whom could I comfortably confide in?   0   1   2   3   4   5   5+

16. Can I trust anybody not to be critical or put me down?   0   1   2   3   4   5   5+

(continued)

Twenty Questions—*continued*

17. Who consistently gives me positive feedback and makes me feel liked and appreciated?   0   1   2   3   4   5   5+

18. Whom could I trust not to reveal anything I might tell them in confidence?   0   1   2   3   4   5   5+

19. Whom could I share an exciting accomplishment with without feeling egotistic?   0   1   2   3   4   5   5+

20. If I had to see a therapist for some reason, is there anybody I would tell?   0   1   2   3   4   5   5+

Socially, a score of 4 or 5 or more on each question is desirable. Practically, 3 or 4 is probably all you can reasonably expect. Emotionally, you're in good shape if you can count on 2 or 3 people—and not badly off if you have one you're really sure of.

7
Is Your Closeness a Comfort?

Is your marriage or relationship offering you the supportive warmth and protection that ideally it should provide?

Nothing is perfect, but in a satisfactory relationship there should be a sense of mutual support that is strongly felt by both partners.

For 30 years Elena had accompanied her husband, a successful physician, to medical conventions whenever he asked her to, willingly listened to his accounts of his day's work, and frequently entertained his colleagues with gourmet dinners. But although she was a highly accomplished artist and often received awards for her work, Julio refused to attend the openings of any of her shows. He considered them "boring"; he'd left the one event he attended, where she won a major prize, before the presentation of awards.

Elena accepted his attitude uncomplainingly on the grounds that his financial success allowed her to pursue her own not very profitable, though highly rewarding, career. "He doesn't mind my being an artist," she commented humbly. "I have to be grateful for that." Actually, Elena's career suited Julio perfectly. He wanted her to be dependent on him and to be free to adapt herself to his schedule, and she was. But her migraine headaches were beginning to interfere with her ability to travel.

"I don't feel Howie really listens to me," Melinda, a young woman involved in a long-time relationship with a professional colleague, told me. "I keep feeling that he's not that interested in me or my problems. If it's *his* problems we're talking about, he expects my undivided attention. If it's *our* problem, he's relatively interested. But when I need help with *my* problem, Howie just isn't there. I'm getting sick of the one-sidedness of our relationship."

And she literally was: at the time she consulted me, her occasional bouts of lethargy and depression were occurring more regularly and seemed more severe.

"Howie's a writer, and I've been very supportive when he's had deadlines to meet or revisions to do," she continued. "My support is just taken for granted. But when *I* need support, it's too bad. Last year I got a contract to write a book—my first. I received the letter of acceptance in the mail on a Saturday when he was home. I was thrilled. When I read the letter aloud to him, he said absolutely nothing. Not a single word. I really wanted to talk to him about it. But every time I brought it up, he changed the subject. It's as if he felt jealous or something."

Your Need for Nurture

A husband's not wanting to listen is a frequent complaint among the unhappy wives I see. Women are traditional nurturers and seem to step naturally into the role. When the support is not mutual and a woman's emotional needs for nurturance are not met, she has a right to feel upset and to ask herself what she is getting out of the relationship.

Wilma's marriage not only provided no support for her, but her husband frequently belittled her both publicly and privately. The product of a broken home, Wilma feared the breakup of her own marriage more than anything else, so she continued to endure Stuart's behavior. She treated him with respect and deferred to his wishes; he viewed her with disdain and behaved accordingly. He had managed to impart the same scathing attitude toward her to their three children, all of whom regarded Wilma as an unwelcome intrusion most of the time. She sometimes felt that when she entered a room all conversation deliberately stopped; she was an alien in her own home.

Sometimes she felt so angry that she literally felt her head pounding, but she never expressed her anger directly.

Although Wilma welcomed Stuart's friends into their home, Stuart was rude to hers. She was not entirely blameless; her self-abnegating manner actually invited the rudeness with which her family treated her. When she did complain, she never did so forcefully enough to bring about any change, but only succeeded in underlining the martyr's role into which she had cast herself.

"I don't have any idea how the children are doing at school," she told me, helplessly, once. "Stu takes the correspondence and report cards out of the mail, and I never see them. The children won't tell me their grades, and when Stu goes to talk to the teachers I'm never included."

Obviously it isn't always the woman in a marriage whose needs are not met. When Ike, a passive young lawyer, came home and needed to talk over the frustrations of the day with his wife, she invariably sided with his boss. Somehow, from Hilda's point of view, everything that went wrong in Ike's day was his own fault.

"Why don't you ever back me up?" he asked her repeatedly. Hilda saw her negativism as "constructive," but in actuality she was only treating Ike in the way she had seen her mother treat her father: with unconditional criticism. After a while Ike stopped trying to confide in Hilda; he learned that doing so only made him feel worse. He found a colleague at the office (female, of course) who was more sympathetic to his needs. Hilda was astounded when he sued her for divorce.

Gale declared that her 20-year marriage was "super," yet she described herself as a recovering alcoholic and an overeater (she'd like to lose 20 pounds) who constantly felt "unable to cope" with her three children. She had seen several therapists, seeking the support she apparently needed, before she consulted me, ostensibly for weight control. But she talked about her personal problems rather than her weight, and cried during most of the first several sessions.

"Don't you think my problem could be hormonal?" she asked me. "I don't like thinking it's in my head."

Her three children were all teenagers, yet none of them helped with any of the household chores. "The counselor I went to when Jerry was having problems suggested we have a family conference and assign tasks to everyone, but that only lasted a little while," she said.

"Now it's back to business as usual, and nobody pitches in but me. I'm sick of doing all the laundry, putting out the garbage, doing everybody's errands, cooking the meals, and washing all the dishes. I used to feel satisfied with my life, but now I'm overwhelmed by the demands. My husband and I went away last weekend, and enjoyed our time together. I was completely relaxed for a change.

"As soon as we were back in the house last night, the tension began to mount. I woke up at 6:00 A.M. this morning and thought of all the nitpicking things I had to do all day. It gave me a tremendous sense of pressure. I'm sick of feeling like the maid. If nobody appreciates what I do, what's the point of doing it?

"Jimmy has absolutely no idea what I'm complaining about."

"We Were Just Kind of Bored"

After 23 years of "not a bad marriage," Lorna became involved in a love affair with a colleague while her husband was on an extended business trip abroad. "When Bud came home I told myself I'd have to stop the affair, but I didn't," she said. "Hank seemed so exciting that it was as if

I'd never been in love before. Even though my daughter suspected—I'm a confirmed shopper, but how many nights a week can you go shopping?— I kept on with it."

Although he never confronted the issue explicitly, Lorna's husband sensed that her attention was elsewhere, and eventually (after more than a year) asked for a divorce.

Lorna accepted eagerly, because her mind was on one thing: Hank. "As the divorce grew close, Bud said several times that he thought we were making a mistake. But my thoughts were elsewhere. I felt so guilty that I accepted a terrible settlement and we sold the house for about half its worth. I moved into a small apartment, thinking it was only for a year or two until Hank could get his divorce and we'd be together."

That didn't happen: when Hank, an Irish Catholic, told his wife his plans, she threatened suicide. He said he couldn't take the chance of having that on his conscience and would just have to stick it out. At the time Lorna consulted me, she was still talking to Hank several times a week and was occasionally seeing her ex-husband.

She was suffering from anxiety and had trouble sleeping. "I'm nowhere with either of them," she said. "If I'd had any idea how things were going to work out, I would have fought to save the marriage. Now Bud has his eye on somebody else, and I've finally accepted the fact that Hank will never leave his wife. I'm on my own, with a terrible divorce settlement, and unless I leave my job I'll keep on bumping into Hank at work. The children blame me for the divorce—no wonder. And there's nobody I can blame for the situation I'm in. I brought the whole thing on myself.

"Our marriage wasn't a bad one," she said. "We were just bored with each other. But after 23 years, who says there'll be fireworks? At least we had a secure family and provided emotional support for each other."

We all need the comfort and security that a warm, nurturing relationship can provide. If we have one and lose it we are devastated and, after a period of mourning, usually start looking for a replacement. Sometimes, like Lorna, we fail to recognize what we have until it is too late.

A Search for Excitement

Oscar did realize what he had: an attractive, supportive, interesting wife who knew instinctively how to meet his needs. Their interests and backgrounds were similar and they had considered themselves "best friends" as well as lovers during their ten years of marriage.

But Oscar was restless and frequently went out on the town with his friends when Elise, a musician, attended evening symphony rehearsals. His rationalization was that all his friends did it—and they did.

The problem was that Oscar fell in love with a young girl and became involved in such a passionate relationship that he literally led a double life for three years. Elise never knew, though he confided in several of his friends; his business took him on frequent trips to the city where Betsy held her first job. Finally Betsy broke off the affair, saying she couldn't take it any longer, and Oscar was miserably unhappy. Betsy occupied most of his waking thoughts, even when he was with Elise. His stomach was in an uproar most of the time and he was experiencing insomnia. Betsy's rejection of him made him want her more intensely than ever and he redoubled his efforts to see her—sending her notes, flowers, and extravagant gifts.

Eventually she relented and the affair was on again. At first he was ecstatic; his physical desire for her exceeded anything he had ever felt, or could remember feeling, for his wife. Yet he recognized her intellectual limitations and knew that if their physical relationship ever paled—though he half believed that would never happen—he would deeply regret leaving Elise, who offered so much more in terms of understanding and intellectual stimulation. In the end, he could not leave his wife; he left his young mistress instead.

In some cases, a need for nurture can go too far—much too far.

Phyllis, badly hurt by two previous relationships that had both ended in rejection, demanded constant reassurances from Ted, the new man in her life. If his statements failed to echo her own thoughts exactly, she obsessively questioned his meanings and berated him for not expressing his feelings.

Not a highly articulate man, Ted was sincerely in love with Phyllis, and as he put it, "hoped they would get married if things worked out." However, her insecurities and constant fears of rejection provoked unending and unnerving discussions that neither seemed able to terminate.

By her insatiable need for reassurance, Phyllis was well on the way to driving away a man she really cared for. She was jealous of his work, his female acquaintances, and his former wife, whom he hadn't seen for several years. They came together for counseling, since both wanted to save the relationship.

"Do you still have feelings for Marcia and wish you were with her?" she demanded one day in my office.

"I have no feelings for her," he replied.

That wasn't enough for Phyllis. "But do you still wish you were with her?" she persisted.

Ted, baffled by her question, replied, "I said I had no feelings for her, so why would I want to be with her?"

Phyllis frequently complained that at times Ted professed love ardently, while at other times his declarations were "chopped liver."

But Phyllis was trying to work it out.

A Fear of Closeness

Melanie had decided, on the other hand, on the basis of some rather similar but apparently more damaging experiences that she could never find the closeness she craved. A divorcee with a 9-year-old child and a gratifying career as a medical social worker, she approached every encounter with negative expectations.

"Ninety-nine percent of people are just not worth bothering with," she declared. "Even the ones who aren't disappointments in the beginning wind up being disappointments in the end. It's obvious to me that I wasn't meant to find a companion. It doesn't seem fair, when some acquaintances of mine who are no more attractive and no more interesting, in my opinion, do manage to find someone. Perhaps I'm too choosy, but I can't help being that way. My efforts just never work out, so the most constructive thing I can do is try to find some peace and comfort without other people. I'll simply try to enjoy my daughter and the few family members I have."

Even these relationships were fraught with conflict; with her daughter, she fluctuated between companionable acceptance and "cuddling" and outright angry rejection. Often she expressed her frustrations over the confinement of being a single parent in such strident terms that her daughter felt totally unwanted. Melanie's relationships with her sister and aunt were frequently disappointing as well. As a child she had felt her mother preferred her sister; now that her mother was dead, her aunt seemed to be continuing the favoritism.

"My aunt completely spoiled my birthday," she complained. "She made eye contact only with my sister, and talked only to my sister. I felt in some weird way that I wasn't even there—as if I had died and was invisible. And it was *my* birthday."

On some occasions Melanie was quite insightful about her problem. "The negative energies I send out are driving everybody away," she said once. "I know that. I have to work hard to send out more positive messages, so that I can get something more positive back. I've seen it work at times. But right now I am feeling so discouraged that it just doesn't seem worth trying any more."

Lew wanted to try, but at 35 he just couldn't get up the nerve to ask a girl for a date. He talked endlessly about his desires to have a girlfriend or a wife, and envied the few friends he had—they were all married. Although he was quite attractive, highly intelligent, and held a high-paying job, his self-concept was negative and his social anxieties overwhelming. He wanted to escape the isolation in which he was living, but initially he seemed unable to carry out even the simplest assignments involving interactions with other people.

Nicole was friendly and related to people easily, but each time a relationship became "serious" or threatened to become so, she found some reason to withdraw. She thought she wanted closeness, yet always found a reason to retreat from it. Since she was popular and had a large circle of acquaintances, she seldom felt really lonely. But she recognized that there was a lack in her life that only a close relationship could fill.

It is quite rare, in my experience, to encounter anyone who actually prefers not to have a close relationship. The rare exceptions are those who have been so badly hurt by rejection that they are afraid to risk it again. Even so, with time they usually do.

If you are alone at the moment, you may find it helpful to think about what you would like to have in a marriage or relationship—and what you are willing to settle for. It is usually better, and healthier, to be alone than to be in an unsatisfactory relationship.

How Does It All Add Up?

If you are presently married or in a close relationship, just how satisfactory is it? There may well be areas that need improvement; the following quiz may help you to identify some of them. Circle the number that most accurately describes your reaction to each question.

	Strongly Agree	Agree	Not Sure	Disagree	Strongly Disagree
1. On the whole, I would rate my marriage (relationship) as very happy.	5	4	3	2	1
2. I have never seriously considered divorce or separation.	5	4	3	2	1
3. If I had it to do over, I would enter the same marriage (relationship) again.	5	4	3	2	1
4. I can rely on my partner to keep his (her) promises.	5	4	3	2	1
5. We are in agreement on most really important issues and values.	5	4	3	2	1
6. My partner respects my beliefs and wishes, even when we differ.	5	4	3	2	1
7. I can trust my partner not to make an important decision or expenditure without consulting me.	5	4	3	2	1

(continued)

How Does It All Add Up?—*continued*

	Strongly Agree	Agree	Not Sure	Disagree	Strongly Disagree
8. Our sexual relationship is satisfying to both of us.	5	4	3	2	1
9. I can count on my partner to be sexually faithful.	5	4	3	2	1
10. My partner is definitely concerned with my happiness.	5	4	3	2	1
11. My partner is considerate of my feelings.	5	4	3	2	1
12. We enjoy spending leisure time together.	5	4	3	2	1
13. We laugh a lot together.	5	4	3	2	1
14. We are tolerant of each other's need for separate activities at times.	5	4	3	2	1
15. If something is bothering me, I don't hesitate to discuss it with my partner.	5	4	3	2	1
16. My partner would sense it if something were bothering me even if I didn't bring it up.	5	4	3	2	1
17. I can trust my partner not to repeat anything I confide.	5	4	3	2	1

(continued)

How Does It All Add Up? — *continued*

	Strongly Agree	Agree	Not Sure	Dis- agree	Strongly Disagree
18. My partner listens attentively when I have something to say.	5	4	3	2	1
19. After talking a problem over with my partner, I feel better.	5	4	3	2	1
20. I can count on my partner for helpful suggestions when they are needed.	5	4	3	2	1
21. My partner never puts me down.	5	4	3	2	1
22. My partner is interested in my daily activities.	5	4	3	2	1
23. My partner is not likely to side with others against me.	5	4	3	2	1
24. If I were sick, my partner would take care of me or make sure somebody else did.	5	4	3	2	1
25. I know my partner will treat my family and friends with respect.	5	4	3	2	1
26. If I wrote a book or article, my partner would be eager to read it.	5	4	3	2	1

(continued)

How Does It All Add Up?—*continued*

	Strongly Agree	Agree	Not Sure	Dis-agree	Strongly Disagree
27. If I won a competition of some kind, my partner would be sincerely thrilled for me.	5	4	3	2	1
28. If I made a mistake, even a serious one, my partner would forgive me.	5	4	3	2	1
29. My partner respects me as a separate individual.	5	4	3	2	1
30. My partner is proud of me.	5	4	3	2	1

To compute your score, simply count the number of questions you scored 4 or 5. If your marriage is a supportive one, you should have answered at least 25 questions this way. Those you scored 3 or less indicate problem areas that need work.

Now turn the tables on yourself and answer the questions again from your partner's point of view, as you believe he (she) would answer. This will give you an indication of how much emotional support you are providing for your partner. In a mutually supportive relationship there should be few 3s on either partner's side.

8
How to Know When It's Hopeless

Peggy, 54, was desperate for relief from her migraine headaches. Since medical efforts to alleviate them had failed, she had reached the point where she thought "talking about it" might help.

Peggy's migraines started at 39, when the first symptoms of an early menopause began to appear. Her periods became irregular and ceased entirely within a few years, but the migraines continued, often as frequently as twice a week.

"I go to bed feeling fine, sometimes exceptionally good in fact, but when I wake up I can tell that my entire day is ruined," she said. "There's nothing I can do but stay in bed. I'm too sick and nauseated to move. It's reached the point where I'm afraid to plan anything; I never know when I'm going to have a migraine and be completely incapacitated.

"It usually begins with a throbbing in the left temple," she continued, "but then frequently moves over to the right. If I stay in bed the throbbing subsides to a dull ache, provided I take my medication; but if I try to get up and do anything the throbbing intensifies and I become more nauseated."

Describing herself as a perfectionist, Peggy admitted that she made matters worse for herself by her endless pursuit of details. "I sweep out the garage four times a week," she commented, "even though nobody cares about it but me. But if I don't do the things I think I have to do, I feel even worse."

She complained that her husband, a New York executive, constantly procrastinated about *his* share of the household chores. "Walter's made me into a nag," she said. "I can't stand it when things don't get done. He does them eventually, but only after I've asked him over and over."

Peggy looked surprised when I asked her if her marriage was a happy one. "If you'd asked me that 15 years ago, I'd have said I wanted a divorce," she replied.

I commented that 15 years ago was also the time when her migraines had started.

At first she denied that there was any connection, saying she'd "just happened" to identify the same time period for the onset of her migraines and her disillusionment with the marriage.

"I resent having to make all the decisions," she said. "I don't know how Walter can function in his job, but he does. He'll call me up and talk for half an hour trying to decide whether he should take the 6:25 P.M. or the 7:05 P.M. It's maddening. I used to be crazy about him, but that was a long time ago.

"To tell you the truth," she said slowly, "fifteen years ago I discovered that Walter was having an affair with a secretary, a silly woman I couldn't stand. She used to call up at all hours of the night. My father ran around on my mother; I always said that was one thing I could never put up with in a marriage. Walter knew how I felt about it, because I told him before we were married. And then he went ahead and did it. That affair ended years ago, but I think there have been others.

"Do you honestly think my anger at him could have something to do with my headaches? The truth is, I'm annoyed with him practically all of the time. And I've never really spoken my piece."

Despite her resentments, Peggy announced that she "got guilt complexes" if she asked Walter to do anything she considered "women's work," such as grocery shopping. She said he was often upset that she was better at "men's work," like fixing the furnace, than he was.

When I asked her to recall when she'd been most symptom-free in recent years, Peggy recalled that when she had remained alone at their summer home, with her husband coming only on weekends, she'd had no severe headaches for three or four weeks at a stretch.

Rob's obsessive, rigid insistence that Camille be punctual for every appointment, run the house like an army regiment (he had been an officer for several years before their marriage), and have every minute of her day (even weekend days) planned was driving her to overindulge in the only comfort available to her: food.

She had gained 30 or 40 pounds in the five years of their marriage, which Rob continually lamented. "If only she would lose those 30 pounds, I think I could put up with everything else," he declared. "I take care of myself; why can't she?"

Since both partners worked, the standard of housekeeping failed to meet Rob's standards, but he was unwilling to take up any of the slack himself. "I feel the house, the cooking, and the children are her responsibilities," he said stiffly. "A part of me feels it isn't quite right to feel that way—but that's how I do feel."

Rob nagged at Camille constantly about her weight. "I don't want a fat wife," he said. "But getting a divorce isn't acceptable to me either." He was trapped by his own demanding standards.

As for Camille, she wanted out. "I can never relax with him around," she said. "Whatever I do, it isn't good enough. The more he tells me not to eat, the more I want to eat. Getting out of this marriage is the only way I can save myself from total collapse—or a weight of 200 pounds."

"My Stomach Can't Put Up with Him"

Judy didn't realize that her marriage was making her physically sick—she would have said it was driving her crazy. Two years before, at 50, she'd married Georgio after being divorced for several years. Judy was a perfectionist and liked for everything to be absolutely neat: her house, her yard, her kitchen, her clothes, and Georgio's clothes. But Georgio had a mind of his own and did not take well to Judy's efforts to reform him.

"He's a careless slob," she declared. "He can't care for me at all. If he did, wouldn't he dress up to please me? He sits around the house in his undershirt. He'd go out to a fancy restaurant in a T-shirt if I'd let him. And he resents it if I tell him what to wear."

Nothing about Georgio pleased her. She'd married him to avoid being alone, and because she felt she needed the financial security he offered. "I've never loved him," she said. "All I'm doing is putting up with him. He embarrasses me when we're with friends or go on vacations. He has nothing to say to anybody unless he's criticizing them or gossiping."

Judy had severe colitis, which had involved an extensive series of medical tests with no improvement in her condition, and was sleeping very fitfully when finally she decided to move out. "I hate to tell anybody I'm getting a divorce again, but I can't stand it any more," she said.

It came as a shock to Judy to discover that she started sleeping soundly once she was in her own place, despite her financial worries. And within a matter of weeks her stomach had calmed down considerably.

Occasionally she talked to Georgio on the telephone; he wanted her back. "While we were screaming at each other one night, I actually could feel my stomach twist up into a knot," she told me. "That settles it. My stomach was telling me I just can't put up with Georgio."

Could a Creative Separation Help?

Not every relationship that seems hopeless *is* hopeless. In some cases, what marital therapists call a period of "creative separation" can help couples who have reached an impasse to rediscover the strengths in the relationship and work out their differences while freed temporarily from the strain of being around each other constantly. "People are moving too hastily as soon as things don't seem to be working out," says Dr. Clifford Sager, clinical professor of psychiatry at New York Hospital-Cornell Medical Center and director of family psychiatry at the Jewish Board of Family and Children's Services in Manhattan.

According to Dr. Norman Paul, a psychiatrist in Lexington, Massachusetts, out of 40 couples who tried "creative separation," 29 stayed together. For some couples the separation gives each a chance to learn to function independently and reflect on his or her own behavior, while maintaining a sense of trust and commitment between the partners.

"If one has just walked out on the other, for a while there is always the fear they will do it again," says Marilyn Henderson, a family therapist with the Marathon County Department of Social Services in Wausau, Wisconsin, another proponent of the technique. "This way it is more of a joint agreement."

When creative separation is used, practical living arrangements, financial arrangements, and other details are worked out informally with the aid of the therapist. Partners must be able to agree on these issues and must both be sincere about using the separation to think through their difficulties. If one partner is definitely committed to leaving the relationship, or is already involved with someone else, obviously the technique will not work.

Creative separation might have helped Noel and Flora, since there were basic strengths in the relationship that both recognized, and since each fulfilled needs that were important to the other. But Flora was not accessible to counseling; Noel came alone.

He was becoming increasingly anxious and irritable as he doubled and redoubled his efforts to please his demanding wife. "I've always loved Flora," he said, "but I often wonder whether she ever loved me, and why she married me. Nothing I do is right. If I'm replacing a washer on the kitchen faucet, Flora tells me how she could do it better. Maybe she could, too. Flora is very competent, and she can't stand anyone who doesn't measure up."

When Noel took care of their two young children, as he often did since he was an artist who worked at home and Flora was an advertising account executive, she complained about how he did it. He tended to be quite permissive, while Flora had definite rules and regulations that she expected to be carried out in her absence.

"As soon as I hear her car drive in, I begin to prepare myself for the onslaught," he said. "I can feel myself tense up as I wonder what she'll find to complain about this time. I think Flora resents the fact that she earns a lot more money than I do, even though we discussed this ahead of time and both thought we could handle it. I can honestly say it doesn't bother *me*—but the way Flora is expressing her anger certainly does.

"I've talked to her about getting help together," he commented. "But that isn't Flora's way of doing things. She can't stand admitting there's anything she can't handle on her own. If things go on this way, I'm headed either for an ulcer or a divorce."

"He Already Has Somebody Else"

Liliane *did* get an ulcer when her husband became involved with another woman. "I wouldn't say our marriage was ever the happiest one in the world," she said, "but we're both Catholic and we do have two kids. My own parents were divorced when I was 7, and I never saw my father after that. I'd always been determined I'd never do that to my own two kids, but if Verne wants to get a divorce there's no way I can stop him.

"I've been trying to look the other way, hoping he would get over it so we could keep the family together," she added. "But I feel that he has abandoned me already. He's never home except weekends when he can see the children. When I try to talk to him, he literally turns away. But when I ask him if he wants a divorce—sometimes I get desperate enough to ask him that—he says he isn't sure. I don't press the point, because I'm so afraid that he'll say that's what he does want.

"Verne can't make up his mind between the two of us," Liliane said ruefully. "And as long as I put up with this situation, he doesn't have to. He can have it both ways. He was away on business for almost a month recently, and when he came home he made a big point of telling me how much he missed the kids. He said nothing about missing *me*.

"I desperately want the marriage to work," she concluded, "but I've reached the point where I wonder how much more hurt I can take. I already have an ulcer; what's next?"

Christine didn't develop ulcers when Brett moved out of the house and into his company's corporate suite in the neighboring city where he worked—for her it was a matter of intense mental anguish that eventually caused her hospitalization.

Although Brett claimed there was no other woman, he said he had to "rethink" the marriage. Christine had married for life; they had three young children, and she had never even considered the possibility that they wouldn't remain together. She deeply loved Brett and could not understand why he was hurting her so much. They had been high school sweethearts and had married shortly after he graduated from college— Christine had gone directly to work to save money for their future.

For months Brett returned home on weekends, bringing his laundry for Christine to do, spending time with the children, and leaving on Sunday afternoon without finding time for a serious discussion with Christine. He found the discussions tiresome anyway.

When they entered counseling, it was obvious that Christine wanted to save the relationship and that Brett only wished to make it appear that he wanted to.

Brett had numerous bones to pick with Christine: she was too meticulous, too house-oriented, too involved with the children. She made heartbreaking efforts to change every behavior that annoyed him, but it was all to no avail. Brett still wouldn't commit himself to the marriage. To make matters worse, he wouldn't commit himself to leaving either, keeping Christine in an ongoing state of suspension. Christine refused to see that "no decision" was a kind of decision.

The stalemate ended temporarily when her nerves snapped and she had to have immediate psychiatric care, but after a brief hospitalization things were exactly the same as before. Brett still could not, or would not, make a decision.

A second psychiatric admission and a second psychiatrist, perhaps more forceful than the first, were required before Christine could make the decision herself in order to regain and maintain her equilibrium. It was a painful way to learn that some relationships are simply too damaging to continue.

A Case of Physical Abuse

In Laraine's case, the damage was not only mental but physical as well. Early in her marriage to a hot-tempered but seemingly loving Italian, there were occasional episodes of violence. On one occasion Mario lost control and slapped her when they argued about what he perceived as her interest in another man during a Saturday night party. He was contrite afterward and immediately became his familiar, affectionate self.

Laraine wasn't too surprised—she had seen her father strike her mother more than once, and considered physical violence a normal part of marriage. When Mario's physical abuse became more intense and more frequent, she continued to accept it, although she was increasingly disturbed at the direction their lives seemed to be taking. At times she thought her own behavior must be provoking Mario's outbursts. Finally she sought counseling, announcing at the outset that she did not want Mario to know she was coming because "he would never understand." To make sure he didn't find out, she paid cash for her appointments.

"I'm afraid of him in a way," she said. "I try very hard not to anger him, but sometimes he gets angry anyway. He's getting more and more violent." She extended an arm that was badly bruised. "I don't think he really *means* to hurt me, but he does, so often. Afterward he's always wonderful—he takes me out to dinner, buys me flowers, and assures me that everything will be different. And for a few days it is—until the whole thing starts all over again. Am I doing something to bring this on myself?"

Despite her problems with Mario, Laraine maintained that she loved him. She'd packed up and left on one occasion, going home to her parents', but Mario pursued her doggedly and she soon relented and returned to him.

"Logically I know my situation is physically dangerous," she said. "At least once a month I have severe bruises or worse—once he fractured my arm. I frequently feel depressed and totally helpless. But I keep overlooking his behavior and focusing on how sweet he can be at other times—and making excuses for him. I'm completely dependent financially," she added. "I married him right out of high school and I've never worked. If I had to support myself, I don't know what I'd do. Mario has his faults, but he's very generous with money."

Like most battered wives, Laraine was a victim of what psychologists call "traumatic bonding."

"Lawyers, therapists, family court counselors, judges, and police are often surprised and frustrated by the apparent loyalty of women toward the men who beat them," say Canadian psychologists Don Dutton and Susan Lee Painter. "It is not uncommon for a woman who has been beaten severely to the point of needing police intervention to save her life, who originally has pressed charges against the man who beat her, and who initiated an exit from the relationship, to change her mind, drop the charges, and resume the relationship."

They present research showing that nearly 70 percent of a sample of 52 women who experienced abuse from their spouses by the end of the first year of marriage (and 15 percent even prior to the marriage) continued to live with their husbands for an average of over 12 years before seeking help.

Among the forces that Dutton and Painter cite as tending to bond women to intermittently abusive partners are family histories of violence in a high percentage of both the abusers and the abused (many abused wives were physically abused as children). And there is an attitude of learned helplessness that leads the victim to believe she has no control over her partner's behavior or in fact over any aspect of her environment.

These authors conclude that "access to social and economic resources may be a factor in some women's inability to leave the abusive relationship, but in general even those with adequate resources appear to remain in the relationship until or unless the abuse becomes so severe as to be life-threatening or comes to involve the children as well."

Emotional abuse, as well as physical, may lead to traumatic bonding if the abuse alternates with periods of warmth, acceptance, and relative tranquility. "I never know what to expect" is a statement typically made by one caught in such a relationship. Intellectual awareness of the reality of the situation usually precedes the emotional readiness to break away.

If you are in a severely abusive relationship, you are likely to need professional help to gain the strength to get out of it. No matter how strong your religious beliefs or your desire to maintain an intact family for the children's sake, the time will come—or should come—when your own physical and emotional well-being must become your foremost consideration.

Obviously there are many situations short of actual physical abuse that are seriously damaging to your health. If you are in such a relationship, it may still be possible to make the changes that will enable you and your partner to live happily and healthily together. But for this to occur, both partners must want to make it happen.

Questions of Abuse

Here are some questions that may provide some realistic information about the toll your relationship is currently taking on your health. Circle the number that most accurately reflects your answer to each question.

	Fre-quently	Some-times	Never
1. My partner abuses me physically.	3	2	1
2. I have had to seek medical help for injuries inflicted by my partner.	3	2	1
3. I have called police for assistance after being abused.	3	2	1
4. Although my partner hasn't abused me, I have been afraid this might occur.	3	2	1
5. My partner abuses me verbally with shouting, insults, or name calling.	3	2	1
6. We have loud, upsetting arguments.	3	2	1
7. I have had to leave the house to end an argument.	3	2	1
8. The neighbors have overheard our arguments.	3	2	1
9. I have been afraid they would overhear.	3	2	1
10. My partner has physically abused our (my) children.	3	2	1
11. My partner is sarcastic toward me.	3	2	1
12. I feel resentful toward my partner.	3	2	1
13. When my partner comes home, I feel myself tensing up.	3	2	1
14. I look forward to my partner's absence from home.	3	2	1

(continued)

Questions of Abuse—*continued*

	Fre-quently	Some-times	Never
15. I prefer to take vacations alone.	3	2	1
16. After a discussion with my partner, I feel physically ill.	3	2	1
17. There are things about my partner that really disgust me.	3	2	1
18. My partner's treatment of me is damaging to my self-esteem.	3	2	1
19. My partner makes me cry.	3	2	1
20. I feel my partner is driving me crazy.	3	2	1

Obviously even one 3 response is unhealthy; 2s are only slightly less so. If you have more than a few 2s or 3s, you are in real trouble and should give serious thought to getting out of the relationship unless you can improve matters significantly.

9
Breaking Broken Records

You don't have to continue exhibiting the behavior patterns you learned in childhood from your parents. You can change or eliminate those that disturb you—if you really wish to do so.

But it's important to recognize the fact that your parents, through their modeling and their teaching, provided you with the framework for your interactions with other people as well as for other aspects of your behavior.

"My mother died when I was 10," a young mother told me recently. "I don't remember much of my childhood *before* she died either, so I feel I grew up without a mother. Consequently, I feel I don't know how to be a mother myself. Sometimes I catch myself talking to my children just the way my father talked to me—even though I hated it at the time."

"I've always been determined not to be the kind of mother mine was," another declared. "She had unlimited time and compassion for her patients—she was a doctor. Her own children were the ones whose needs were not met. She was always too tired or too busy to give me and my sister the attention we craved. If I asked her for something when she *was* available, I was made to feel it was an imposition. At times I sense that I'm almost as unavailable to my own children. I find myself more interested in things that don't involve them. I frequently lose my temper and yell at them. I don't want to, but I do—that's why I'm here."

Like Mother, Like Daughter

The influence of parental modeling was made crystal clear to me during a recent session with a 35-year-old divorced mother and her 10-year-old daughter. Both mother and daughter were having social difficulties. Chloe, herself the child of a rejecting mother, felt she could not find enduring love, or even acceptance, from anyone. Her feelings of self-worth were so low that she lacked the perspective even to put ordinary human errors into perspective. If a friend or acquaintance failed to return a telephone call immediately, Chloe was certain that the person wanted nothing further to do with her. She never considered the possibility that he or she was out of town or failed to receive the message. She felt unappreciated and ignored even by her own family, and frequently confided these feelings to her daughter.

Nina, at 10, was already expressing the same attitudes—hardly surprising, since she both felt and heard her mother's isolation. "You don't look very happy," Nina reported that a teacher had said to her on the day of one of our sessions. "Is something the matter?"

"I told her *everything* was the matter," Nina said dramatically. "Just take a look at me eating my lunch in the cafeteria any day. I'm there all alone—*nobody* is eating with me."

Further questioning revealed the fact that Nina's classmates ate their lunch in a smaller room outside the cafeteria, but that she refused to accompany them, stating vehemently that the cafeteria was "the right place" to eat. Nina finally conceded, somewhat reluctantly, that her own behavior was a major factor in her isolation.

Nina also complained bitterly that she had not been given the lead role in the school play. "My teacher doesn't like me," she said. "I was the best of those who read the part, but she wouldn't give me the chance." Five others who tried out had also failed to get the part, but Nina felt singled out for rejection. "I won't even attend the play," she declared. "I would feel so bad I might embarrass myself by crying."

"My mother was always very impatient with my father," a 40-year-old woman told me not long ago. "In my heart I sympathized with Dad and felt sorry for him, even though I never said anything. He didn't have much of a life. He was a sweet, easy-going, passive man.

"I can see that my husband is quite a bit like my father," she continued. "But that isn't the problem. The problem is that I'm impatient with Gardner just the way my mother was with my father. I hear the same tone and sometimes even the same words. And until recently I didn't think I was like her at all."

Myra's mother had been unfaithful. She'd had an ongoing affair with a man in the office where she worked, and everyone there knew about it. When she consulted me, Myra had just become involved with a man in the office where *she* worked.

When she wanted to meet him for a weekend, she arranged for her mother to "cover up." "I didn't like to ask her to lie for me," she confided, "but I knew I could count on her to do it."

Anita discovered when she was very young that her father's secretary was also his "girlfriend." "I felt humiliated and embarrassed," she said. "We lived in a small town where everybody knows everything about everybody. When I married Chet, I told him that if he did that to me, I'd leave him—that infidelity was the one thing I could never put up with. I was determined not to be put in the position my mother was in."

But when she was in her mid-forties, she discovered that Chet was involved with *his* secretary. "I was furious," she said. "I should have left him—the pain and anger of it has literally ruined my life. Half the time I'm sick from it. But I didn't leave—I stayed in the marriage just like my mother, getting angrier and angrier with every year that passes."

Amy, 32, called for an appointment after reading an article about me in a local newspaper. "I don't know where to begin," she said when she arrived. "I've never talked to anyone except my mother and aunt about this, but I need an objective opinion. My husband and I have been married ten years and we have practically no sex life. He says I don't appeal to him sexually and I'm not a good lover. My mother and aunt say marriage is like that. They say I should be glad I have a nice house and a family and forget about sex—that's what they did."

As she continued to talk, Amy admitted that her "good" husband frequently abused her verbally, and often threatened her physically as well. "He threw me against the wall in front of my mother and she told him I deserved it because I was a spoiled child," she said. "My mother and aunt think I'm crazy to think of leaving such a good husband, and I'm scared to death to be alone. Maybe I'm too old to find anybody else."

During her childhood, Amy had heard frequent bitter quarrels between her parents, and occasionally her father had beaten her mother. "When I was 12 years old my mother confided in me that my father abused her sexually," she said. "She showed me her breasts—he had almost mutilated them. My parents were divorced when I was 16, and I left home to escape the turmoil. I was scared of men for a long time. Lenny was the first man who hadn't insisted I go to bed with him right away, so I thought he was nice and married him. I got cold feet the night before the wedding but when I called my mother, she said, 'Go ahead—you can always get a divorce.'"

Like Father, Like Son

It wasn't Seth who found his stinginess a problem—it was his wife. "Seth's father was the tightest man I've ever met in my life," she said. "He collected every food coupon he could find, and went from grocery story to grocery store to get the best bargains. At Christmas his presents were the cheapest available, and he complained that his wife bought frivolous things for the children (with her own money). When she died, at 75, she'd never had a chance to enjoy life at all, though Seth's father was a wealthy man.

"Seth is just like him, and he's driving me crazy," she declared. "He visited six stores Saturday to find the best buy on a new ironing board. It took all day. I've given up on grocery shopping—I can't stand going with him. I earn almost as much as he does, but he expects me to account for every penny I spend. He thinks buying books and magazines is a total waste of money—I'm supposed to get them at the library. I simply can't go on living with such a miser."

Though he had a wife and two children he loved, Charles started to "fool around" when he was in his late thirties, at exactly the same age his father had been when *he* became involved with another woman.

"I always thought my father's behavior was callous and unfeeling, and I hated the way he humiliated my mother," Charles said. "Yet I'm doing exactly the same thing to Penny, though she doesn't deserve it any more than my mother did. I'm disgusted with my own behavior, but I keep on doing it. It wasn't so bad when it was just an occasional night on the town while traveling on business. Now, though, I've become quite involved with a very attractive lady—just like my father did. Occasionally I think of leaving Penny for her—and my father thought of leaving my mother too. He could never make up his mind. Finally, when it was too late for her to start a new life, my mother left him."

Since our early experiences are so important in shaping our behavior, it's quite possible that you, too, are repeating patterns that you would prefer to eliminate. Perhaps you are not even consciously aware that you are acting as your parent acted. It is frequently a surprise to patients to discover, in therapy, that a certain behavior or pattern of behavior is a direct reflection of what they observed in childhood.

Even when behavior patterns similar to those of a parent are not obviously manifested, the origins of what psychologists call "styles of loving" can be traced back to childhood experiences.

The Antecedents of "Styles of Loving"

In a recent study of 540 people between the ages of 15 and 82, Phillip Shaver, a psychologist at the University of Denver, found that about half fit into "a secure style of romantic love, and the others split evenly between anxious clingers and those who tend to avoid romantic ties." In recalling their childhood, the anxious lovers—"those who frequently become obsessed with their lovers, are prone to intense jealousy, and undergo extreme emotional highs and lows"—reported that their parents had an unhappy relationship, and that their mothers were emotionally intrusive, while their fathers were distant and demanding.

Another psychologist, Carl Hindy of the University of North Florida in Jacksonville, also investigated the pattern of "anxious attachment." That is a term coined by John Bowlby to describe extremes of depression when a relationship ends, exaggerated feelings of dependence on the partner, and the feeling that one never receives enough love and attention.

According to Dr. Hindy, chronic anxiety over rejection results from the failure to develop stable expectations for love and affection in childhood. Such people are entirely dependent on their partner for emotional stability, and their moods fluctuate with their sense of acceptance or rejection. Since they feel unloved as children, they feel no one will love them or even like them, which leads to a constant search for reassurance.

According to Dr. Hindy, the anxious lovers and those who maintain a posture of detachment (more often seen in men than in women) when a relationship is threatened or ends share a common childhood background. They both had parents who were rejecting or hostile, or who were inconsistent and unpredictable.

In setting the stage for successful adult love relationships, it seems to be interaction with the opposite sex parent that is most important.

Overinvestment in relationships is also often observed in people whose opposite sex parent died when they were quite young, especially if the relationship before death was less than ideal.

Agatha, 35, lost her father when she was 10. Even before that, she hadn't felt secure in their relationship. He was ill for a while before his death, and not up to active fatherhood. In addition, Agatha felt that he preferred her brother.

In her adult love relationships, Agatha manifested all the typical signs of anxious attachment. She had the greatest difficulty at the end of a relationship, when she simply could not let go but would persist in initiating telephone conversations and meetings long after the end of the affair. She brooded indefinitely over her lost lovers, obsessing about what she could have done differently to produce a happier and more enduring relationship.

Carlton's mother ran away from home when he was 11, leaving Carlton's father to cope with him and two younger brothers. When he reached adolescence, he was desperately eager to "find somebody to love," but his eagerness was a turn-off for most of the girls he encountered. Eventually he became involved with a girl who lied to him and took advantage of his generosity. They had frequent fights about her behavior, but Carlton continued to put up with it.

"I know she isn't ideal," he said, "but at least now I have a girlfriend. If I break up with her, I'll be alone again."

Olivia *was* alone, and had never had a boyfriend. She was literally living out Carlton's nightmare. Since she was very young Olivia had been compared unfavorably to her attractive older sister. Olivia was quite attractive too, but in her own eyes she was plain and dumpy. Her divorced mother and sister constantly criticized her appearance.

"You can't go out in *that!*" they would shriek when she came downstairs dressed for the day. She had reached the point where she voluntarily solicited her sister's help before dressing for an important occasion. "Edyth's taste is *much* better than mine," she declared.

In addition to criticizing her appearance, Olivia's mother constantly accused her of being "selfish" and "irresponsible." She was neither. But she had listened to her mother's complaints so long that she constantly berated herself for what she viewed, not surprisingly, as her shortcomings. When I pointed out to her what she was doing, she insisted that her mother was *right.*

When she went to a party, Olivia approached only the "nerds" whom she judged insecure enough to be interested in anyone as unworthy as she felt herself to be. But after spending an hour or so with one of them, she quite naturally felt disinterested—she was a very intelligent girl—and walked away. Since she didn't allow herself to be exposed to anyone who might interest her, Olivia never got to first base with the opposite sex. The old tapes she was playing in her own head were standing between her and the opportunity to establish a relationship with someone she could respect.

The Role of the Family Myth

Sometimes patterns of behavior, or family expectations or myths, can actually be traced back through generations. According to David F. Musto of Yale, a psychiatrist and historian, one well-known American family—the Adamses—"passed on a destructive family myth about its own place in history, a myth that contributed to serious psychological difficulties, including a suicide, over successive generations."

Abigail Adams, wife of John Adams, the second American president, was responsible for the creation and propagation of this myth, says Dr. Musto. Left behind to suffer loneliness and hardships while her husband rose to fame, "she justified her sacrifice by glorifying her husband and the cause for which he fought," and developed grand expectations for her children, especially John Quincy Adams, who she believed was destined to be "a hero and statesman."

Dr. Musto believes that the family self-image, which required moral superiority, outstanding success, and aloofness from the shabby side of business and politics, created such an impossible situation for later generations that one of John Quincy's sons, George Washington Adams, defeated by his inability to live up to expectations, committed suicide at age 28.

"If you look back in your family, you are often able to find a psychological twin or near-twin," says Professor Monica McGoldrick, a clinical social worker in the department of psychiatry at Rutgers. "For example, a patient of mine thought of herself as a total oddity in her family, because she is gay and has a wry sense of humor in a family that is otherwise straitlaced and tightlipped. But she recently found out about a grand-aunt who was rarely mentioned by the family. The grand-aunt had the same sort of sense of humor, and lived all her adult life with another woman, with whom she 'shared a bed,' as her family put it."

Professor McGoldrick also cites the pattern of estrangement over three generations in the family of Eugene O'Neill. "Both Eugene and his oldest brother Jamie felt estranged from their father, and all of them blamed each other for the mother's drug addiction," she comments. "In the next generation, the playwright was totally estranged from his oldest son and had nothing to do with his daughter Oona after she married Charlie Chaplin."

Of course, family histories may exert positive as well as negative influences, and often—perhaps more often—do so. Carl Jung, for example, came from a family in which virtually all the males for three generations had been either physicians or ministers, and many family members—including Jung's mother and a cousin whose seances Jung attended in his youth—believed in the supernatural.

And for three generations the family of Alexander Graham Bell had a preoccupation with problems of speaking and hearing. His paternal grandfather, an actor and elocutionist, wrote a book on phonetics and invented a cure for stammering, and both his father and uncle taught their father's technique. In addition, both his mother and his wife were deaf.

If your family history is leading you in a positive direction, be thankful, for those who preceded you have made your life an easier one. But if you find yourself playing destructive old tapes in your head, or acting in accordance with some outmoded scripts that are interfering with your life and your relationships, you can change.

Playing the "Parent Tape"

A first step is to identify the problem; the following quiz may help you. Take a few minutes to consider each question carefully before circling the number that best describes your reaction:

	Often	Some-times	Never
1. I put myself down just the way my parents, or one of my siblings, used to.	3	2	1
2. I catch myself doing things I especially disliked in my parents.	3	2	1
3. When I'm cross with the children, I recall the way my parents spoke angrily to me.	3	2	1
4. My partner reminds me a lot of one of my parents.	3	2	1
5. My partner complains that I'm just like my mother (father).	3	2	1
6. I suffer from the same physical complaints as one of my parents.	3	2	1
7. I recognize negative attitudes in myself that are like my parents'.	3	2	1
8. My partner makes the same complaints about me that my mother (father) used to make.	3	2	1
9. There's a psychological twin in my family history who manifested all or most of my worst failings.	3	2	1
10. I'm very afraid of winding up like my mother (father).	3	2	1

A score of 20 or more indicates that you are playing some broken records that need to be discarded. If you scored under 15 (and answered the questions both thoughtfully and honestly), you are doing better than average in this department.

PART 4
First Aids

1
Becoming Yourself

It's impossible to overstate—for your peace of mind, your health, and your relationships—the importance of you being *you*.

No one said it better than Shakespeare:

"To thine own self be true."

Or, as Kierkegaard paraphrased it:

"Be that self which one truly is."

Carl R. Rogers, the psychologist who originated client-centered therapy, elaborated on the same point in his book, *On Becoming a Person* (Boston: Houghton Mifflin, 1961). Rogers stresses the fact that in a genuine relationship, it is essential to express your own personality and your feelings openly.

Relationships can only be real if *you* are real, and accept and recognize your own feelings. In the course of learning to accept your own feelings and attitudes, you grow in your capacity to understand and accept the feelings and attitudes of others.

Many clients enter therapy because, whatever the presenting issue, they are beginning to ask, "Who am I? How can I become myself?"

Traditional marriage has in many cases represented a complete loss of independence and selfhood for women. Yet often they are not even aware of it until years after the erosion began. And several more years may pass before they enter therapy or take some other step to develop a sense of autonomy.

Sometimes, more often than the partners think, the changes dictated by a wife's need to become herself can be worked out within the marital relationship. But sometimes her resentment is so great that she no longer wants to work it out; by the time she recognizes her predicament, all she wants to do is leave.

"I'm doing this for *me*," a patient said recently. After a lifetime of responsible, selfless behavior toward her husband, her 14-year-old son, and her elderly parents (whom she cared for until their death), she had decided to leave her husband and son and begin a new life on her own. Though her husband wanted to compromise his stereotyped behavior to save the marriage, she had no strength or motivation to work things out. She had "had it."

Before you can become a loving person, you must love yourself, and this means becoming your own unique self. It's an exciting process, but seldom an easy one because being yourself does not mean staying the same. All of life is a process of growth and change, of trusting your own experience and intuitive feelings to lead you in the direction that will allow you most fully to become yourself. As a result, your relationships will become deeper and more meaningful.

Because when you give yourself up for someone else—to be a good wife or husband, or to live up to someone else's perfectionistic standards—your resentment will express itself psychologically or somatically.

2
Relax and Live Longer

While it's essential to confront the stressful conflicts and relationships in your life and do everything you can to resolve or minimize them, there are certain basic steps you can take to deal with the physical and emotional effects of stress—whatever the cause.

The most important of these is meditation.

Whether you suffer from headaches, insomnia, backaches, chest pain, nail biting, stuttering, or generalized feelings of anxiety, this simple procedure is certain to help—and it doesn't involve drugs or doctors' visits. (Naturally, it shouldn't be expected to take the place of prescribed medical approaches, but it can enhance their effectiveness.)

The regular practice of meditation (Transcendental Meditation is the form most commonly used in this country) or relaxation, as described by Dr. Herbert Benson in his books *The Relaxation Response* (New York: William Morrow, 1975) and *Beyond the Relaxation Response* (New York: Times Books, 1984), for 15 to 20 minutes twice a day will significantly relieve whatever problem you are having by interfering with what Dr. Benson calls "the anxiety loop."

I have never seen a patient who failed to obtain some relief through meditation, provided he or she could be induced to practice it faithfully twice a day.

If your problem is a relationship conflict that has not yet manifested itself in the form of physical or psychological symptoms, meditation will still help. You'll be calmer and better able to deal with issues as they arise. Because you are more relaxed, you'll have better control over whatever *you* have been doing to escalate the conflicts.

And even if you have no problem, relationship or otherwise, meditation can help you achieve higher levels of creativity than you thought possible, because the process makes you aware of unconscious thoughts and feelings otherwise accessible only in the dream state.

During relaxation or meditation, the heart rate is lowered, the rate of breathing decreases, blood pressure (if elevated) is reduced, brain waves become slower, and the rate of metabolism is lowered.

When we are stressed, worried, or too concerned about our health, we experience anxiety. And the anxiety soon becomes part of an ongoing, and vicious, anxiety cycle. The initial anxiety activates the sympathetic nervous system (the "flight or fight" response), which responds to emergencies or stress by releasing adrenaline and noradrenaline (or epinephrine and norepinephrine).

These hormones are useful in emergencies. In fact, they may save our lives. But excessive amounts, activated by repeated stress, may lead to chronic anxiety, hypertension, backaches, tension headaches, and a variety of other symptoms.

When an already anxious individual becomes conscious, through bodily sensations, of the effects of adrenaline and noradrenaline, the result is more anxiety.

Practicing meditation or relaxation, as Dr. Benson explains, interrupts the vicious cycle by blocking the release of these hormones.

Practitioners of the ancient meditative techniques of yoga and Zen Buddhism have long been observed to have a remarkable capacity for voluntary control of certain mechanisms of the autonomic nervous system. During the 1960s the Maharishi Mahesh Yogi, a guru, brought a simplified form of yoga to the West, which he called Transcendental Meditation.

Controlled observations of Transcendental Meditation at Harvard's Thorndike Laboratory proved conclusively that meditation produced a marked decrease in the body's consumption of oxygen, while alpha waves increased in intensity and frequency. There was a decrease in blood lactate (associated with anxiety states); heart rates decreased, and the rate of breathing slowed.

More recent studies show that, along with these changes, relaxation produces shifts in hormone levels that have beneficial effects on the immune system. For example, relaxation training in medical students during exams was found to increase their level of the helper cells that defend against infectious disease.

Relaxation in Combating Illness

Cardiovascular problems can be significantly ameliorated by relaxation training, which has been found to decrease the body's response to norepinephrine. It seems to mimic the action of beta-blocking drugs used to control blood pressure. In addition, relaxation can lower cholesterol levels and lessen the severity of angina attacks.

Diabetics can profit from relaxation, since it improves the body's ability to regulate glucose in patients with adult-onset diabetes. And it offers relief to many asthmatics by diminishing the emotional upsets that can trigger attacks and by widening restricted respiratory passages.

Finally, sharp decreases in pain and related symptoms have been reported after relaxation training.

How to Meditate

While other relaxing techniques (autogenic training, progressive relaxation, and hypnosis) produce similar physiological changes to those observed during meditation, most people find Transcendental Meditation or the relaxation response the easiest to employ.

The ancient meditative practices historically involved a religious or philosophical purpose. Dr. Benson initially isolated only four elements that he believed to be necessary for the elicitation of the relaxation response, regardless of the cultural source. These were:

1. A quiet environment, indoors or out, free of external distraction.
2. An object to dwell upon, whether it is "the mantra" used in Transcendental Meditation, another word or syllable, or a visual symbol.
3. A passive attitude, which allows unwelcome thoughts to be casually, not forcefully, dismissed, while the mind returns to the contemplation of the chosen object.
4. A comfortable position, not one conducive to sleep.

Dr. Benson's original instructions for inducing the relaxation response, which is similar to the method used in Transcendental Meditation, were as follows:

1. Sit quietly in a comfortable position.
2. Close your eyes.
3. Deeply relax all your muscles, beginning at your feet and progressing up to your face.
4. Breathe through your nose and become aware of your breathing. As you breathe out, say the word "one" silently to yourself.

5. Continue for 10 to 20 minutes, opening your eyes occasionally to check the time. (Do not use an alarm.) After meditating, sit quietly for a few minutes before standing up.
6. As you meditate, maintain a passive attitude and allow relaxation to develop at its own pace. If distracting thoughts occur, simply dismiss them gently and return to repeating "one" on each out-breath. Practice relaxing once or twice daily, but not within two hours after any meal, since the digestive processes interfere with relaxation.

A few years after the publication of his first book, Dr. Benson discovered that the effects of relaxation were more beneficial if one of the aspects he had originally eliminated—a religious or philosophical purpose—was reintroduced. He now recommends that "a person's deepest personal beliefs," which he calls the "Faith Factor," be incorporated into the practice of relaxation.

To add the Faith Factor to the basic technique as previously described, select a word or phrase that reflects your own basic belief system. It should be brief enough to be repeated silently as you exhale normally. Some examples are: "Hail Mary"; "Our father who art in heaven"; "Love one another"; "Shalom"; and "Allah."

Since it is essential to maintain a passive attitude, do not choose a directive word or phrase such as "heal" or "get better."

In recommending the use of the relaxation response, I have found that the greatest difficulty is convincing people to do it—and keep doing it. Many feel they are too busy to spend 15 or 20 minutes twice a day "doing nothing." But if you meditate regularly for four to six weeks, you will note a definite improvement in your health and general well-being.

When you are feeling better, it's tempting to cease the practice of meditation. However, if you really want to continue your sense of well-being and continue to enhance your creative potential, you will meditate regularly as a part of your daily routine.

3
Exercise and Feel Better

The benefits of exercise, like those of meditation, are universal.

According to recent medical studies, including one of 16,936 Harvard graduates, physical activity significantly reduces your chances of suffering a heart attack by increasing oxygen supply to the heart muscle, increasing blood flow to the heart, reducing irregularities in heart rhythm, and lowering blood pressure.

Exercise lessens fatigue, clears arteries of cholesterol, and enhances the ability of the blood to dissolve clots. It diminishes the risk of osteoporosis (a major problem for post-menopausal women) and is effective in combatting mild to moderate depression. According to Dr. Edward D. Greenwood of the Menninger Clinic, exercise also promotes well-being by increasing ego strength, dissipating anger and hostility, relieving boredom, and resolving frustrations.

What is the biochemistry of exercise?

Endomorphins, morphinelike secretions produced by the brain, create a feeling of well-being when they result from pleasurable activities. Although the sudden discharge of epinephrine (adrenaline) can disrupt the rhythm of the heart under circumstances of extreme anxiety or panic, the same hormones can have a cushioning effect—and lift your mood—when they result from exercise you enjoy.

The circumstances of physical effort are often more important than the amount of effort. Being late for an important appointment, or rushing through a crowded airport, for example, might produce a feeling of chest pressure, while ten times as much exertion could be sustained comfortably during an enjoyable game of tennis.

Those who exercise regularly sleep better and experience less anxiety and tension. Introducing regular exercise into your life can help dissipate the effects of stress, regardless of how these effects are produced or expressed. Yet most of the patients I see who have serious anxiety problems do not get any regular exercise at all, and it is often quite difficult to convince them to do so.

It is also clear from recent evidence that exercise, even more than diet, is the ultimate answer to weight control, but all but the most serious weight-loss candidates resist the intrusion of a regular exercise program into their lives. They'd rather eat grapefruit.

If exercise is so beneficial, why isn't everybody doing it?

Like meditation, exercise is one of those activities that most people can dismiss with the rationalization that they're too busy. But the fact is: exercise can add years to your life and can inestimably improve the quality of the life you lead for as long as you lead it.

Naturally, you must choose an exercise program that is appropriate for your age and general physical condition, as well as one you have a reasonable chance of carrying out. If you are over 40 and have been leading a sedentary life, or suffer from any chronic illness such as diabetes or heart disease, you should have a medical checkup before beginning to exercise. Even then you should begin gradually, and work up over a period of weeks or months to your desired exercise level.

There is no one exercise that is right for everyone. Certain exercises build muscle strength and tone, while others relieve tension, help you lose weight, or condition your cardiovascular system.

For cardiovascular conditioning, the exercise you choose must be aerobic, which means it promotes the use of oxygen. Aerobic exercise can change your metabolism and bring about permanent weight reduction as no amount of dieting can do. Walking, running, cycling, jumping rope, rowing, crosscountry skiing, and swimming are among the most common aerobic exercises.

For aerobic exercise to do the job you want it to do, most authorities say you must bring your heart rate to 60 to 70 percent of its maximum. (Pushing yourself beyond this can be damaging.) To estimate your maximum heart rate, subtract your age in years from 220. Your target rate for exercise is between 60 and 70 percent of that number.

You can take your pulse (heart rate) by counting the beats in six seconds (by placing a finger on your wrist or on your neck) and multiplying by ten. While exercising, unless you are riding a stationary bicycle, you will have to stop for six seconds to check your heart rate. It's important to do this to make sure you are doing enough, but not overdoing, while you are establishing a regular exercise routine.

Though the choice of exercise is a personal matter, there is one exercise that is available to all during every season, costs nothing, and is beneficial even to the elderly and those with heart disease. Walking for half an hour a day, five days a week, at a pace of three miles an hour, while carrying a six-and-a-half-pound load can, according to an Israeli study in the *Journal of the American Medical Association,* produce a significant improvement in physical fitness in just three to four weeks.

Although it is less stressful than almost any other conditioning exercise, walking provides all the advantages of more demanding activities.

Exercise with a Partner

As beneficial as exercise is to everyone, boredom often prevents all but the most devoted physical fitness enthusiasts from following through on a long-term basis. One way to combat the loss of motivation engendered by boredom is to exercise with a partner.

"I find more and more people exercising with a partner," says Alfredo Racano, director of the aerobics program at the Vertical Club in Manhattan. "As more people exercise and as training habits become more strenuous, you find that if you're going to push yourself you need incentive. The buddy system has always been a training ritual."

Joan Fields, a real estate broker, works out twice a week at a gym with her daughter Pam. "Exercise is a lonely thing, but it gets me out. I think I'd do it even without my daughter, but with her I enjoy it more."

Pam comments that exercising with her mother "gives us a chance to get together. We rarely get a chance to see each other otherwise. We have a good time without sitting down to dinner. We usually work out for about an hour, then we go our separate ways."

Working out with a spouse not only helps people stay with a fitness regimen, but also helps couples stay with each other, some experts believe.

Exercise physiologist Ellen Kushner, who helps people design their own fitness programs, points out that it's essential to choose the right activity for shared exercise. It won't work if one partner is very proficient and the other is taking it up to please him or her. Too great a disparity in skill or experience will lead to frustration on both sides.

If they are both at the same level of accomplishment or are both starting from scratch, their chances for enjoying the experience together are much greater.

Two of my former patients, who happen to be married to each other, find that their afternoon jogs provide an opportunity to exchange ideas. Since both are writers, they talk over their plans for books and articles while jogging together, which they do five or six times a week. They agree that this shared physical activity has enhanced their relationship.

Despite the potential psychological benefits for the relationship, Covert Bailey, author of *Fit or Fat* (Boston: Houghton Mifflin, 1978), cautions that men and women should be careful about exercising together because of their basic physical and muscular differences.

He advises women never to let a man push them into exercising at his rate. He thinks exercising alone or with another woman is a better solution. The only exception, he says, is if the man is several years older than the woman, or if she is in much better physical condition than he is.

Obviously, if you enjoy playing a game of tennis or going for a swim with your spouse or lover, this, like other activities you share, will enhance your relationship.

But it is probably best if you get your *serious* exercise, the 30 minutes a day designed to keep you fit, by yourself—or with someone whose age and exercise requirements closely approximate your own.

Some recent studies suggest that "soft aerobics" such as walking or bicycling rather than running or aerobic dance put less stress on a woman's muscles and joints, and that aerobic fitness can be achieved at a somewhat lower level of exercise intensity.

According to Richard Stein, M.D., director of the exercise laboratory at SUNY Downstate Medical Center and chairman of the New York Heart Association Exercise Committee, working out at only 65 percent of maximum heart rate will improve cardiovascular fitness.

While it will take six to nine months rather than three to achieve fitness at this level, working out at 65 percent of maximum heart rate, rather than a much higher percentage, greatly improves the average person's enjoyment of and motivation for exercise. For women over age 60, activities that increase heart rate to only 30 to 45 percent of maximum are just as effective as more intense exercise, according to one recent report.

Being physically active can add as much as three hours' worth of energy to every day. Late-day fatigue, rather than being the normal effect of a busy day, often indicates that you haven't been active *enough*. Regular exercise can provide several hours of additional energy every day.

One warning: total-body exhaustion (still feeling tired the day *after* exercise) is a symptom of exercise overload. It's a sign that you've done too much.

4
Eliminating Nervous Habits

Even though a nervous habit is a result of anxiety or tension, if it has persisted long enough or is severe enough the chances are that by now it is also a *cause* of anxiety.

Perhaps you've been teased or laughed at because of a nervous habit, or have been afraid you would be. Perhaps you struggle to conceal it from a boss or lover. The hair pullers I've seen, for example, have all been fearful that someone—even a doctor or a hairdresser—would discover the bald spot they'd created.

Stutterers worry endlessly not only about public speaking, but even about expressing themselves in ordinary conversation, and answering the telephone is a source of continual anxiety. Those who suffer from tics or hand tremors are afraid to drink a cup of coffee or a glass of wine in public.

To strengthen your motivation to overcome your habit, make a list of all the ways in which it has embarrassed you, inconvenienced you, or caused you anxiety.

While psychoanalytic theory suggests that if a symptom is removed another will arise to take its place, there is little or no evidence to support this supposition. Instead, eliminating a nervous habit leads to increased feelings of self-esteem and lessened anxiety as well, since one cause of tension, the symptom itself, has been removed.

This is especially true if someone in your life is nagging at you about your habit, or if you are constantly struggling to conceal it from someone whose opinion you value.

Since your nervous habit occurs more frequently under stress, it will probably vary in intensity from one period of your life to another. Even if you feel you have overcome it completely or drastically reduced it, it is possible that there will be some recurrence during times of severe stress. But you can go a long way toward overcoming it completely, and doing so will make you feel much better in other ways.

You have nothing to lose, then, and everything to gain, by attacking your habit directly. Most people who seek treatment for a nervous habit have already tried a few direct attacks on their own, without success. Painting the fingernails with bad-tasting preparations or sitting on the hands are typical home remedies for nail biting.

I've already suggested that you observe, record, and describe your habit or problem behavior. In doing so I'm sure you discovered that, as I've been saying, your habit occurs more frequently when you are nervous.

When you recognize increased feelings of anxiety, begin to breathe deeply, evenly, and slowly, inhaling and exhaling at a regular rate. Relax your posture as well, making sure not to hold yourself rigidly erect. Make it a practice to check your breathing and posture regularly; if you are tense, relax.

Just breathing deeply and saying "calm . . . relax" to yourself will help a great deal.

If nail biting or hair pulling is your problem, make sure that when you are seated at a desk or in a chair reading, studying, or watching TV you are sitting and breathing in a relaxed way. If you are a stutterer, relax yourself before you enter a situation in which you are likely to stutter.

Many nervous habits respond quickly to hypnotic suggestion, sometimes after only a visit or two. But if a reliable hypnotist is not available in your area, or if you prefer to try to solve the problem on your own, you can try what Nathan Azrin and R. Gregory Nunn, authors of *Habit Control in a Day* (New York: Pocket Books, 1977), call "the competing reaction" for nervous habits.

To be effective the competing reaction must be incompatible with the habit. In other words, you must choose a reaction that makes it impossible for you to carry out the habit at the same time.

The competing reaction should not be obvious to anyone who is watching, should not interfere with your normal activities, and should increase your awareness of the absence of your habit.

As soon as you realize that the habit is occurring or is about to occur, immediately begin the competing reaction and continue for three minutes. Practice the competing reaction in front of a mirror until you can do it unobtrusively. Continue to practice until the reaction appears perfectly natural.

Nail Biting and Hair Pulling

To overcome nail biting and hair pulling, Azrin and Nunn suggest the clenching reaction—making a fist or grasping a convenient object with pressure great enough "that you can distinctly feel the pressure on your fingers, but not so great as to cause tension or strain."

If you are driving and become aware of an urge to bite your nails or pull your hair, grasp the steering wheel tightly with both hands. If you must remove a hand to shift or for any other purpose, return it to the wheel and continue the clenching reaction for approximately three minutes in all.

If you are seated in a chair when the habit or urge occurs, grasp the arms of the chair; if you are reading, hold the book tightly with both hands; if writing, hold the pen tightly with one hand while pressing down on the paper with the other; when speaking on the phone, grasp the receiver tightly with one hand and a pen, pencil or other object with the other hand. If there is no convenient object to grasp, simply clench your hand into a fist.

Begin your competing reaction as soon as you become aware that you are experiencing the urge to carry out your habit, that you have started the habit itself, or that you have indulged in any associated or anticipatory movements, and continue the reaction for three minutes.

For Nervous Tics

For nervous tics, the competing reaction Azrin and Nunn recommend is a hard tensing or "isometric contraction" of the opposing muscles for that tic. If your tic is a head jerk, place your chin on your chest and press downward, or press your chin against a hand instead of against the chest.

For shoulder jerking, push both shoulders downward while pressing the elbows against the body. For head shaking, contract the neck muscles slowly with eyes forward and head centered.

Considerable practice may be required to learn to perform the competing reaction naturally enough that it will not attract attention.

For Stuttering

The competing reaction for stuttering is maintaining a relaxed posture while controlling the rate of your breathing. Inhale before speaking, begin exhaling as soon as you have inhaled, and then begin to speak. Do not hold your breath even briefly.

Practice controlling your breathing while reading aloud. For more detail on the control of breathing, see *Habit Control in a Day*.

For Other Nervous Habits

Some suggested competing reactions for other nervous habits are:

- For teeth grinding: relax the jaw and make sure your teeth do not touch, separating them with the tongue if necessary.
- For eye blinking: voluntarily blink your eyes every five seconds or so while keeping them wide open between blinks.
- For hand tapping: use the clenching reaction.
- For lip biting: close the mouth and hold the teeth tightly together.

In addition to practicing relaxation and using the competing reaction, it is helpful to visualize yourself, while deeply relaxed, in various situations in which you have been likely to exhibit your nervous habit. See yourself in these situations *without the habit*. I use this procedure with my hypnotic patients in conjunction with suggestions for competing reactions.

5
Interrupting Problem Behavior Patterns

If you have a behavior pattern that is interfering with your life or your relationship with someone else, it—like the nervous habits discussed in the last chapter—is undoubtedly affecting your anxiety level and your health.

All too often, people rationalize an undesirable behavior like procrastination or losing their temper by saying, "That's just the way I am." But you can change any behavior pattern you really want to change. The key is your *motivation.*

A woman telephoned me last week to ask if I could make her *want* to stop smoking. Of course, I told her that I couldn't—I could only help her stop if she wanted to stop.

Sometimes it's possible to help a patient increase the motivation to change by emphasizing the disadvantages of his or her behavior pattern—or by encouraging the patient to do so. If you have identified a behavior pattern you don't like, list the disadvantages of continuing it. Write down everything you don't like about it and all the ways your life would be improved without it.

Many of my patients have recognized a pattern they'd like to change, but have not been successful in doing so on their own. Often a therapist, especially one who is interested in brief symptom-oriented therapy, can help you to bring about a desired change. But there is no reason why you cannot change your own behavior if you really want to.

One of the easiest ways of changing problem behavior is through hypnosis, and I usually try this approach first if the patient is willing. But not everyone is hypnotizable enough to benefit from this method, and it is almost certain to require professional help.

Another technique for bringing about rapid behavior change, which will work for absolutely everyone, is one Jay Haley, a well-known family therapist and author, details in his book, *Ordeal Therapy* (San Francisco: Jossey-Bass, 1984). Haley was a student of the late Milton

Erickson, a leading medical hypnotist who was famous for finding brief solutions to his patients' problem. He often did so by prescribing ordeals for them, though Haley was the one who coined the term.

Haley's concept of ordeal therapy is that if it is more unpleasant to keep a symptom or a problem than to give it up, you will give up the symptom or solve the problem.

Usually it is the task of the therapist to impose the ordeal and that of the patient to carry it out. But you can choose your own ordeal.

In doing so, keep in mind that the ordeal should cause as much distress as the symptom itself, or more. If the first ordeal isn't severe enough, another should be selected. For maximum effectiveness, the ordeal should also accomplish a beneficial result. And, of course, it must be something that is not harmful to anyone involved.

One standard ordeal that both Erickson and Haley frequently recommend is some form of exercise in the middle of the night. Almost everyone would hate getting up for an hour at 3:00 A.M. to carry out a prescribed exercise, yet this is not harmful and can easily be done. The only equipment needed is an alarm clock—and the motivation to overcome the problem behavior.

Haley cites one case in which a man with insomnia was told to get up and wax the kitchen floor if he could not sleep; after a few days, he recovered. When the same prescription was given to a woman suffering from anxiety attacks that caused her to perspire excessively, she too soon overcame her symptom.

A young man with a bed wetting problem was instructed that if he woke up during the night with a wet bed, he was to go out for a one-mile walk, return, and sleep the rest of the night without changing the sheets; if he awakened in the morning with a wet bed, he was to set his alarm clock for 2:00 A.M. the next night and take his one-mile walk then. The bed wetting diminished immediately, and within a few weeks had ceased entirely.

If the problem recurs *at any time,* even years later, the ordeal should immediately be reinstituted.

Before an ordeal can be selected, you must clearly define the behavior so that there is no ambiguity about when the consequence is to be carried out. If the problem behavior is binge eating, for example, you must specify exactly how much food constitutes a binge. Then you must carry out your ordeal conscientiously every time you binge—with no exceptions.

If you choose an ordeal that is sufficiently unpleasant (but not merely punitive—remember it must accomplish something worthwhile) and carry it out faithfully, you will be successful. The greatest problem encountered by a therapist in using ordeal therapy is getting the patient to do it. And this is the greatest difficulty you will have in using the technique yourself. When you select the ordeal, you must make a firm commitment to yourself to carry it out.

Most effective ordeals are what Haley refers to as "straightforward tasks" that have some self-improvement benefit. A standard Ericksonian prescription for insomnia, for example, was to require the patient to get out of bed and spend an hour or more reading books he or she needed or wanted to read, but hadn't read (for a scientist, he suggested technical journals)—and do it standing up.

Sometimes, rather than a straightforward assignment, a "paradoxical task"—more of the problem itself—is chosen, but it is defined in such a way as to become annoying. A thumbsucker might be encouraged to suck several fingers rather than just a thumb; a person with an explosive temper might be instructed to have a tantrum every day at 8:00 P.M. I once suggested to a woman who was a chronic complainer that she schedule her complaining for 9:00 P.M.—a time that wasn't convenient because she preferred to relax with her favorite TV show at that time.

When the behavior is carried out deliberately, it becomes voluntary rather than involuntary. That is an important distinction.

Another possibility is to literally make yourself pay for indulging in your problem behavior. If you habitually lose your temper or go on eating binges, for example, you can decide that each time you do so you will pay a prearranged fine that doubles each time ($1 for a first offense, perhaps, $2 for the second, and $4 for the third).

You might donate the money to your favorite charity, or pay it over to a spouse or friend on a preagreed basis each time the problem behavior occurs. This tends to work best if both of you are trying to overcome a certain behavior—not necessarily the same one.

Whatever consequence you choose, the important thing is that you impose it faithfully *each time*. If you do so and the problem behavior continues, change the consequences until you are successful.

If you doubt what I say about the effectiveness of consequences, just consider for a moment what would happen if a police officer automatically appeared *every time* you were driving over the speed limit, and fined you $50. If that didn't bring your speeding under control, the fine would be raised to $100—and so on.

Sooner or later—probably sooner—you would develop total control over your tendency to drive over the speed limit.

Wouldn't you?

6
Changing Someone Else's Behavior by Changing Your Own

Perhaps a behavior pattern that is making you anxious isn't your own but someone else's.

And perhaps there is something you are doing that is reinforcing that pattern. If so, you may be able to change the behavior by changing your own.

Behavior doesn't occur in a vacuum, but within a family system. Therefore, if you change what *you* do, you will automatically affect the behavior of those in your family system. In most cases, nagging about a behavior or calling attention to it, even in an ostensibly helpful manner (unless the person has requested you to do so), will automatically increase it.

I see this often in my patients with weight problems. "My husband tries to tell me what to eat and not to eat," one complained recently. "We went to the movies last week and I bought a box of candy. He took it from me forcibly. I knew I shouldn't have it, but I was furious—and determined to get back at him by eating more later."

In general, your best chance of changing a behavior pattern that disturbs you in someone close to you is to *do something different* in response.

In *Healing in Hypnosis* (New York: Irvington Publishers, 1983), Milton Erickson relates the case of Anne, a student at Wayne State University, which dramatically illustrates this point. Her behavior was changed by changing the response. There was no effort to determine the underlying cause of her problem, which was a long-established behavior pattern that had continued all through school, college, and into medical school.

Anne never managed to get to class on time. By the time she was scheduled to attend Erickson's 8:00 A.M. lecture she had already been publicly reprimanded by practically every professor in the medical school for her repeated tardiness. Her procedure was well known: 15

minutes after the class started, she would walk across the front of the room, down a side aisle, across the back of the room, halfway up the other side aisle, then to the middle aisle.

When Anne marched in at 8:20 A.M., Erickson signaled all the students to rise. He then salaamed Anne, as did every member of the medical class. Everybody who encountered Anne that day did an elaborate salaam. The next morning, Anne was the first one in the lecture hall, and that was the end of her difficulty.

Steve de Shazer, director of the Brief Family Therapy Center in Milwaukee, and author of *Keys to Solutions in Brief Therapy* (New York: W. W. Norton, 1985), literally instructs patients to "do something different," without telling them what the something different is.

Since no particular action is prescribed, the clients can choose their own. And this may lead to a greater level of involvement and cooperation.

Usually, when someone comes to a therapist complaining of a child's or a spouse's irritating behavior pattern, they've already tried all the different ways they can think of to alter the situation. The problem is that what they've been doing is *not different enough*.

For example, the parents of an 8-year-old boy tried controlling his tantrums with time-outs, lecturing, and spanking; nothing worked. Instructed to "do something different, no matter how strange or weird or off-the-wall what you do might seem," the father handed his son a cookie when the next tantrum occurred. When the mother next witnessed a tantrum, she danced circles around him while he kicked and screamed. Both consequences were effective; not knowing what to expect from his parents, the child stopped his tantrum behavior.

Dr. de Shazer relates another case in which a young woman complained about her husband's depressed, down-and-out manner when he returned from a business trip. She'd tried cheering him up, drawing him out, and inviting friends over, but nothing changed. When instructed to "do something different," she decided that what he would be least expecting would be for her not to be home. She went out, leaving a note saying she would be home late.

When she returned, he had cooked his own dinner and seemed in good spirits. She concluded that it was *her* behavior—appearing overly concerned about him and unduly upset by his absence—that was causing his depressed manner. By changing her own behavior, she changed his.

Leah, 35, was upset because her husband frequently stopped off at a local bar on his way home from work for a few beers with his friends. She'd tried complaining and reasoning with him to no avail.

When Leah found a place to stop on *her* way home—and stayed there even longer than he did—his behavior changed abruptly.

Myron, a young social worker, was having trouble with his wife because of her unreasonable jealousy. If he talked to a female acquaintance on the telephone—a colleague or someone with whom he'd been in graduate school—she would fly into a rage and accuse him of being unfaithful. If he conversed with a woman at a party, she made his life miserable for days.

They were on the verge of separating when Myron came to see me. (His wife refused to come—she was jealous that he was consulting another woman.) When he stopped debating and reasoning with her, and began firmly stating his right to maintain his friendships in one brief sentence (and then refusing to discuss it further), matters improved dramatically.

Sometimes people manage to sabotage their own efforts to do something different. I suggested to Matt, a 40-year-old lawyer, that instead of reacting angrily to his wife's tempestuous outbursts (which usually occurred immediately after breakfast) he simply leave the house.

"That works," he conceded. "I tried it a few times on my own. But I refuse to have to leave my own house because of someone else's behavior." Matt was determined to deal with his wife's temper tantrums by doing exactly the same thing he'd always done—but it wasn't going to work.

If, like Matt, you find yourself unwilling to change your own part in a destructive pattern of interaction, perhaps you actually prefer the status quo. Because when you do something different, the situation will become different as well.

PART 5
Be Nice and Be Healthy

1
The Affectionate Touch

One of the most frequent laments I hear from married women—and sometimes, though less often, from married men—is that their mates aren't affectionate enough.

"His family wasn't affectionate, and he doesn't know how to be either," one young wife told me recently.

"If my husband comes in and gives me a hug, I immediately feel suspicious," said another. "He can only be affectionate if he wants sex, but sometimes I'd just like to be held."

When romance is new and sexual desire at its peak, it's unusual to worry about a distinction between affection for the sake of sex and affection for its own sake. The urge to touch and be touched is usually so strong during the early phase of a relationship that no one bothers to analyze it.

It's usually later, after a few years (or more) of marriage that women begin to complain of a lack of affection. Often they report that they are no longer affectionate with their husbands either—they're afraid of being rejected or fear that an affectionate gesture will be taken as an invitation to sex.

Because physical contact is so important in establishing and maintaining emotional bonding, it's unfortunate that so often we neglect this source of comfort and closeness within a relationship.

Touching can make us feel warm, secure, and loved. And it is highly probable that physical contact also provides important health benefits.

I say "highly probable" only because it is difficult to sort out the contribution of physical contact from other beneficial aspects of close personal relationships.

Research evidence on the importance of physical contact per se is limited, though common sense tells us that it is effective in relieving anxiety and providing emotional comfort. We all know what a hug or a touch of the hand can do when we're feeling down.

Dr. James Lynch and his colleagues at the University of Maryland Hospital have investigated the effect of human contact on one aspect of physical functioning—the heart rate. One of their studies of over 300 coronary care patients provided conclusive proof that the simple act of touching significantly influences patients' heart rate and rhythm. In some of the patients, pulse taking by a nurse had the power to completely suppress arrhythmias.

Dramatic changes in heart rate were also observed in another study in the shock trauma unit of the same hospital. Human contact seemed to be even more important under traumatic circumstances, whether the patients were very young, very old, or in between, and regardless of their cardiovascular pathology, physiological states, and their medication.

While the information we have concerning the effects of physical contact on the hearts and health of humans is relatively limited, laboratory research documenting the effect of human contact on animals is quite extensive. As Dr. Lynch reported in *The Broken Heart: The Medical Consequences of Loneliness* (New York: Basic Books, 1979), at Johns Hopkins, W. Horstly Gantt began to study the reactions of dogs in Pavlov's isolation chamber to human contact. In one observation he noted that as soon as an investigator entered the room, the animal's heart rate would decrease 20 to 30 beats per minute. When the person approached more closely, the heart rate would fall even more and fell to its lowest value during petting.

Cats and horses, as well as dogs, react to human petting. In one study at the University of Pennsylvania, horses' heart rates slowed so precipitously while the animals were being petted that they began dropping heartbeats.

"The Laying on of Hands"

Outside the laboratory, clinicians are also beginning to experiment with "the laying on of hands." Dolores Krieger, a registered nurse at New York University Medical Center who has written about her own experiences with the use of therapeutic touch, believes that the beneficial results come from a special kind of humanized touch that lets the patient know the healer's intent to help. The patient also feels the healer's strength and responds to it.

Therapeutic touch is now included in the nursing curriculum at New York University Medical Center and in some other in-service hospital programs.

Most of us know from experience that a mother can readily comfort a terrified infant by her touch. And an older child who has been hurt physically or emotionally wants comfort from a parent, most often the mother.

But we may forget that the need for physical contact continues throughout life—unless we are suddenly without it. I often hear a single or divorced person state sadly that "What I miss most of all is someone to hold me."

Yet those who are married—some of them reasonably happily married—often fail to take advantage of the opportunity they have to give and receive this very real source of comfort.

Are you one of them?

2
The Power of Positives

Positive thinking is a big topic—and an important one.

You probably already realize that thinking positively can affect your chances of reaching a goal that is important to you, help you overcome anxiety and depression, and significantly affect the outcome of serious illness.

But you may not have considered the importance of positive thinking and positive actions in your relationships with others.

If you've ever been around a person who was constantly pessimistic, sad, or critical, you know how it makes you feel. "When Mack is in one of his gloomy moods, he enters the room like a black cloud," a patient told me. "As much as I struggle to maintain my own equilibrium, he pulls me right down with him every time."

I remember a former friend whose conversation consisted almost exclusively of dreary recitals of the illnesses, problems, and difficulties of everyone she knew, coupled with dire predictions for the future. I say "former" because I finally became so tired of her depressing monologues that I began to avoid her entirely.

Short of bowing out of the relationship, you may have more control than you realize over the negative communications of those in your life. You may be able to produce significant change in another's behavior by doing something different yourself.

If someone you know is prone to hypochondria, asking how he or she feels is an open invitation to a discourse about his or her illnesses. And instead of listening patiently to a friend's ongoing expressions of self-doubt, you could say, pleasantly but firmly, "I really can't sit back and listen to you putting yourself down that way."

If you are involved in a relationship or friendship with someone who is openly critical of you, you don't have to put up with it—and you shouldn't. Nothing is more damaging to self-esteem than a constant barrage of criticism.

Perhaps you are inviting criticism by expecting it. When I encounter a patient whose spouse is consistently critical, almost invariably there is a negative parent in the background who undermined that individual's self-esteem so thoroughly that he or she came to expect criticism as a matter of course.

Often we behave in such a way that we bring about the very behavior we dread or fear. Lily, 40, was a case in point.

"I'm so sensitive to rejection," she declared repeatedly, both to me and to the man she was living with. "My experience in the past has conditioned me to fear being rejected again." She continually demanded reassurance from him that he wanted to marry her, even though she was not sure that she wanted to marry *him*.

By her constant harping on the subject, Lily was setting the stage for another rejection. She was obviously afraid that it would happen again but, rather than behaving in a way that might prevent the expected result, she was actively helping to bring it about.

We've all had certain interpersonal experiences, beginning in childhood, that have conditioned us to act and react in certain ways. Extreme social anxieties usually have their roots in childhood rejection or ridicule—a child who was put down by parents, siblings, or teachers for being "stupid" often grows into an adult who would rather remain silent than risk being unfavorably evaluated by others. One who felt rejected by peers in adolescence may avoid social events in later life to protect himself or herself from the anticipated rejection.

Similarly, a stutterer instinctively expects to stutter in situations that have produced that response in the past; a blusher anticipates blushing; and one who suffers from shaking hands worries for hours before attending a cocktail party.

Naturally, the expected behavior almost always does occur, because thinking about it is enough to bring it on. In other words, expect the worst and the worst is sure to happen.

In contrast, *positive* expectations are likely to lead to positive consequences. A person who expects to be successful—whether in a career or in interpersonal relationships—has a much greater chance of succeeding than one who expects failure.

I often help patients develop positive expectations by showing them how to change the way they talk to themselves and visualize themselves. From the very first visit I try to communicate my expectation that patients will be successful in attaining their goals. Recently I was told by a woman who'd lost 4 pounds after her first session of hypnotherapy that she attributed her success to my positive expectations.

If you tend to expect the worst, you can change. *You must believe that you can change.* Without this belief, change is very unlikely to occur.

For example, if you are trying to enlarge your circle of friends, you must believe that there are people out there who will accept you and respond favorably to your overtures of friendship. If you do not, you will unconsciously sabotage your own efforts to make friends. Something in your demeanor will proclaim, "Don't bother with me. I don't deserve your friendship."

If you are trying to improve a relationship you already have, you must believe that you can change your own contribution to the problem. Thinking "That's just the way I am" will absolutely prevent progress.

I try to have patients rephrase statements such as "I can't control myself" as something that allows space for change to occur, such as "Until now, I haven't been able to control myself."

A simple rephrasing can bring about the expectation that, although change hasn't yet occurred, it will occur in the future.

I encourage patients to practice "thought-stopping" for negative thoughts: "I can't do it"; "No one will like me"; "I won't be able to think of anything to say;" "I'll feel like an idiot"; "I'm just a bad-tempered brat" and so forth.

The procedure for thought-stopping is extremely simple. Mentally (silently) yell "Stop!" while jabbing a finger (hard) with a fingernail. That's all there is to it.

If the negative thought recurs, or another comes to mind, repeat the treatment.

To counteract the negative thought, immediately substitute a positive image—a scene you can visualize clearly. You might choose an interpersonal situation in which you felt very successful. A friend gave you a sincere compliment, for example, or told you how much you'd helped him or her overcome a particular problem; or you attended a party where you felt at ease and conversed fluently with people you hadn't met before.

Visualizing in a positive way, seeing yourself as you'd like to be, is one of the most effective ways I know to bring about the changes you desire in your ways of interacting with others.

Define Specific Goals

But there is another important step you may need to take prior to visualizing, defining the specific goal you'd like to accomplish.

- "Making more effort to meet people," for example, is too vague. "Go to at least four new events each month" would be better.

- "Try to see friends more often" could be restated as "Have lunch with a friend at least once a week."
- "Be more affectionate with my spouse" might become "Surprise my spouse with a hug at least twice every day."
- "Stop complaining so much about my aches and pains" could be rephrased, "Confine my symptom discussions to my doctor's office."

Defining goals specifically may be sufficient to give you a start in behaving more positively. But you will probably find, like most people, that visualization helps you see your goals more clearly and makes it easier to begin working toward them.

Visualization works best when you are in a very relaxed state, so before beginning sit down (lying down is not recommended, as you might fall asleep) in a comfortable chair. If you are aware of tension anyplace in your body, tense up those particular muscles and then relax them.

Now relax further by turning your attention inward and focusing on some aspect of your body—a tingling feeling in a fingertip or the sound of your own breathing. Sit quietly for a few minutes and let yourself sink deeper and deeper into a state of complete relaxation.

Only this morning a patient told me that she can quickly put herself to sleep or induce a state of numbness and tingling, which she described as "half awake, half asleep," by chanting to herself, "I want to go to sleep, I want to go to sleep, I want to go to sleep."

The state you are striving for is similar to the state produced by meditation, except that—and this is an important distinction—when visualizing you are directing your thoughts toward a goal rather than passively repeating a word or phrase.

When you feel thoroughly relaxed, visualize yourself succeeding at the goal you have stated. If you want to meet more people, see yourself at a social gathering or a discussion group. Visualize yourself talking freely and spontaneously, having a good time, looking poised and self-confident.

If you are working on being more affectionate with your partner, visualize yourself doing so in a relaxed, easy manner, and see your partner responding.

Not long ago a patient complained that she frequently forgot the names of people she knew well, especially when she had to introduce them. One day she was feeling very apprehensive because she was having a party on Saturday—and feared she would have problems introducing her guests.

I had her relax and visualize herself introducing each guest to every other guest, and the next week she reported that she'd remembered every single name with no difficulty. In the past she'd sabotaged herself by visualizing herself *forgetting* names. When she imagined herself remembering them instead, she did remember.

Simply by seeing yourself do something you want to do, you make it possible for it to begin happening. It's almost impossible to succeed at anything without first believing or imagining that you can do it.

You can work on developing self-confidence and self-esteem by relaxing comfortably and deeply, and visualizing yourself with the interpersonal skills you would like to have. As you do so, think back to some situation that gave you a feeling of interpersonal success and self-confidence. Deliberately recall as much of that feeling as possible.

In your daily interactions with others, constantly keep in mind the way you'd *like* to behave. When you notice that you are not measuring up, deliberately change your behavior. It may not sound easy—but you can do it.

Imitate Someone More Successful

Dr. Arnold Lazarus, a leading behavioral psychologist, recommends "exaggerated role-taking" as another way of bringing about more positive interactions with others (as well as for overcoming fears or anxieties). To use this technique, picture someone else coping easily and effortlessly with situations you would ordinarily find difficult. Then simply imitate that other person.

For example, suppose that every time your spouse walks in 15 minutes late you react by blowing up irrationally, setting off a debate that lasts all evening. You've found this reaction to be unproductive and damaging to your relationship, and you want to change it.

Think of someone you know who would handle the situation calmly. When your spouse next arrives a few minutes late, immediately picture that calm, serene person and imagine how he or she would behave. Imagine exactly what this person would say and do. *Then go ahead and imitate him or her.*

Practice the desired behavior ahead of time in the usual manner—that is, by visualizing it while in a relaxed state. Visualize your spouse coming in a few minutes late and visualize yourself reacting as the model you've selected would react.

Let Go of Old Resentments

Many people I see in my practice are full of resentments over how they've been treated in the past by parents, siblings, peers, ex-lovers, or spouses. While it's helpful to express these resentments initially to get them out in the open and laid to rest, continually recreating the painful events that caused them can produce extensive physical and psychological damage.

One young man, a freelance writer, repeatedly lamented his parents' failure to adequately support him, emotionally or financially, when he was young. He was still bitter over the fact that he'd dropped out of college because they couldn't afford to continue paying his tuition. His feeling, often expressed, was that if only they had helped him get off to a better start he wouldn't be in the financial difficulty that seemed to be an ongoing part of his life.

But despite his anger at his deceased father and his mother, he continued to turn to his mother for "a temporary loan" whenever his bills got the better of him.

Eventually, no matter how justified such resentments may have been, they simply must be put where they belong—in the past. Doing so is not easy, but once again visualization may help.

In his book *Sermon on the Mount* (New York: Harper & Row, 1934), Emmet Fox suggests a specific process for forgiving that involves becoming aware of the person you resent and picturing good things happening to him or her.

Initially, it may be difficult to see good things happening to a person toward whom you feel anger and hostility. But eventually, as you repeat the imagery process, you will be able to picture good things happening to that person and feel better as a result. In addition, your face-to-face dealings with the other person will become more relaxed and pleasant. This imagery process can help relieve stress that you might have carried around for much longer to the detriment of your physical and psychological well-being.

If you are nursing old wounds, are reexperiencing painful episodes from the past, or continually feel aware of resentment and hostility toward another person, try this imagery technique.

1. Sit down comfortably, close your eyes, and relax.
2. Clearly visualize the person toward whom you feel resentment.
3. Visualize good things—accomplishment, love, or attention—happening to that person. If at first you find it difficult to see good things happening to the person you resent, keep trying. You'll become more successful with practice.
4. Think of what you yourself may have done to create the original problem and try to imagine the situation from the other person's point of view.
5. Notice how much more relaxed and less resentful you feel.
6. Open your eyes and resume your normal activities.

Since this entire process takes only a few minutes, you can easily employ it whenever you discover yourself dwelling on unpleasant, painful, or upsetting incidents or relationships from the past.

"But I don't *want* to picture good things happening to my boss," a patient told me recently. And your initial reaction may be that you don't want to either. But remember that the purpose of dealing with your old resentments in this way is to *protect your health*.

By actively working to develop positive expectations of yourself and your relationships, and by giving up unproductive resentments, you will be relieving yourself of much unnecessary stress and anxiety and starting on the path to greater happiness and better health.

3
Laughter Can Save Your Life

King Solomon (Proverbs 17:22) may have been the first to express the sentiment that "a merry heart doeth good like a medicine."

But he certainly wasn't the last.

Thomas Sydenham, the famous 17th-century physician, commented that "The arrival of a good clown exercises more beneficial influence upon the health of a town than twenty asses laden with drugs."

Apparently this statement is more than speculation: Raymond A. Moody, Jr., M.D., in his book *Laugh after Laugh: The Healing Power of Humor* (Jacksonville, Florida: Headwaters Press, 1978), reports several cases in which the arrival of a clown produced a documented improvement in health among individuals as diverse as a child diagnosed as catatonic and a 95-year-old man suffering from depression.

Numerous American Indian tribes, among them the Pueblos, Hopis, Zunis, and Crees, had ceremonial clowns whose sole purpose was to provoke mirth among their tribesmen. They were called in to entertain and heal the sick with their hilarity, frightening away the demons of ill health.

William McDougall, a psychology professor at Harvard, proposed that the biological function of laughter was to maintain psychological health and well-being by increasing the circulation and respiration and raising the blood pressure, thus producing a condition of *euphoria* or general well-being.

According to an account by writer-editor Norman Cousins in his book, *Anatomy of an Illness as Perceived by the Patient: Reflections on Healing and Regeneration* (New York: W. W. Norton, 1979), Albert Schweitzer "employed humor as a form of equatorial therapy, a way of reducing the temperature and the humidity and the tensions.

"Life for the young doctors and nurses was not easy at Schweitzer Hospital," Cousins writes. "Dr. Schweitzer knew it and gave himself the task of supplying nutrients for their spirit. At mealtimes, when the staff came together, Schweitzer always had an amusing story or two to go with the meal. Laughter at the dinner hour was probably the most important course. It was fascinating to see the way the staff members seemed to be rejuvenated by the wryness of his humor."

Cousins set out to prove to himself what philosophers and a few discerning physicians have always known intuitively when, in 1964, he laughed his way "out of a crippling disease that doctors believed to be irreversible."

Stricken after his return from a tiring European trip with a serious disease of the connective tissue, he was told by physicians he had one chance in five hundred for a full recovery.

Not one to passively place his recovery in the hands of others, Cousins carefully analyzed the events leading up to his illness. As he thought over the frustrations and demands of his visit to Russia, he arrived at the conclusion that his illness was a result of adrenal exhaustion, which made him—but not his wife, who had accompanied him—susceptible to the infection he had contracted in Moscow.

Knowing that adrenal exhaustion could result from emotional tension, frustration, or repressed rage, he wondered if positive emotions like love, hope, confidence, faith, and laughter could produce the same chemical changes in reverse.

After consultation with his doctors, he determined to put his plan into effect. Concerned about the toxic effects of the drugs that had been prescribed for him as pain-killers, he decided instead to combat the pain with laughter.

"Nothing is less funny than being flat on your back with all the bones in your spine and joints hurting," he comments. "A systematic program was indicated. A good place to begin, I thought, was with amusing movies."

With the aid of a movie projector, some old Marx Brothers films, some "Candid Camera" films, and a cooperative hospital staff, Cousins discovered that his idea worked. "Ten minutes of genuine belly laughter had an anesthetic effect and would give me at least two hours of pain-free sleep," he wrote. "When the pain-killing effect of the laughter wore off, we would switch on the motion picture projector again and, not infrequently, it would lead to another pain-free sleep interval. Sometimes, the nurse read to me out of a trove of humor books. Especially useful were E. B. and Katharine White's *Subtreasury of American Humor* (New York: Random House, 1948) and Max Eastman's *The Enjoyment of Laughter* (New York: Johnson Reprint Co., 1971)."

Curious about the effect of laughter on his body chemistry as well as on the felt experience of pain, Cousins arranged to have readings of his sedimentation rate—the speed with which red blood cells settle in a test tube (affected even by relatively minor illnesses such as grippe)—taken just before and several hours after each laughter episode. The results indicated small but consistent drops each time, which held and were cumulative.

After a few months Cousins confounded his doctors by recovering sufficiently to return to his work as editor of the *Saturday Review*, and his mobility continued to improve year by year until, in 1980, again following a hectic travel schedule of speaking and conference engagements, he was once more hospitalized with a life-threatening illness—this time a heart attack.

His recovery, again facilitated by his positive attitude and self-participation in his rehabilitation, was recounted in *The Healing Heart: Antidotes to Panic and Helplessness* (New York: W. W. Norton, 1983).

Even against strict doctor's orders, he kept laughing.

"No laughing," his doctor told him. "You yourself have said laughing is a form of internal jogging. You're not up to any jogging right now, especially internal jogging. No spoofing. Stay flat on your back and just be a vegetable."

A little later, when his wife came in to see him, he told her he was under orders not to laugh. Then, at his request, she read to him from the morning paper. One of the items she read caused him to let out a roar of laughter.

"You're not supposed to laugh," she said, laughing.

"The laughter hadn't hurt one bit," Cousins wrote. "In fact, I felt warm and relaxed. Right then, I knew I was going to make it all the way. Laughter was still a friend."

Cousins commented that since the physical pain that was such a major feature of his collagen illness was not present, following his heart attack "my need for laughter was not as pronounced as it had been earlier. But I had a generous supply of laughter nevertheless. I swapped stories with the nurses, residents, interns, and visitors. My reputation had preceded me in the hospital. And I suffered no shortage of staff personnel wanting to try out their favorite stories."

While Cousins' therapeutic use of humor—deliberately inducing laughter by watching comic films or reading humorous essays—was chiefly a solitary one, for most of us the experience of laughter is usually a social event.

In fact, it's often contagious. While we might laugh aloud while watching a humorous movie alone, we almost certainly would do so if watching the same movie in a room where several other people were laughing.

Get Laughter into Your Relationships

We share laughter when we tell jokes or humorous stories or make light of ourselves. (Making light of others, while it may provoke laughter, is not humor but sarcasm.) A well-developed sense of humor that allows us to see the funny side of things is an undisputed social asset—as well as good medicine.

Just think for a moment of your own mood after being with a friend with whom you shared some laughter, compared with the way you feel after listening to someone's problems for an afternoon. My own mood is depressed after spending an hour with a chronic complainer. I try to keep complaints to a minimum in therapy sessions because they are seldom productive if allowed to continue unchecked.

You can interrupt a woeful recital by tactfully introducing a more cheerful topic. Unhappy feelings do have to be expressed, and I am not suggesting you deny this need, but I urge you to interject touches of humor into your relationships with others as often as it is appropriate.

After leaving the *Saturday Review* to accept a faculty position at the UCLA Medical School, Cousins had the opportunity to carry out "a little laughter experiment" with a group of cancer patients at a California VA hospital.

During his first visit with the group, Cousins told some of his favorite stories and played a cassette laughter track. "The effect on the patients was that of being on a toboggan that had reached the steepest part of the hill and continued to accelerate," he wrote. "They were on a runaway laughter course and couldn't stop. Some of them couldn't stay in their chairs. The contagion of all the laughers was such that I was rolling along with the rest."

After ten minutes' laughter, many of the patients said that their pain had receded—just as Cousins had experienced himself during his own illness.

He suggested to the group that they work on creating a more upbeat atmosphere by staging one-act plays, obtaining cassettes of stand-up comics and videotapes of funny movies, and starting every meeting with a report from each person about the good things that had happened since the previous session.

When he returned to visit several weeks later, the experimenter found that the most effective feature of the program was the requirement that each patient report on happy events. Since they didn't want to turn up empty-handed, they made a point of making certain that something good *did* happen—which you can do yourself if you resolve to begin every conversational encounter on an up note.

While no one would recommend that laughter and other positive emotions be regarded as substitutes for necessary medical treatment, their beneficial effects on the body as well as the spirit are no longer in question. Medical research, much of it sparked by Cousins' efforts, suggests that pleasurable emotions actually cause the brain to release its own pain-killing secretions.

You don't need to wait for a serious illness to strike to bring the healing power of laughter into your life and your relationships. It may seem contrived at first if it represents a dramatic change in behavior, but if you are determined to begin every conversation with a joke or good news, you can do so.

You'll feel better as a consequence, and so will each person you talk to—who will probably respond in kind. Just the act of *looking* for a funny story every day will help to raise your spirits, and you'll enjoy laughing all over again each time you repeat the story.

4
To Tell the Truth

Can you remember the last time you had a guilty conscience because you felt you had to conceal something from someone close to you?

Just thinking about that experience now may be enough to raise your blood pressure, decrease the electrical resistance of your skin, increase your rate of respiration, and make your heart beat faster.

These physiological changes that accompany intense emotion are the basis for the polygraph, or lie detector. The polygraph measures changes in heart rate, blood pressure, and skin resistance while a subject is relaxed and while he or she responds to a variety of both neutral and critical questions.

Because some people show physiological changes while answering certain questions for reasons other than lying, and because sociopathic individuals may not show physiological changes when they do lie, the method isn't foolproof and its findings are not admissible as court evidence. Nevertheless, it's the basic idea that is important here. Concealing the truth, for those of us with a firmly ingrained notion that lying is wrong, is one behavior that is guaranteed to wreak havoc with our nervous systems.

There are obviously degrees of guilt, and a "little white lie" may occasion little or none of that interior commotion that tells us when we've transgressed our own moral code. However, you can probably recall some relatively minor lie that caused you uneasiness. Suppose your spouse asked you to do a certain chore, for example, and you forgot to do it or just didn't find the time. But you didn't want to admit the truth and lied instead. Or maybe you overlooked paying an important bill, as we all do occasionally, but didn't want your spouse to know. So you said the bill never arrived—knowing it must be at the bottom of a stack of papers on your desk.

Almost every week I see one or more patients who've deceived a spouse into thinking they've stopped smoking. They come for hypnosis to stop smoking because they *have* to stop—they can't live with their guilt feelings any longer. It isn't the smoking they feel most guilty about—it's the lying.

Sometimes lying is necessary.

Working mothers may have to lie to their bosses about their family responsibilities to manage the conflicting demands of career and home. "I never tell anyone I'm taking the children to the doctor. *Never.* I always have another reason for being out," declares one career woman.

"If your children are sick, call in and say *you're* sick," advises another executive. "Sometimes you have to say you're sick even if nobody is, just so you can attend your child's play at school or have a conference with the teacher."

But this kind of lying creates ongoing stress. "In the long run, it's self-defeating," says Dr. Sheila Akabas, director of the Center of Social Policy and Practice in the Workplace at Columbia University School of Social Work. "You're always living inside the lie, always on guard and worried that you'll be found out."

People who "live a lie" are subjecting their bodies to long-term stress. Not telling a child he or she is adopted, for example, means living with the constant threat that the truth will somehow be discovered. If you've ever had an extramarital affair, you know how much guilt and suffering you experienced as a result of the lies you told to cover it up.

Often a person will confess an affair to relieve his or her own guilt at the expense of his or her partner's peace of mind. (In most cases, I don't think confession of an extramarital relationship that has been terminated is advisable; the damage it may do to the marriage may be greater than the damage of concealment.)

In *The Language of the Heart: The Body's Response to Human Dialogue* (New York: Basic Books, 1985), James Lynch cites the case of a 51-year-old woman suffering from high blood pressure who "had carefully concealed from her 32-year-old daughter the fact that she had been an illegitimate child. The woman said that her life with her daughter had always been a lie, and she lived in fear that some day her daughter would find out." Only after she confessed the truth to her daughter did her blood pressure drop from its hypertensive levels.

Obviously, long-term concealment of a secret like this has far greater consequences for mental and physical health than a relatively inconsequential lie told easily and quickly forgotten.

The toll exacted by lying also varies tremendously from one

person to another. We each have our own unique moral code, the result of our life experience and especially our childhood training. And just as pain warns us that the body is endangered, guilt lets us know when we are in trouble psychologically.

Guilt can be an ally of mental health because it tells us when we've done something our psyches can't tolerate. What matters is your own moral code, for it is your own conscience, not anybody else's, that will make you miserable—or sick—if you disobey it.

The fact that lying runs counter to your moral code obviously does not mean that truth is *always* the best policy. There are times when lying or omitting part of the truth is necessary to spare the feelings of someone you love.

I do not recommend brutal honesty. But I do believe you will feel better and avoid emotional turmoil, with its physiological concomitants, if you lead your life in such a way that you have little (or nothing) to lie about.

5
"You Must Have a Guilty Conscience"

If lying can cause so much physiological damage, it seems reasonable that other transgressions against your moral code will also result in insomnia, headaches, upset stomachs, and possibly even more unfavorable consequences.

My father, the possessor of a considerable amount of folk wisdom, used to remark when I complained of not sleeping well: "You must have a guilty conscience."

As a country lawyer who tried both civil and criminal cases, he was well aware of the psychological repercussions of guilt.

Unfortunately, some people feel guilty about something practically all of the time, and they torture themselves incessantly. Their early experiences and upbringing predisposed them to view their own behavior so harshly that there is no pleasing the punitive parent they have internalized.

I do not advise such individuals to modify their behavior to soothe their superego. Instead, I advise them to modify their expectations of themselves so guilt will not remain the ruling passion of their lives.

Although Zelda never actually had an affair, she experienced a very strong sexual attraction to the principal at the elementary school one of her children attended. She felt extremely guilty and lost over 10 pounds within a month after acknowledging her feelings to herself. "I never admitted my feelings for this man to my husband, though he could tell that something had changed," she said. "Since it was never openly discussed, I continued to punish myself for it for years. And when Norris was cruel to me or humiliated me in public, I accepted it because I felt I deserved the punishment. I felt like I was just walking around dead for a long time."

Zelda was the victim of an overzealous superego.

For most of us, though, guilt is a useful signal, and we can—and should—learn from it.

Cynthia carelessly revealed a friend's confidence to her husband, rationalizing to herself that "we tell each other everything." But she awoke during the night feeling very disturbed that she had betrayed her friend, and vowed to herself that she would never again repeat something told to her in confidence.

Nona forgot her best friend's birthday, though her friend had never forgotten hers. When she remembered, she rushed over with a bouquet of flowers and a more than generous birthday gift. She decided to avoid similar problems in the future by writing all important birthdays and family occasions in her appointment book at the beginning of each year.

Jetta, furious at her 14-year-old son when informed by the school principal that he had started a fight at school, lost her temper and told him he was grounded for two weeks without giving him a chance to tell his side of the story. Later, when the principal called to say that he had been mistaken, Jetta felt extremely guilty for not defending her son and determined not to make the same mistake again.

During the last few years of his mother's life, when she was terminally ill with cancer, Leo was extremely busy with the demands of his work as partner in a prestigious law firm. He conscientiously carried out his responsibilities in terms of making financial decisions for his mother, but left it to his sister to continue the close personal contact they had all had in earlier years. After his mother died, he felt so guilty and depressed that he gained 20 pounds, lost interest in his work, and spent many evenings staring blankly at the television set.

Dina was literally tied in knots with guilt because she had had an affair with her husband's best friend. They had realized simultaneously that their involvement couldn't continue, and had terminated it after a few months. Her guilt, however, remained with her. She couldn't confess and didn't want to hurt her husband or her marriage. But she had learned that she couldn't handle extramarital affairs—the price was too high.

Roger was torn between his wife of ten years, whom he loved, and the young mistress with whom he'd been hopelessly *in* love for almost three years. He had reached the point where he felt guilty toward both women; his inability to reach a decision about what to do made matters even worse. He knew he would continue to feel guilty no matter which decision he made.

The superego just never gives up.

If during your formative years you internalized a moral code, as most of us did, you will have to follow it, modify it (if you can), or suffer the consequences.

6
"Do Unto Others"

Being secure in the knowledge that you are needed and valued by others is one way of minimizing stress.

Hans Selye, the Canadian physician who is known throughout the world for his work on the body's physiological response to stress, recommends "Earn thy neighbor's love" as a sound biological law.

By love he means all positive emotions, not only the love between a man and woman or parents and children, but also the feeling of gratitude, friendship, admiration, compassion, and respect.

In Selye's view, man's ultimate aim in life should be to develop his own potential as fully as possible.

He urges the pursuit of excellence (rather than perfection)—a goal that he believes will enable us to earn the respect and love of our neighbors.

Selye advocates the philosophy of egotistic altruism in which man's objective is to amass a fortune to assure personal freedom and the capacity for survival—but the fortune consists not of money but of friends.

A skillful doctor, an effective teacher, or a first-rate electrician rarely has trouble finding work.

If your services are in demand by others, you will never be out of work. And if you are a good friend and neighbor, you will never be without friends yourself when you need them.

As one of my patients puts it, "I have to outflow more positive energy in order to get more back. When I give more to other people, I find I always receive more in return, and it seems to happen almost immediately."

It's not necessarily even a matter of receiving more in return from the same person you're giving to—though that is certainly likely to happen—but just a matter of getting more back *in general,* almost as if some natural law of physics were involved.

A friend of mine, upset by the prospect of an unwanted and imminent divorce, received a pair of opera tickets from another friend. She called and wanted to reciprocate with dinner in a restaurant. But her friend kindly, and wisely, said, "You're going through such a bad time right now that a lot of people are going to want to do things for you. Don't feel you have to pay them back—just pass it along later when things are better in your life."

Of course, my friend had numerous people who wanted to help her because she had been helpful to others in the past. Making sure that you "outflow energy," as my patient put it, is one way to ensure a current of energy in your own direction.

You don't need to be religious to be a good Samaritan. This is especially true if you can envision a worldwide bank of goodwill on which each person is entitled to draw proportionately to his or her deposits. Of course, performing valuable services for others—and feeling needed and valued as a result—has rewards of its own entirely apart from any specific tangible returns the investment may provide in the future.

Simply look around at the elderly people you know, and compare the emotional, intellectual, and physical state of those who are still working productively with that of those who have retired or given up.

My own father kept emotionally and intellectually fit by practicing law until six weeks before he died at 83, and my friend, Ida Davidoff, a New Canaan marriage counselor, is still going strong at 83 with a schedule of engagements that would exhaust some people half her age.

The feeling that one has important work to do that is valued by others keeps many artists, writers, and musicians functioning productively and creatively well past the age when many of their contemporaries have died or retired. Picasso was still creating art at 90, and Pablo Casals was still a virtuoso on the cello at the same age.

We can't all be artists, but we can all learn to do something well that will enhance our value in the eyes of others. I find my own work extremely gratifying, as scarcely a day passes without some very strong positive feedback from a patient whom I have helped to lose weight, stop smoking, overcome a phobia, or improve a marital relationship. These experiences validate my sense of personal worth and reinforce the security of knowing that I am useful to others.

And you can be useful no matter what your age. I recall reading about one 83-year-old man who was on the board of a hospital, raising money for a center for abused children, and had time for golf only once a week.

"I must say that a lot of people think I am silly at my age to be doing all these things," he declared, "yet I see so many of my friends who have nothing to do. I feel the hospital needs me."

Few things are as frustrating or as depressing as complete inactivity. Among people suffering from incapacitating, painful, and incurable diseases—and among the elderly—those who withdraw from normal activities suffer most because they cannot avoid thinking constantly about their hopeless situations.

It is not just keeping *busy* but keeping busy productively and contributing something to others that is conducive to your physical and psychological well-being.

Of course, it is possible to be *too* busy, and doing unto others can be overdone, either within the family or in taking on too many assignments in the community or at the office. Pure altruism can be counterproductive in terms of personal welfare and satisfaction. We all know some self-sacrificing person who tries to do everything for everyone, and loses himself or herself in the process.

Probably every mother—at least every mother of several children—has felt at times that too many people were dependent on her for too many things. Working mothers, in particular, attempting to balance the demands of a career with those of home and children, may simply feel stretched too far.

But even this condition, stressful though it admittedly is, is probably healthier than the feeling that one isn't needed at all. Just a few days ago a woman of 52 came to see me because she wanted to stop smoking. A woman of limited education and resources, she had raised her children and she and her husband, a factory foreman, had moved into a small apartment.

"It seems like there's nothing I have to do any more," she recounted. "I'd like to get a job, but I'm not trained for anything. The housework in my apartment doesn't keep me busy and I keep putting it off anyway. I guess I'm wondering what I'm going to do with myself for the rest of my life."

This woman had reached a stage in life where she felt she didn't matter. Her greatest pleasure during the day was sitting down (repeatedly) with a cup of coffee and a cigarette. No wonder she couldn't bring herself to stop smoking.

It's never too late to begin doing things that will ensure you matter to others. If you don't know where to start, begin with any worthwhile volunteer activity. The choice is up to you.

7
Listening Is Therapeutic

It's well known that "being a good listener" is an important social asset that is essential in forming and maintaining close relationships.

Listening attentively to others has major health benefits as well. In developing the habit of listening more closely, you will also be lowering your blood pressure!

In a study of medical and nursing student volunteers at the University of Maryland, it was found that blood pressure and heart rate rose rapidly when subjects read aloud (whether alone in a room or when the experimenter was present), or spoke to the experimenter. When the students remained quiet (that is, not talking), either alone or with an experimenter present, blood pressure readings were significantly lower even if the experimenter was talking.

When hypertensive patients were studied, blood pressure and heart rate also rose significantly when they began to speak, despite a frequent appearance of calmness and a lack of awareness of these bodily changes. The higher a patient's resting blood pressure, the more it tended to increase during vocalization. These changes occurred during relaxed conversation that did not include discussion of emotionally provocative topics.

In all 40 subjects observed, blood pressure and heart rate increased when they talked about their daily lives and decreased immediately when they became quiet.

Interestingly enough, when human beings talk to their pets blood pressure either does not change or actually decreases. In *The Language of the Heart,* Dr. James Lynch observed the contrast between the way people talk to their pets and the way hypertensive patients talk to their doctors. He began to experiment with changing his reactions in order to modify his patients' styles of communicating.

Hypertensive patients, he noted, tend to be defensive even while listening: "they appeared to decode our messages as a radar operator interprets the sudden blips from the direction of an enemy's territory."

Since Dr. Lynch's work with hypertensive patients involves continual computer monitoring of their blood pressure during therapy, he is able to detect changes of which the patients themselves are unaware. He soon discovered that when he related a personal anecdote or read aloud from a medical text or a book of poetry, patients seemed to drop their defensive posture and truly listen.

Dr. Lynch related these episodes—when his hypertensive patients were attending to something outside themselves—to the calming effect of stroking and talking to a pet.

As his work with computer monitoring of blood pressure responses during therapy continued, Dr. Lynch observed that blood pressure decreased during listening, often even below baseline levels.

In conversations between normotensive individuals, the normal give and take of conversation allows blood pressure to rise and fall to baseline levels. But hypertensive patients' typically defensive mode of listening does not induce this compensating drop in blood pressure.

It seems clear that people who listen—truly listen—are helping their bodies maintain healthful equilibrium. I often suggest listening attentively to others, or attending closely to some other aspect of the environment, as a way of helping a phobic patient cope with fear and anxiety.

Dr. Lynch quotes a psychiatric colleague who remarked, during a discussion of the rise in blood pressure during speech, that "It's clear Sigmund Freud knew what he was doing when he got the patient to talk! By remaining quiet, at least he spared his own cardiovascular system. Maybe he unconsciously felt the vascular stress of face-to-face dialogue and thus opted for the only personally healthy method available to him."

But you don't have to be a therapist to improve your own health, as well as your relationships, by listening—*really* listening.

8
Keep in Touch

Listening attentively to others is one way to improve your relationships with people who are close to you, as well as your own physical and mental health.

Deepening your relationships by doing things to bring you closer to those you care about is equally important. My first suggestion to help you accomplish this goal is very simple: keep in touch.

Some people always find time to nurture relationships with old friends and relatives by writing leisurely letters, visiting occasionally, and making telephone calls, while others never seem to bother. As a result, old friendships weaken and eventually disintegrate.

Fortunately, most women do form and maintain close friendships and are able to share personal feelings and experiences with other women. Among men, though, except for homosexuals, close friendship appears to be relatively rare.

One man I know tried to reach out toward other men at a time in his life when he felt lonely and isolated following a divorce. He found that men had networks of business associates and tennis partners, but that they confided in their wives or mistresses and not in other men. Most seemed unwilling or unable to form a close relationship with another man.

Men in our culture are probably less conditioned than women toward close friendships with others of the same sex, but they are not the only ones who may let friendships wither through lack of nurture.

As I write this, I can name at least four people with whom I've had extremely close friendships at various periods of my life, and would still have much in common if we should meet again. Yet because I did not make the effort (and they didn't either) we have drifted apart.

Right now I'm thinking of reestablishing these contacts. I don't like the feeling that I am too busy for friendship.

One of Meyer Friedman's behavioral prescriptions for Type A

patients who have experienced a coronary attack, or are prime candidates for doing so, is to begin to write letters again, on a regular basis, to relatives and friends.

Often Type A's must make a conscious effort to rekindle their interest in other people. Hard-driving, competitive people tend to be so preoccupied with their own activities that they promptly erase from their minds anything others tell them.

If you suffer from this preoccupation with your own affairs, you can overcome it. After every encounter or telephone conversation with a friend, make a deliberate effort to recall what he or she discussed with you. If she mentioned the possibility of her daughter's getting a divorce or her husband's early retirement, spend a few minutes thinking about these things and wondering about the outcome. Then, before talking with your friend again, think about them once more so that you can ask about them. This will help you stop the process of instantly forgetting what others tell you.

Don't wait for your friends to call you. Make the effort to pick up the phone yourself just to talk, or to make plans to get together.

Naturally, each of us has a finite amount of time and energy to expend, and that means that we can develop and maintain only a few truly close relationships. But perhaps you have more time, and more energy, for friendships than you thought.

After all, how many things are really more important?

9
Hold that Temper

Woodrow Wilson once wrote: "If you come at me with your fist doubled, I think I can promise you that mine will double as fast as yours, but if you come to me and say, 'Let us sit down and take counsel together'... we will presently find... that the points on which we agree are many."

Among the most difficult couples I see in marital therapy are those in which one partner is a clear-cut Type A personality—manifesting irritation and hostility over the most trivial matters—and figuratively, if not literally, approaching every encounter with a doubled fist.

Free-floating hostility, one of the traits that is typical of the Type A personality, leads to critical impatience, contempt, obscenity, and angry outbursts of temper out of all proportion to the stimuli that evoked them.

Some things are worth getting angry about, of course, and deepfelt anger or resentment toward an important person in your life needs to be expressed. But swearing and fuming because you are stuck in traffic, or because your mate forgot an item on the grocery list or neglected to put a glass in the dishwasher, are not helpful and are actually harmful. Such actions obviously hurt relationships, even though many of these seething, easily irritated people are curiously oblivious to the interpersonal havoc they are creating.

"I didn't mean anything by what I said," a Type A personality may comment after the explosion has passed. "Why can't she just forget it?"

And the constant expression of anger adversely affects your health as well. Just as laughter causes the brain to release pain-relieving endomorphins, Type A behavior with its associated angry outbursts results in the extra production of norepinephrine and ACTH.

"We believe that it is the excess discharge of norepinephrine—the hormone manufactured by the sympathetic nervous system, and employed as its messenger agent to control the correct functioning of the heart and the degree of constriction or dilation of the body's large and small arteries—that is chiefly responsible for the development of arterial diseases," Dr. Meyer Friedman writes.

It is his contention that Type A behavior, through the production of excess norepinephrine, initiates or exacerbates three arterial diseases: migraine, high blood pressure, and coronary heart disease. The exact physiological process by which these changes occur remains to be more definitely described. One factor, however, seems to be the interference of excess norepinephrine with the liver's ability to rid the body of unneeded fat.

Type B personalities, in contrast to Type A ones, rarely lose their tempers over traffic tie-ups, trivial errors of subordinates, or the inevitable problems of family life. They have the ability to overlook the minor errors and shortcomings of their wives and children. They are free to give and receive praise and to express affection both verbally and physically.

While women as well as men may suffer from Type A behavior, their expressions of hostility are usually less dramatic, less obscene, and less abrasive. They show fewer facial signs of hostility, seldom tap their fingers on tables or desks, and are less likely to suck in their breath while speaking. Like Type A men, however, they try to hurry the speech of others, and may pretend to listen while actually thinking of something else.

One Type A woman consulted me because she was having increasing difficulty tolerating her second husband, an easy-going Type B with a casual attitude toward the niceties of life that Molly considered of the utmost importance. She often complained that Pat had "messed up my kitchen." He would walk over a floor she had recently waxed and wasn't good about cleaning up the dishes if he prepared something to eat.

He ate sloppily and wore pants and shirts that didn't match. "Why can't he try to look nice to please me?" Molly continually lamented. "He knows how much I care about things like that." She didn't like the way he spoke to guests and criticized his interactions with his children, his grandchildren, and his elderly mother.

As she barked out her complaints, punctuated with occasional obscenities and grimaces, Molly recognized that her seething anger was entirely out of proportion to Pat's misdeeds. Yet everything he did continued to irritate her. "Molly picks" was Pat's view of things.

When she became extremely angry, or when her inhibitions were released by a few drinks, Molly sometimes threw dishes, even dishes full of food, against the wall of the kitchen she cared for so meticulously. "I'm ashamed to tell you what I did this week," she often began.

Eventually she gained considerable control over her behavior, but she could find only one way to rid herself of her seething irritation with Pat. She left him.

If you are afflicted with the kind of free-floating hostility that typifies the Type A personality, you do not have to go through the rest of your life irritating, and being irritated by, everyone around you. You can change.

With the assistance of a grant from the National Heart, Lung and Blood Institute and additional financial support from several private corporations, a group of 1,012 volunteers who had experienced one or more heart attacks, and a staff of specially trained psychiatrists, psychologists, nurses, and cardiologists, Dr. Friedman initiated the San Francisco Recurrent Coronary Prevention Project in the fall of 1978. The objective of the study was to determine whether the modification of Type A behavior prevented recurrent heart attacks.

Volunteer participants were randomly assigned to two groups that both received identical cardiovascular counseling, but Section II was given Type A behavior counseling as well. A third group, composed of post-infarction patients who volunteered for yearly follow-up examinations only, served as a control. The cardiovascular counseling was provided in 90-minute sessions every two weeks for three months, monthly for three months, and then at two-month intervals for the remainder of the study.

At these sessions counselors stressed the dangers of eating even a single meal loaded with excessive fat, of severe physical exercise, of the excessive use of caffeine and alcohol, of very high altitudes, and of prolonged exposure to cold—physical conditions that have all been found to exacerbate coronary heart disease. (Smoking was not a factor, since volunteers were not accepted unless they had stopped smoking at least six months previously.)

In addition, the Type A behavioral counseling group met for 90 minutes each week for the first two months, every other week for the next two months, and then monthly for the remainder of the study.

At the end of four years, questionnaire and interview data indicated that statistically significant changes in Type A behavior had occurred in Section II participants. And they had experienced significantly fewer heart attacks than those in Section I.

Since this investigation so conclusively proved that altering Type A behavior can reduce the likelihood of recurring heart attacks in those who have already experienced one or more, it seems reasonable to assume that modifying Type A behavior can also prevent coronary heart disease from occurring in the first place.

Dr. Friedman recommends this type of behavior modification for several particular groups of individuals: those who suffer from irregularities in their heartbeats or angina, those who have had a positive treadmill test (showing electrocardiographic abnormalities or having to discontinue the test due to angina or a pronounced drop in blood pressure), those with maturity onset diabetes (which has been found to accelerate the course of coronary disease), those with a family history of coronary heart disease or hypertension, and "triple risks"—individuals who smoke 10 or more cigarettes per day, suffer from hypertension, and have a high cholesterol level. In addition, he points to those not in immediate physical danger in whom Type A behavior "has created a wasteland of character and personality."

Anyone who has been closely involved with an individual with severe Type A manifestations knows that this is no exaggeration. "The aggravation, irritation, anger, and impatience which are the main exterior signs of Type A behavior are unlovely at best and truly hateful when present to a high degree," Dr. Friedman writes. "They usually evoke a negative reaction in others at both the conscious and the unconscious level. For example, the Type A's impatience, which habitually leads to the attempt to finish other people's sentences for them, to interrupt and make them speak faster, may very well come across as an attempt to dominate. . . . The Type A's habit of criticizing other people, often in foul language, is equally repellent even to other Type A's."

If you recognize the signs of Type A behavior in yourself and realize that these are interfering with your relationships with others, you will be happier and healthier as soon as you decide to change the aspects of your behavior that are causing problems. Recognizing the behavior and making a decision to change is the first step.

Shortly after the publication of Dr. Friedman's book, *Treating Type A Behavior: And Your Heart* (New York: Knopf, 1984), I attended a two-day medical conference at which he was one of the speakers. The most useful thing I learned at the conference was a technique that Dr. Friedman described (but does not mention in his book) for learning to subdue the constant irritability that is the hallmark of the Type A.

Don't Explode . . . Say Hook!

This technique is called "The Hook," and I have found it to be extremely helpful for Type A's. (I have used it occasionally myself, since along with Dr. Friedman and the majority of psychologists, physicians, attorneys, and corporation executives, I too confess to some Type A characteristics.)

If you are easily irritated, I'm sure you will readily agree that by noon on a typical day you have already experienced a dozen or more (possibly *many* more) potential irritants. Think of each of these potential irritants as a hook—one that you can choose to bite or not to bite. The choice is up to you.

Since humor is a good way of dissipating anger, it may help to visualize yourself as a fish with a big mouth at the same instant you say "hook!"

The objective is to swim past as many hooks as possible.

"I've managed not to get angry, I mean not *really* angry, for over three weeks," a divorced mother told me yesterday. "I feel positively victorious that I have managed to ignore so many things that would have hooked me in the past. As a result, I feel a lot better in every way, and my relationship with my daughter has improved 100 percent. I realize now that I have been quite abusive verbally in the past. For the first time in years, I feel that I can give her my unconditional love."

The search for the underlying causes of such anger, like the search for the underlying cause of most behavior problems, it seems to me, is largely unproductive. Much time and effort can be expended in sifting through the past to allocate blame, which needless to say can usually be attributed to one or both parents. Although there is some value in pointing out the probable antecedents, after a reasonably thorough (but not excessively time-consuming) discussion of a patient's childhood, going over and over it tends to make the problem worse rather than better.

Some patients are worse off after extensive psychotherapy than they would be if they had had none at all. They are well informed, they tell me, about the causes of their problem, but they are no closer to getting rid of it than before. In fact, their tendency to ruminate unnecessarily about their neglectful, ungiving, or downright abusive parents gets in the way of constructive action.

Nowhere is this more apparent than in the case of the hostile outbursts of the Type A personality. As long as he or she justifies such behavior by feelings of anger toward a parent (who by now may have been deceased for many years), little progress can be made.

If you suffer from free-floating hostility, you must take responsibility for the behavior yourself. And you must take responsibility for changing it. The more you express this senseless hostility, the more, not less, angry you become. Exploding over nothing causes further damage to your self-esteem as well as raising your blood pressure and alienating those around you.

I don't believe in suppressing all anger, or in striving for a bland, lifeless personality. But I do believe in changing those things that are seriously interfering with your health and your relationships.

To help you identify Type A behavior in yourself, Dr. Friedman's list of tell-tale signs is helpful:

"(1) If you become irritated or angry at relatively minor mistakes of your family members, friends, acquaintances, or complete strangers or find such mistakes hard to overlook; (2) if you frequently find yourself critically examining a situation in order to find something that is wrong or might go wrong; (3) if you find yourself scowling and unwilling or unable to laugh at things your friends laugh at; (4) if you are overly proud of your ideals and enjoy telling others about them; (5) if you frequently find yourself thinking or saying that most people cannot be trusted, or that everyone has a selfish angle or motive; (6) if you find yourself regarding even one person with contempt; (7) if you have a regular tendency to shift the subject of a conversation to the errors of large corporations, or various departments and officers of the federal government, or of the younger generation; (8) if you frequently use obscenities in your speech; (9) if you find it difficult to compliment or congratulate other people with honest enthusiasm."

You can't possibly avoid all the irritants in your life, but you can change your reaction to them. While you are working to do so, it will be helpful to keep an ongoing daily journal in which you record every angry outburst *at the time it happens*. Later, when you have cooled down, reread what you have written and ask yourself whether the stimulus justified the outburst. In other words, was it worth it?

Try to put things into rational perspective and simply overlook unimportant irritants. And deliberately eliminate obscenity from your conversations. This doesn't vent hostility but often intensifies it. Finally, summoning your sense of humor will help.

You know what responses are healthy. Even if you feel angry over some minor episode, you don't have to act that way. Change your actions first, and your feelings will follow. Behave as if you feel the way you would like to feel.

If you are accustomed to exhibiting hostile behavior, you may need some practice in summoning a smile easily. You can do this by regularly recalling happy or amusing events, and by deliberately practicing your smile in front of a mirror, observing all the facial changes that accompany it.

Then get out there and start smiling.

PART 6
Speak Up for Your Health's Sake

1
Get It Off Your Chest

Being the strong silent type doesn't pay off. At least, not where your health is concerned.

Confiding in others has definite benefits in terms of your physical and emotional well-being. Studies of Blue Cross members in the United States and of several thousand patients in national health plans in Europe have found that individuals undergoing psychotherapy consult physicians for medical problems less frequently than those who are not in therapy. This isn't surprising when you consider that a high percentage of visits to doctors' offices—some estimates place the figure as high as 50 percent—are due to psychological rather than physical problems.

Why is the act of confiding so beneficial? Some psychologists attribute it to the availability of comparison information, others to the help it provides in organizing, structuring, and meaningfully interpreting the experience. In addition, financial assistance, medical treatment, or practical advice may result directly from the act of telling someone about the problem.

Studies of confiders versus nonconfiders have found that nonconfiders, or repressors, have higher cancer rates, higher mortality rates following breast cancer diagnosis, elevated blood pressure, and more physical disease in general. In laboratory tests, repressors exhibit significantly higher blood pressure, skin conductance, forehead muscle tension, and higher cardiovascular responses.

James Pennebaker, a Southern Methodist University psychologist, has carried out a series of research studies of the long-term health benefits of confiding in others. He believes, based on his investigations, that if you experience a severe trauma and inhibit your natural impulse to confide in someone, you are more likely to obsess about it for several years or decades. And in the long run you are more likely to develop some major or minor diseases as a result.

While confiding in others is something almost everyone does following upheavals such as death of a spouse, childbirth, and divorce, certain other less acceptable experiences such as rape or the commission of a serious crime are less likely to be discussed. Even rather minor events that cause embarrassment or make people "look bad" are frequently concealed.

I have often found patients reluctant to disclose episodes they consider shameful—rape, incest, or criminal activity (of their own or a family member)—even in the therapeutic situation. Often these events are revealed after a solid bond of trust has been established.

Bulimia, alternate binging and vomiting, is a problem that many young women conceal for years, even from members of their immediate families. "I've never told this to anyone before" is a frequent preface to a confession of a habit felt to be extremely shameful. One young woman finally told me she was bulimic after I had been seeing her for several years.

Yesterday, while interviewing a young girl I had not seen before, I suspected from her statement that she was frightened of men that she had been the victim of rape or incest in the past. When I questioned her about it, she said, "That's something from my past that I would rather not discuss. I want you to help me and I'm afraid that if you knew about that, you wouldn't want to."

The act of *not* confiding or not discussing is regarded by Dr. Pennebaker and his associates as behavioral inhibition, since confiding is the more usual course of action. When inhibition occurs on a short-term basis, it is reflected in such changes as blushing, heart rate, and blood pressure. Long-term inhibition, according to psychologists with this point of view, is associated with stress-related diseases such as heart attacks, cancer, and ulcers. Confiding the feelings associated with a traumatic event allows a person to integrate and assimilate the event and put it behind him or her.

Every therapist has had patients who have failed to complete their "grief work" following death or divorce, due to a refusal to face painful feelings. To move forward, these patients must complete the mourning process. Many are significantly depressed until this is accomplished, even though the precipitating event may have occurred years before.

A Case of Not Confiding

A few weeks ago I saw a couple whose marriage had been in serious trouble since the death several years ago of the young man's mother, who had lived with them. She had departed abruptly, after an argument with her daughter-in-law, to visit a son who lived in the Midwest.

Before leaving, she telephoned several family members and announced to them that "If anything happens to me, it's Angela's fault." Shortly after her arrival at her son's home in Cincinnati, she died of a heart attack.

Unlike the rest of his family, Eugene didn't blame his wife for his mother's heart attack; he blamed himself. But he talked to no one about his feelings; instead, he ate. He had gained over 30 pounds when the couple came to see me.

"It's as if he doesn't care about me, the kids, or himself any more," Angela complained. "He wears sloppy clothes and won't even get a haircut unless I tell him to." Refusing to discuss his feelings of guilt, sadness, and anger after his mother's death had led to a prolonged period of depression and interpersonal difficulties.

To investigate his hypotheses about the links between traumatic experience, behavioral inhibition, and disease, Dr. Pennebaker and his students have carried out a number of surveys which have borne out his contention that certain types of events are unlikely to be discussed, and that repression is frequently correlated with disease later in life.

A survey of 115 students enrolled in medical psychology classes at SMU found that those who reported extremely upsetting traumas before the age of 17 and had not confided in others took more over-the-counter medications, and had more symptoms and diseases, than subjects who had experienced no trauma or those who had confided in others about the traumas they had experienced.

A Written Confession

The results of another experiment suggest that expressing feelings can be effective even if they are not spoken aloud to another person. Volunteers who spent 15 minutes writing about personal traumas during four consecutive evenings made fewer visits to doctors' offices in the next six months than did subjects who wrote about insignificant matters.

Of course, there are certain instances where confiding, regardless of its physiological benefits, may be maladaptive. Confessing a crime of your own or your spouse's, for example, obviously could lead to arrest. And repeatedly talking about a trauma, with no resolution of the feeling involved, may lead to higher rather than lower levels of anxiety.

On the whole, though, inhibiting the confiding of problems isn't healthy. A series of studies at Harvard University under the direction of psychologist David McClelland indicates that people who generally keep their feelings to themselves tend, under stress, to release hormones that lower their immune system's resistance to disease. If you belong to the majority for whom confession is good for the body as well as the soul, you may find that writing in a diary or journal is the best way of expressing your feelings at times.

Sometimes it is unwise to reveal too much. It's not always a good idea to say whatever is on your mind. Confiding can be mischievous or even hostile if its purpose is to make the listener feel guilty or cause trouble for a third party.

Talking too freely about one's personal problems can also reveal a self-centeredness that can alienate the listener. Some people take advantage of sympathetic listeners who have difficulty interrupting a monologue and more generally in asserting their rights in a relationship.

Are Women Better Confidantes?

Does it matter whether your confidante is a man or a woman?

It may.

Research studies suggest that most husbands do not perform the "mental hygiene" function of marriage. Almost a third of 731 husbands in one survey were reported to respond to their wives' problems with criticism, rejection, or indifference. Women are generally expected to fulfill the nurturing, expressive role—and they do.

In a three-year survey of 1,000 adults in the Albany, New York, area, people with a confidante of either sex reported feeling less anxious and depressed than people who had no confidante. Dr. Nan Lin, the sociologist who conducted the study, speculates that friends of the opposite sex are better psychological complements for one another.

He attributes this to the fact that women are usually better at communicating than are men. When their male friends are depressed, it's natural for them to get the men to express their feelings.

On the other hand, men are generally more practical, and tend to go out and do things when they feel depressed. When their women friends are depressed, they encourage them to be more active.

There may be times when there is no friend, male or female, who can provide the understanding or advice you need. Then you must seek out a special confidante—a therapist.

Confiding in a therapist is considerably different from confiding in a spouse or friend.

You don't have to worry about a therapist's feelings, and you can be free to express whatever is on your mind without fearing that it will be held against you. You know the therapist will have your best interests in mind, and that he or she will accept you no matter what you say.

2
Healthy Speech

Some kinds of speech are healthier than others. And it isn't entirely, or even primarily, a matter of *what* you say. It's how you say it.

As everyone who has been closely involved with hypertensive patients knows, they speak more quickly and more intensely when discussing an emotionally laden topic. They often breathe irregularly while speaking; some literally keep on talking until they run out of breath. Even when hypertensive individuals speak softly and slowly, they may not breathe properly.

Dramatic changes in blood pressure are experienced by hypertensives during speech, but they are seldom felt. In fact, those patients whose blood pressure fluctuates the most are likely to feel it the least. Even when their blood pressure is dangerously elevated, they feel nothing.

In the course of the therapeutic technique devised by Dr. James Lynch at the University of Maryland Medical School, patients learn to recognize changes in their bodies by observing a computer monitor during therapy. They are instructed by the therapist in modifying their speech patterns to keep blood pressure at acceptable levels.

Among the patients Dr. Lynch describes is Karl, 54, a typical Type A personality who had been taking hypertensive drugs for almost a decade before coming to the clinic for treatment. During his first psychiatric session, Karl's blood pressure averaged around 155/95, with significant fluctuations during speech. He initially resisted watching computer tracings of his blood pressure, but by the sixth session he had become intrigued with the changes he observed.

On one occasion, when Karl made an emotionally significant statement and his blood pressure then soared from 145/90 to 195/140, he declared: "I didn't feel anything. I didn't feel a damn thing! I didn't feel that damn pressure go up, and I didn't feel it go back down. Nor do I now feel anything other than a bit lightheaded."

"What do you think that means?" his psychiatrist asked. "Does it tell you anything about your feelings?"

"Christ!" he exclaimed. "I must be totally disconnected from my body and my feelings."

In the course of the next six months Karl began to connect his blood pressure changes to certain topics of conversation. He actually started to sense his own feelings for the first time in his life.

Observation of computer tracings of blood pressure during therapy and instruction in slow talking versus fast talking, listening versus talking, breathing and relaxing while talking, and being attentive to the emotional content of speech are key factors in the therapeutic program for hypertensive patients at the University of Maryland. Patients are taught how to communicate effectively without dangerously elevating their blood pressure.

You don't need to wait until you have a heart attack or are diagnosed as hypertensive to improve the way you communicate with others. Even if you have not developed physical problems—or are not aware of them—you may be conscious of the fact that your communications are causing interpersonal problems.

Most Type A individuals I see do not come because they have health problems, but because their explosive personalities and their angry communications are getting them into interpersonal difficulty, most often with a spouse.

Here are five simple rules that will make your own communications more effective as well as better for your health:

1. Stop to listen—give the other person a chance to talk. And listen *attentively*, don't just pretend to listen.
2. When you catch yourself racing your words, slow them down.
3. Stop to relax and breathe deeply.
4. Curb your tendency to interrupt. If necessary, ask a family member or a friend to remind you when you do it.
5. Before embarking on a long story, stop to ask yourself whether anyone really wants to hear it. If not, you'll find yourself in a race to finish before you lose their attention completely.

It may seem difficult at first to remember these rules, but you can in time. You, your friends, your spouse, and your heart will all be glad you did.

3
Happy Talk

Happy talk—any conversation that makes you, or someone else, feel happy—is an extension of positive thinking and has stress-reducing effects similar to those produced by laughter. Humor is, in fact, one aspect of happy talk, but there are others as well.

Take compliments, for example. I don't mean flattery, which tends to be insincere, but genuine praise. How often have you "thought" a compliment without saying it? Every time you do that, you're depriving someone you know of an opportunity for happiness.

If you're attuned to the idea of being complimentary, you'll find more things to comment positively about. It's a way of thinking as well as a way of talking, and it's a way of thinking you'll enjoy.

People often get in the habit of pointing out all the flaws and negatives in others without stating the positive—which is so much more effective. This happens between married couples and between parents and children. One of the first things I try to do in such cases is to interrupt the flow of negative communication by helping them to focus on the positives.

Sometimes, a patient will say, "but there's *nothing* about his behavior that I like!" If the relationship in question is a troubled marriage, a completely negative appraisal by either partner usually signals the beginning of the end.

When a parent makes that comment about a child, I try to convince her (it's usually her) that there must be *something* about the child that pleases her. Children do go through difficult stages when most of what they do is unattractive or unappealing. But you can't divorce your child; you'll feel much better if you start focusing on the positives.

Eloise, who lost her own mother at an early age, was almost sick over her relationship with her teenage daughter. She frequently cried when she talked about it. Since she'd never really known her own mother, she had very unrealistic expectations of her relationship with her daughter. She didn't realize that teenage rebellion is a normal part of growing up and developing independence.

Because she expected that things would always go smoothly between them, she was frequently disappointed, and became increasingly critical of Wendy's behavior. It was difficult for her to say anything positive about Wendy—despite the fact that Wendy did well in school, held an after-school job, and had never been in any kind of trouble.

Their interactions were so tense that mother and daughter avoided each other. Eloise was extremely angry about Wendy's sullenness and her lack of interest in participating in family activities.

When she eased up on her criticism and demands and started relating small pleasant pieces of her day to her daughter, she noticed an improvement almost immediately.

"For the first time I feel that I'm making some progress with our relationship," she said. "And for the first time I feel that Wendy is trying too. Things are much happier around the house. She says goodbye when she leaves and hello when she comes in. One morning she even asked my advice about what to wear."

If you have subordinates at work or have household help, your relations with them will improve if you look for opportunities to express your recognition of a job well done. This idea seems so simple and basic that I wonder why anyone has to be reminded of it. Yet I often hear the complaint that "My boss never gives me any positive feedback."

Obviously there are times when complaints and negative statements are necessary. But the more sincere positive comments you can make, the happier you and those close to you will be.

A social worker I know came up to me at a recent art opening to say, "I just had to tell you that a patient came in last week carrying your book. She said, 'Do you know this book? It's really good!' I told her I knew not only the book, but the author."

I was pleased that Mildred went out of her way to relate this positive comment to me—and I told her so.

How Do You Respond to Compliments?

It's possible that, without even meaning to do so, you have been discouraging positive feedback. How do you respond to compliments?

Here are some reactions that are certain to discourage further efforts to praise you:

- Saying nothing.
- Replying, "Oh, it wasn't much."
- Declaring, "I was just lucky, that's all."
- Changing the subject immediately.
- Comparing yourself unfavorably to the speaker or someone else: "Oh, you could have done it much better."

These responses make the speaker feel ridiculous and put down by your failure to acknowledge the compliment. In effect you've destroyed both his or her pleasure in giving the compliment and your own in receiving it.

When the compliment involves some aspect of your appearance or clothing, avoid saying, "Oh, *this* old dress?" or "It was a bargain" or "I don't *feel* like I look nice," or, even worse, "You can't really mean that?"

Even if it seems unnatural at first, practice acknowledging a compliment with a simple "Thank you" or "That makes me feel really good." This will add enormously to your own good feelings and the pleasure of those around you who have gone to the trouble to say something nice.

Compliments, of course, aren't the only kind of happy talk. How often do you tell your husband, parents, and children that you love them?

It's sad that there are so many people around who never directly and verbally express their love. "I always knew my father loved me by the things he did for me," women often say. "But he never said so." It really isn't enough to say, "He knows I love him." Why not tell him now and then to be sure?

Between friends, too, there are many opportunities for a direct positive statement of feeling, yet these are often missed. One of my patients turned back at the door of my office the other day. "I had a 'Gee, I like you' I wanted to say today," she declared.

Sharing positive experiences is another aspect of happy talk. I'm very pleased that my children seem eager to let me know when something good happens to them. When I received a message recently to call one of my daughters at her office, I was afraid she might be upset about something. She'd been in her first professional job only six months and, being quite a perfectionist, often didn't feel sure of herself.

"I got a $4,000 raise!" she exclaimed when I reached her. "And when I had my review they didn't say one bad thing about me!" You can't go around telling the world that you received a raise, but you can certainly tell the people who care about you.

And there are many other positives that most of us experience every day that we could relate to others. I'm not advising you to turn into Pollyanna, but reporting on the pleasant side of life can't hurt, and it can help.

Norman Cousins relates the story of his visit to a group therapy program for cancer patients he organized at the Sepulveda, California, VA hospital. At the beginning of the meeting, each person was required to report some auspicious personal happening.

"I hadn't realized that I was expected to talk about something good that had happened to me," he related. "Fortunately I was not without material."

Here is the story he told:

" 'Something happened to me last Thursday that was indescribably wonderful,' I said. 'Never again, as long as I live, do I expect it to happen again. It was unforgettable. What happened was that when I arrived at the Los Angeles Airport from Chicago, my suitcase was the first one off the baggage carousel.'

"An ovation.

" 'That was not all,' I said. 'I went to the telephone to call the office and promptly lost a dime when an operator came on and asked for a quarter. It was a recording. I put in another dime, got a live operator, told her what happened, and she said the phone company would be glad to send me the dime if I would give her my name and address. It seemed absurd that the phone company would spend 20 cents in stamps, to say nothing of personnel expense, just to refund a dime—and I said so. I also pressed the coin-return lever.

" 'At that point, all the innards of the machine opened up and quarters and dimes tumbled out in magnificent and overflowing profusion.

" 'Operator,' I asked, 'are you still there?'

" 'Yes.'

" 'Operator, something quite remarkable has just happened. All I did was press the coin-return lever and the machine is giving me all its earnings. There must be more than three dollars in coins here and the flow hasn't stopped.'

" 'Sir,' she said, 'will you please put the money back in the box?'

" 'Operator,' I said, 'if you will give me your name and address, I'll be glad to mail it to you.'

"Cheers, applause, standing ovation."

Not a bit involved with self-praise, either of these stories.

Yet, undeniably happy talk—the kind I urge you to become accustomed to. Happy things happen to everybody some of the time. When you develop the habit of looking for them—and talking about them—they have a way of happening more often.

4
Assert Yourself

Depressed people are not assertive.

And assertive people are not likely to be depressed.

Depression results from, or leads to, what one writer has called "learned helplessness." Animals and humans who believe they have no control over their own lives lose hope and become apathetic.

If you feel that what you say has no impact on those around you, or if you fear expressing your feelings because you are afraid to upset others, you are not in control of your life. You may think that going along with the wishes of others is taking the easy way out. But in the long run it isn't.

Yesterday I heard the ultimate story of nonassertiveness. A bright and successful young man sat in my office and told me and his wife that he had married her ten years before because he didn't want to hurt her feelings.

"I knew that getting married was a mistake," he said. "And I tried to convince you that it would be too difficult financially. I told you how hard you'd have to work while I was in graduate school, and you did."

"But," she objected rationally, "you put it all on financial grounds. You never said you didn't want to marry me."

"It was too hard to break the engagement," he said diffidently. "I just couldn't do it. I figured that we were good friends and that we both liked sports and that it would work out OK."

But it didn't. Now, ten years and two children later, Bart had reached the point where he could no longer continue in the marriage.

"You didn't want to hurt me," Ilona repeated incredulously. "What do you think you're doing to me now?"

He shrugged his shoulders helplessly.

"What about the children?" she demanded. "We talked about having children."

"I just went along with it," he said miserably. "It didn't seem like such a bad idea at the time."

Bart's nonassertiveness had cost him ten years of depression, not to mention the agony his wife was suffering and the pain his children would experience as a result of the divorce. And he had thought he was taking the easy way out.

Leslie was depressed too. An appealing 19-year-old college sophomore, she spoke desperately about her lack of success with boys, her tendency to be an academic grind, her jealousy of her younger sister, and her inability to make real friends as opposed to acquaintances.

"My parents are absolutely perfect," she declared on her first visit. "They're supportive, they're fair, they're my best friends. And yet," she continued with a sob, "it seems like my perfect parents have managed to screw me up pretty badly."

Despite their alleged perfection, it soon developed that Leslie's parents were extremely critical. She related being labeled as "selfish, inconsiderate, cheeky, and thoughtless" on various occasions. Her clothing was under constant scrutiny. "But," she added, "they're always right. If they say I'm being selfish, I realize that I am. And if they say I'm cheeky, I realize I was talking back."

"What's wrong with talking back?" I inquired.

Leslie looked shocked. "You don't talk back to your elders," she stated categorically.

And Leslie literally never had. "Haven't you ever rebelled against your parents?" I asked.

"There's never been any need to rebel," she said defensively. "My parents are absolutely fair. My sister rebels all the time. They expect that from her, but not from me."

"I think it's time for you to start speaking up for yourself," I told her. "The next time one of your parents tells you you're selfish, why don't you tell them you disagree?"

Leslie stared. "You don't know my father," she said. "Nobody disagrees with my father."

"I suppose you're constantly telling *yourself* that you're selfish and inconsiderate and don't have good taste in clothes," I said.

"How did you know?" she replied. "They're with me even if they're not with me. If I don't get up to give an old lady a seat on the bus, I tell myself I'm being selfish. And I'm never satisfied with how I look."

"Leslie, you're not going to feel better until you stop trying to be a good little girl all the time," I said emphatically. "How could you *not* be depressed when someone is constantly criticizing you for being selfish, inconsiderate, cheeky, or poorly dressed—and you don't even defend yourself?"

Studies show a positive relationship between depressive symptoms and nonassertive behavior. Depressed people either avoid interpersonal contact entirely or function ineffectively in their interactions with others.

Assertiveness training is one of the most effective behavioral techniques for treating depression. Taking control over some aspect of one's behavior, however small, decreases feelings of hopelessness and helplessness.

Nonassertive people typically put everyone else's needs ahead of their own because they fear that disagreeing will cause others to dislike them, or because they feel their own rights are not important. Nonassertiveness is almost always a characteristic of my phobic patients, who have to be taught how to function more independently and speak up for themselves more forcefully as well as be helped to deal directly with their phobic symptoms. The helpless, dependent, giving-up attitude is apparently conducive to the development of certain physical diseases as well as of depressive, anxious, and phobic states.

Although the topic is still controversial, research studies point to a relationship between the psychological state of "giving up" and the development of cancer. Dr. Lawrence LeShan, a psychologist who is the author of *You Can Fight for Your Life: Emotional Factors in the Treatment of Cancer* (New York: M. Evans, 1977), identifies four typical components in the life histories of over 500 cancer patients.

One of these components is a feeling of despair following the loss of an important role or relationship, which was not expressed but bottled up. These patients simply couldn't let others know how they felt. Others described them as "wonderful," "saintly," or "good"; they tended to put others' needs unfailingly ahead of their own.

According to O. Carl Simonton, a pioneer in the psychological treatment of cancer, "most of our patients acknowledge that there was a time prior to the onset of their illness when they felt helpless, unable to solve or control problems in their lives, and found themselves 'giving up.' . . . They saw themselves as 'victims'—months before the onset of cancer—because they no longer felt capable of altering their lives in ways that would resolve their problems or reduce their stresses."

Dr. Simonton says that most of the cancer patients he has treated "recall having had feelings of helplessness or hopelessness some months prior to the onset of the disease. This process does not *cause* cancer, rather it permits cancer to develop. . . . It is this giving up on life that plays a role in interfering with the immune system and may, through changes in hormonal balance, lead to an increase in the production of abnormal cells. Physically, it creates a climate that is right for the development of cancer."

It is by no means certain that a passive, nonassertive, helpless stance will lead to cancer or some other life-threatening disease. But this attitude will, at the very least, lead to marked feelings of anxiety or depression, or a combination of the two.

Beginning to Assert Yourself

So I suggest that if you have assertive problems, you begin now to correct them. This is one of the most rewarding changes you can possibly make in your behavior.

In the past women have been culturally conditioned to the passive, dependent role—and they still generally receive conflicting messages or outright disapproval when they choose not to act in a traditionally feminine way. It's no wonder, then, that more women than men complain of depression.

When women become assertive, they are often accused of being aggressive or masculine. (It's all right for men to be aggressive, of course; in fact, it's expected.) I've been told on more than one occasion that I was "too direct." I know I am not abrasive or harsh in manner. It's just that women are somehow expected to be *indirect*.

I don't believe in expressing every feeling or thought you have without regard to its practical consequences or its effect on others. There are times when thoughts and feelings should be suppressed rather than expressed. Blurting out untactful or hurtful remarks is not what assertiveness is about.

If you are trying to become more assertive, it's possible that at first you may occasionally go a step too far and end up sounding aggressive. Up to a point this is all right—things will level out. But watch out, even in the beginning, for angry outbursts that may alienate you from others.

Actually, I don't find that this happens often with my nonassertive patients. Whether working with them individually or in a group, the greatest problem I encounter is resistance to changing *enough*. It's quite difficult for a passive person who's accustomed to going along with everyone else's wishes to suddenly begin speaking up for herself. But since people don't want to come back next week and say they didn't carry out the assignment, I can usually start producing gradual changes fairly quickly.

Role playing is the most effective way of teaching assertiveness, whether individually or in a group. I used to feel somewhat uncomfortable with the technique, as many patients do when it is first introduced, but now it comes very naturally.

Sometimes patients will say, after role-playing a particular situation, "but I could never think of that!" I tell them not to worry about simply using my words in the beginning, but that their own will come to them easily as they become more experienced and more comfortable with asserting themselves.

In the next several chapters I'll be talking about various aspects of assertiveness. I'll be giving you my words for handling the kinds of assertive problems I've found to occur most frequently among my patients.

I want to stress the fact that *how* you say them is extremely important, at least as important as the words themselves.

Assertive words delivered in a whisper will not get the message across, nor will assertive words delivered in a menacing tone create the impression you are after. It's essential to sit (or stand) erect (but not stiffly), to make comfortable eye contact, and to speak firmly but pleasantly. And now for some specifics.

5

Say What You Really Mean

Countless books have been published about how to communicate.

My own feeling is that communication should be direct and to the point (unless this course of action is going to produce unnecessary hurt feelings or some other undesirable consequence). Yet, as linguistics professor Deborah Tannen points out in her book *That's Not What I Meant* (New York: William Morrow, 1986), some people prefer to be indirect.

"I took it for granted that I would come out and say what I wanted, and that I could ask my husband what he wanted, and that he would tell me," she writes. "But he assumed that people—even married people—don't go around just blurting out what they want. To him, that would be coercive because he found it hard to deny a direct request. So he assumed people hint at what they want and pick up hints."

In Dr. Tannen's marriage (which, not surprisingly, didn't work out) her husband kept taking something she'd said "as a hint about what I wanted, and I mistook his agreement with what he thought I wanted for being what he really wanted. He kept acting on hints I hadn't thrown out, and I kept missing hints he had."

Indirect communication includes statements like "I don't think we should go out to dinner tonight because I know you're really tired" when what you mean is "Let's don't go—*I'm* tired."

Some people feel more comfortable with hints and excuses. They view these as polite ways of communication, while they see direct statements as blunt, possibly even rude. I've been accused of being *too* direct, even though I do all I can to avoid being rude. I don't say everything that comes into my mind, but I refuse to communicate through hints and nuances. That is, I refuse to do it *often*.

There are times when all of us, including myself, are not entirely direct. It just doesn't seem like the right thing to do. Suppose you've arranged with a friend to go out to dinner and you've been looking forward to it all day. At the last minute she calls and says, "I'm really exhausted. Do you mind if we don't go out tonight?" She's being direct and honest.

You have an equal right to say, "Yes, I do mind—I'd been counting on going out." But wouldn't that be rude, to insist on what *you* want? Most of us would say, martyrlike, "Oh, no, that's OK"—even though that isn't what we mean.

Sometimes indirectness is socially or culturally dictated. If you're having dinner at someone's house and are offered seconds, in some societies you would be considered rude if you eagerly accepted, and in others rude if you refused.

There are vast cultural differences that affect styles of communication and our expectations of others. Dr. Tannen relates the story of a Greek man who accused his American wife of speaking in an irritating monotone. He was accustomed to the extreme fluctuations in pitch typical of Greek women; her expression of emotion seemed highly unnatural to him.

Similarly, a young Protestant man I know found his Jewish wife's intense and volatile expression of anger extremely upsetting. "I come from a family of screamers," she explained. "It doesn't *mean* anything." But to him it did.

The pitch of your voice can change the meaning of what you say. "*What* did you say?" is obviously not the equivalent of "What *did* you say?" or "What did you *say*?" It's important to be aware of the stresses or inflections that modify the words you speak.

Similarly, what some people view as an encouraging or sympathetic response—"Wow!" for example, or "Oh, my God!"—might be startling and disconcerting to another. And if someone relates an experience and you say sympathetically, "That's *crazy*," your companion may think you mean *he's* crazy!

Asking a lot of questions seems friendly to some people, nosy to others. Of course, some questions are intrusive no matter when you ask them. But, while simply being conversational and trying to show an interest in another person, you may be perceived as behaving like the FBI.

It's true that there are differences in conversational styles. And it's true that there always will be some people who just can't bear to say what they mean, but prefer to communicate exclusively by innuendo, body language, and manipulation, expecting others to learn to read between the lines. But if you are having difficulty communicating with someone you are close to, I think you should learn to say what you mean and do all you can to encourage the other person to do the same. I believe that faulty styles of communication can, and should, be altered, so that people can understand each other clearly without constantly resorting to guessing games.

Yes, I *can* read between the lines, and I often do. It will always be necessary when dealing with certain patients, at least in the early stages of therapy. And I'm more than willing to try to understand and respect cultural differences with regard to communication.

Personal relationships are something else. If the subtleties of indirect communication are working well for you and your partner, and both of you enjoy playing this particular game, there's no need to change. But since you are reading this book I suspect that you are having some difficulties in interpersonal relationships. If so, I think learning to say what you mean may help.

6
Expressing Your Needs

Learning to express your own feelings and your needs is absolutely essential in working out a satisfactory relationship with another person.

That doesn't mean that you're going to have a "me first" attitude and not consider anyone else's feelings. But it does mean that you will give at least equal consideration to your own.

"He never tells me how he feels" is a frequent complaint I hear from my married women patients.

"I just don't know where this guy is coming from," a young woman declared this morning to me and the man she is living with. "He never tells me how he really feels. I have to keep asking and asking. It may take me 24 hours to get a perfectly simple answer that anybody else could come up with in five minutes."

She attacked him angrily, accusing him of concealing his feelings from her to try to present himself in a more favorable light.

"I grew up thinking it wasn't right to express any feelings," Barry said. "Even if I had a complaint about a friend, my mother would advise me to let it blow over. She didn't want to cause a scene. And at home if I expressed any feelings she didn't like she became very angry with me."

"Well, you still seem to be expecting Mother to get angry again if you let me know what you're feeling," Bea snapped back.

Barry really *didn't* know how to express his feelings. He'd never been taught how to do so. He needed help not only in expressing his feelings but in recognizing them.

In general, women are encouraged to express certain feelings more readily in our society than men. It's all right for women to cry (but not on the job!), although men who do are regarded with suspicion.

But in many families the verbal expression of feelings is not encouraged, either by men or women. Enlightened young couples are trying to facilitate more open discussions these days. Many of my clients who are young parents seem to me to be doing a very good job of helping their children learn to express themselves.

There are many people, though, who are not sure how they feel at any given moment. And there are even more who know how they feel, but wouldn't dare say so—or haven't dared to say so until now. These are the people who can most easily help themselves by learning to be more assertive.

Can You Say This?

Let's consider some of the feelings that most often need to be expressed:

- "I feel very angry."
- "I'm annoyed."
- "I'm bored."
- "I'm excited!"
- "I'm depressed."
- "I'm simply delighted."
- "I'm so frustrated."
- "I feel too rushed."
- "I feel a lot of pressure."
- "I feel very anxious."
- "I'm so happy right now."
- "I feel content."
- "I feel so relaxed."
- "I feel rested."
- "I'm upset."

How many of these feelings can you recall experiencing in the past week? How many have you expressed directly (in words) in the past week? How many have you felt but not expressed?

As a preliminary exercise, try to make a habit of sharing these feelings with the people closest to you. For the moment, just *imagine* yourself openly expressing them. As I've explained elsewhere, visualizing yourself doing something is the first step toward doing it successfully.

Naturally, you're usually annoyed or angry or excited *about* something, or as a result of something somebody did. This adds another dimension to the expression of feelings, and makes the problem a little more difficult. How many of these statements could you make to someone close to you? How many have you actually made?

- "It really bothered me when you . . . "
- "I don't like it when you . . . "
- "It makes me angry when you . . . "
- "You hurt my feelings when you . . . "
- "I like it a lot when you . . . "
- "It made me feel good that you . . . "
- "I don't agree with you that . . . "
- "I felt insulted when you . . . "
- "I felt rejected when you . . . "
- "I almost cried when you . . . "
- "It made me jealous that you . . . "
- "I resent it when you . . . "
- "I want you to . . . "

You've probably had occasion to make many of these statements within the past month. Did you? If not, what was stopping you? Do you often choke it all back and reply, "Nothing!" if someone asks you what's the matter—when something obviously *is* the matter?

Being able to say "I want you to . . . " or "I'd like for you to . . . " is especially important. I often ask patients to make sure they use these phrases several times each week.

"There's Something I'd Like to Talk to You About"

Patients frequently tell me that they have trouble initiating a conversation about a negative feeling. I suggest they do so by saying simply, "There's something we need to discuss" or "There's something I'd like to talk to you about," and then go right ahead and get to the point. One of the preceding phrases might follow this introduction.

People who aren't accustomed to being direct are usually surprised to discover that the expression of feelings can be so effective when it is done simply and openly. Often a patient expresses a feeling very directly to *me* about an important person in her life—usually a spouse, a parent, or a child, but sometimes a friend as well—and when I say, "Have you ever told him just how you feel?" she replies, "Oh, no! I couldn't" or "No, I guess not, not in those words." Sometimes she adds, "But he *knows* how I feel!"

I always ask how she can be so sure if she's never expressed the feeling openly. Don't expect to guess at anyone else's feelings, and don't make anyone else guess at yours.

I have one patient who constantly tries to second-guess me. Conditioned by her early experiences to expect rejection, she frequently says, "I *know* you're angry with me!" or "Now I've really done it. I know you won't want to see me again" or "You're thinking that I'm really a jerk." She's always wrong, but she's convinced that she is right.

To be understood clearly and correctly, feelings must be clearly expressed.

I'm talking about your personal relationships now, and not your relationships on the job. On the whole, I think you are better off keeping your emotions under control at work. Not always, perhaps, but most of the time.

Within a personal relationship, important feelings simply must be expressed. A fleeting annoyance or irritation about some trivial episode that may never reoccur is probably best ignored. You don't want to get in the habit of complaining about *everything*.

A young married woman told me yesterday that her husband is disgusted with her "nagging." As a result of overcoming a phobic problem that paralyzed her psychologically for years, she has developed the self-confidence to express her numerous dissatisfactions with her husband's lack of attentiveness, his constant "going out with the boys," his habit of falling asleep in front of the TV set immediately after dinner, and his failure to help her divorced mother with the yard work.

The list goes on and on; the problem is that Melanie's complaints are not leading to constructive changes. She has failed to recognize the fact that, having expressed her feelings clearly on several occasions, she now has the choice of accepting her husband the way he is or terminating the marriage, since he seems unwilling to change.

"He didn't even remember our anniversary—the first time in 13 years," Melanie declared. "I waited and waited. I'm always the one to bring it up. We usually go out the weekend before to celebrate. He was planning to go to the club on Monday. I couldn't believe it. Saturday came and went and he didn't say anything. Finally Sunday night I couldn't stand it any more. 'You're going out tomorrow?' I asked.

" 'We have anything planned?' he said.

"I looked at him kind of funny. 'I guess not,' I said. Then he knew. He got this sheepish look on his face. 'Oh, it's our anniversary,' he said. 'Why didn't you say something?'

"I blew up," Melanie continued. "Why do I always have to be the one? Why can't *he* remember?

"I was hurt, really hurt. I felt so bad all day at work Monday that I gave myself a headache. Then he came home with an anniversary card and a box of candy, and I felt better. But it still hurt that he hadn't said anything on his own.

"Sometimes I think the new me is too much for him to take. Maybe he liked me better when I was so obsessed with my problem that I didn't have the energy to complain about anything *he* did."

Melanie is dealing more successfully with her siblings. "I've always been the one they assumed would take care of Mom," she declared. "It's like I don't have any feelings and don't have a life of my own. They can make their own plans for holidays or move out of town because they know I won't leave Mom to sit home alone if she doesn't have plans. But I'm sick of it. I've told them they're all grown up now and it's time for them to take their turn. I'm not putting up with this any more—and I mean it! I'll do my share, but I won't do theirs too."

Is there some important feeling in your life right now that *you* need to express?

The first step, as always, is to identify the problem. The second is to figure out what you'd like to say, and the next is to rehearse the scene in your imagination.

Then do it.

For maximum peace of mind, improved relationships, and better physical and psychological health, your goal should be to express yourself openly and directly—unless for some reason it is not appropriate or desirable to do so.

7
Learn to Say "No"

Sometimes being assertive simply means being able to say "no."

If you frequently do things you don't want to do because you're afraid of upsetting someone else, or because you think being feminine means being meek and agreeable, you know how angry this can make you feel inside.

Some people, most of them women, will go along with someone else's wishes at the time, and later declare furiously that they didn't want to do so. "You *knew* I didn't want to!" they may say accusingly.

But maybe the other person didn't know. Indirect communication is usually faulty communication.

If you've somehow acquired the idea that it isn't feminine or nice to say "no," it's time to give yourself permission to use this small and very important word. It can make all the difference between being in control of your life and *not* being in control, between saying what you mean and *not* saying what you mean.

I sometimes assign patients the task of saying "no" at least three times a week—just to learn that they can do it. It's amazing what a big effect such a small change can produce.

I'm not advocating that you make a habit of saying "no" when you don't mean it—only that you refuse to do things you really don't want to do.

In general, I think women have become more assertive and better able to say "no" in recent years. I see fewer patients whose major complaint is that they have difficulty saying "no." But I still see them.

One of the most obvious and most potentially serious consequences of not being able to say "no" is getting more involved sexually than you wish. I still encounter women, both young and middle-aged, who have trouble saying "no" to men sexually. The threat of herpes and AIDS is forcing many women to assert themselves in this area for the first time.

But among high school- and college-age girls there are still many who say, "I was afraid if I said 'no' he wouldn't like me." (And the number of teenage pregnancies is still rising.)

Despite the dangers, some women are still so dependent on men's opinions and so lacking in self-confidence that they can readily be pressured into sexual submission. It isn't rape, because they agree to it. And often it doesn't even require much in the way of persuasion.

The emotional consequences of unwanted physical intimacy, quite aside from the possible complications of pregnancy or sexually transmitted infections, can be devastating. You cannot maintain feelings of self-esteem when you fail to exercise your right to control the intimate activities of your own body.

It is not only young and inexperienced girls who sometimes find it difficult to resist unwanted sexual advances. Newly divorced women in their thirties, forties, and even beyond may not know how to act or what to say when a man makes a sexual advance.

At the simplest level it is essential to protect yourself by avoiding intimate situations with strangers. If you accept a date with someone you don't know, unless he is well known to a friend you trust, arrange to meet him on safe territory like a restaurant or bar. Be sure you know whom you are dealing with before you place yourself in a situation where a difficult-to-resist sexual advance can occur.

Even if you are strongly attracted to a new romantic interest and *want* to get involved, you have the right to say, "You're going a little too fast for me" or "I'm not quite ready for that yet." Some women ask me how fast they should let matters progress.

"I'm completely out of practice," one divorcee said to me recently. "Just how fast is too fast?"

There's no easy answer. But if you feel it's too fast, then it *is* too fast, and you should refuse to let matters go any further. If in doubt, don't.

Often women have difficulty refusing dates with a man they don't want to go out with. They're afraid to hurt his feelings. I think, though, that this is changing as women gain more respect for themselves and value their own rights more highly.

But suppose you *are* invited out by someone you're not interested in dating. What can you say?

I think it's kindest to make an excuse the first time—and the second. There's no point in being brutally direct if it isn't necessary. If he asks a third time you could say, "I'm awfully busy right now. If I find I have some free time, I could get in touch with you."

That's about as far as politeness will carry you, but 99 out of 100 times that will be far enough. There may be a time when you'll have to say directly, "I'm sorry, but I'd really rather not." But this is quite unlikely to happen.

However, there are certainly going to be occasions when someone you like asks you to do something you don't want to do. There's nothing wrong with saying you don't care for war movies or you don't feel like going out to dinner or you don't want to go skiing this weekend. Of course, you must realize that a certain amount of compromise is involved in every relationship.

There's another category of request that is unreasonable. If you find yourself feeling uncomfortable or upset when someone asks you an inconvenient favor or wants you to take on an added chore you don't want, you have a perfect right to refuse. And it isn't necessary to add elaborate excuses, explanations, or apologies.

Some people, especially women, feel guilty when they say "no," regardless of the circumstances. If the "no" must be said to a lover or family member, the feeling of guilt increases.

Monica was very fond of her new grandchild but, having raised three children of her own and enjoying her new-found freedom to be alone with her husband, resented being treated as an always-available babysitter. Initially, she acquiesced to every request, feeling angry and put upon as she did so. When she began saying "no" to requests she didn't wish to accept, she was surprised to find that her daughter understood and respected her for speaking up.

Lisa resented the fact that her sister Judith, whose 5-year-old daughter enjoyed playing with Lisa's child, often asked if she could drop Ginny off for a few hours. To make matters worse, Judith used the time to go shopping or out to lunch with their other sister, Eve. Judith and Eve had always been close, while Lisa felt left out. Her feelings of annoyance at being used as a babysitter finally became so strong that she was angry enough to say "no." But she began to feel better about herself only after establishing a safe distance between herself and her sisters.

Eileen was married to a man several years her senior who had a college-age son from his previous marriage. Because he had divorced his first wife when his children were quite young, Art felt extremely guilty and could never say "no" to his son. When Art, Jr., began having increasing difficulties with his mother and decided to move in with his father and Eileen, she suddenly found herself "playing the heavy."

"It's so hard being a stepmother," she said. "I didn't want him living with us, but the poor kid had no place else to go. But when Art refused to tell him he couldn't help himself to our liquor supply, borrow the car without asking, and have his friends over for all-night parties when we were away, I had to be the one to say "no." We've worked most of it out fairly well now, but it hasn't been easy."

Fran finally managed to break away from Marvin, a man she'd lived with for almost two years. They'd decided to share an apartment rather impetuously after a brief acquaintance. Marv was temporarily, or so Fran thought, down on his luck. Significantly, it was Fran's apartment they shared. Marv had left the corporation he worked for, so he told her, and was looking for a simpler, more agreeable way of life. He was evasive about his divorce and his relationship, or the lack of one, with his children.

Several times Marvin asked Fran to lend him money, and each time she did. He always paid her back, but she began to feel she was being used. She became concerned, too, about Marv's inability to hold a steady job or make realistic plans for the future. He seemed to be drifting. As a result, Fran's feelings changed, and she finally told Marv she wanted him to move out of the apartment. Reluctantly, he did.

Then the inevitable happened. Marv lost his job again and couldn't pay his rent. When he turned up one evening, suitcase in hand, and begged her to take him in "for just a few days," Fran had to summon all her resolve to avoid a rerun of the scenario she had finally ended with so much difficulty.

She said "no."

"We've moved eight times in the last few years," said Mary Ellen, a corporate wife. "At first I even convinced myself that I enjoyed seeing different parts of the country. But I thought this move would be our last," she continued. "We've lived here three years, the longest we've been in any one place. I've started putting down roots and made some friends I'm really fond of, and I've started a master's degree program.

"But last week the bubble burst," she declared. "Ron came home one evening all excited and happy and told me he'd been offered a new post in South Africa. The challenge appeals to him tremendously, and I understand that. It isn't even that he thinks what I'm doing isn't important, exactly. But obviously he thinks what he's doing is so much *more* important. The children are all in college now, so I can't use them as an excuse. The fact is I simply don't want to go. I've had my life disrupted too many times. I love Ron, but I feel like I just can't do it again."

When I asked her if she'd told him exactly how she felt, she said she hadn't. But for the past week she'd experienced severe insomnia and her stomach was "tied in knots."

With some support, she was able to tell Ron that she couldn't go along with the move. Somewhat to her surprise, when she explained how strongly she felt he willingly agreed to decline the position.

Sherry was the one every member of her family turned to for support. The oldest and the only girl in a family of five children, she listened to her brothers' problems and provided whatever help they needed. She'd inherited the role of parent when her mother and father moved to Belgium, where he was an executive for an international company.

Unfortunately, Sherry's brothers were not as responsible as she was. One of them was married and doing well, but two had drug dependencies and one couldn't hold a job. In fact, he didn't even bother to look for one. When Sherry's father called her from Brussels and instructed her to "have a talk" with Stevie, she put her foot down.

"No," she said. "I've had it with doing all the dirty work in the family. I'm not Stevie's mother or his father—you are. I'm tired of being the bad guy. Stevie can go without a job for another few months until you can get over here and have a talk with him yourself."

Finding the strength to say "no" to someone you care about, or whose love and support you need, is the most difficult part. Finding the *words* is easy, once you have made up your mind.

Just say, "No, I can't do that because . . . " or "No, I really don't want to do that" or "No, I don't have time to do that right now."

In dealing with strangers—people who call on the telephone to sell you something, for example—it's enough to say, "No, I'm not interested." But someone you're closely involved with may be hurt by an abrupt refusal with no explanation.

You should say "no" if you want or need to do so, but when refusing a person who is important to you, I think, you should explain your feelings—briefly.

But don't apologize.

8
Necessary Negatives

"You can't take constructive criticism!" There's probably not a person around over the age of 25 who hasn't had this phrase directed pointedly at him or her more than once, under the guise of constructive criticism, of course.

Just how constructive *is* constructive criticism anyway?

Often it isn't helpful, or constructive, at all. Frequently it isn't even meant to be. It is often intended to intimidate, ridicule, or diminish the person to whom it is addressed, possibly motivated by the speaker's need to bolster his or her own flagging self-esteem.

When you state a negative feeling such as "It bothers me when you . . . ," you are, in a sense, criticizing another person, but this differs drastically from harsh attacks such as "How could you do such a stupid thing?" or "You always make a horrible mess in the kitchen!"

Labeling a person's behavior with some perjorative term is never constructive. And criticism should be directed not at the whole person, but at the specific behavior that concerns you. It's one thing to say, "I don't like what you did"; another to declare, or even imply, "I don't like *you*."

Most of us experience distinct physical symptoms, perhaps a sinking feeling in the pit of the stomach or the sensation of being hit below the belt, when we are severely criticized. The harsher the criticism, the more pronounced the physical sensation is likely to be.

And when we criticize others, especially when we do so in a deliberately mean or inconsiderate manner, we produce the same uncomfortable reactions in them. Since these feelings are so unpleasant, it's only natural to try to escape from anyone who is habitually critical.

Some kinds of criticism not only produce that sinking, injured feeling, but literally inspire the recipient to get back at you by continuing the behavior that elicited your criticism in the first place. Criticizing an overweight person for overeating is the number one example of this reaction. I hear variations of it several times each week from obese (and slightly overweight) patients: "When my husband criticizes me for what I'm eating I feel furious, and determined to eat even more. I know it's childish, but I react that way every time."

Picking on the one flaw in an otherwise perfect or highly satisfactory performance is guaranteed to deflate the ego and prevent further efforts to please. It's far more effective to praise the desirable aspects of the behavior, and ignore or minimize the negatives.

But there are times when you do have to speak up and tell someone close to you that you don't like something he or she did—or did not do.

When it is necessary to express negative feelings about some situation or behavior, it is helpful to question your motive for speaking up. There's seldom any point in criticizing people "for their own good." (This doesn't apply to raising children, of course.) Unless the behavior you're complaining about is upsetting to you in some way, in most cases I don't think you should be making the criticism. Naturally, if your opinion was solicited, the situation is a little different.

When you have a complaint to make, *be specific*. A vague, general statement such as "You don't ever show consideration for me" may leave the listener wondering what is meant. But if you say, "It bothered me a lot that you forgot our anniversary," there's little room for doubt about exactly what is on your mind.

In addition, there's no reason to complain about something that can't be changed. If the behavior *can* be changed, it may help to tell the other person how the suggestion you're making would benefit the relationship. For example:

"If you did things occasionally that made me feel you really loved me, I'd feel more appreciated and life would be a lot more pleasant for both of us. I wouldn't complain so much and you wouldn't feel as though I were nagging all the time."

Suggesting something specific you'd like the other person to do is much more helpful than berating him for not doing it. Suppose you're rushing around preparing for a dinner party and your spouse is leisurely reading the newspaper. Instead of exploding, it would be more productive to say: "I could use some help. Could you set the table, lay a fire, and help me clean up the kitchen?"

Keep in mind how your complaint is going to make the other person feel (but don't disregard how *you* are going to feel if you don't say anything), and choose a time when your discussion will not be overheard by others. It is much more humane to voice your negative comments in private.

When You're the One Who's Criticized

Unless you're superhuman or superperfect, there are times when someone you care about is going to criticize you.

How do you respond?

Many typically nonassertive, self-effacing people react by immediately saying to themselves, "I'm wrong. This just proves it all over again. I'm no good!" It never occurs to them that maybe the other person's criticism is wrong. They become so accustomed to criticism that they expect it, and hear it, even when it doesn't exist.

Others respond angrily, striking back with whatever counter-criticism comes to mind—and something nasty usually does.

Whatever the outward reaction, almost everyone feels upset and hurt. But it can be less painful, and less upsetting, if you stay calm, breathe deeply, and try to remember that it's some specific behavior that is being criticized, not you yourself. Instead of thinking despairingly, "He doesn't love me any more!" tell yourself to relax and listen. Maybe there's something in the criticism you're hearing, even if it hurts.

Perhaps after listening you'll feel the criticism is unfair. Then you should say so, or just disregard it.

Perhaps you'll feel especially hurt because you know the complaint is valid. You may have elicited the same criticism often in the past or you may simply be aware that this is a problem you have. In this case, you should give some serious thought to what you can do to change the behavior.

Or you may feel that even if the criticism is valid, the results, in terms of an improved relationship or personal growth, simply do not warrant the effort required to bring about the change. Maybe you're satisfied with things the way they are and want to leave them that way.

You are not obligated to change your behavior just because someone asks you to do so. But if it is someone you care about and you want to maintain and deepen the relationship, it is in your best interest to consider negative comments in as open-minded a way as you can—even though it hurts.

9
Assertiveness at Work

Assertiveness at work is a little different from assertiveness in a personal relationship. It's not so much a matter of expressing feelings as of being able to stick up for your rights, communicate clearly by letting others know exactly what you expect of them, and being both tactful and direct when you have a criticism or a request to make.

Often women have trouble suppressing their emotions on the job. If they are upset they may cry, and then they are more upset. This is a case where it isn't all right to cry. And it's not all right, as a general rule, to go around telling people you work with that they've hurt your feelings.

It's necessary to consider not only what you'd like to express but what the immediate and long-term consequences will be. If you have a difficult boss, you simply may not be in a position to speak up about his or her unreasonable demands or sarcastic manner. You may have to choose between leaving the job or putting up with the boss.

I remember an engineer who consulted me because his irate, irrational supervisor was making him miserable. He had developed a stomach ulcer, couldn't sleep at night, and was becoming irritable with his wife and children.

He asked me if I could desensitize him to his boss's outbursts. I suggested that he look for another job, but he was determined to stay. He couldn't bring himself to give up his seniority, his pension, his benefits, or his ulcer. He stayed on the job and kept the ulcer.

Andy, a medical researcher, was a nervous wreck because his company was moving to New Jersey. There had been some cutbacks, but most of the staff who wanted to go would be transferred. However, Andy's expectations changed weekly in accordance with the constantly fluctuating plans of the manager of his department. Andy would be going in September; he wouldn't be going until December; he wouldn't be going at all.

Since Andy had a wife and two children to consider as well as himself, he finally decided to confront the manager directly and made an appointment to discuss the problem.

"I can't continue to live with this indecision," he said. "If I am moving to New Jersey, I'll have to sell my house here and buy one over there. I'd like to go—it sounds like a good opportunity—but I have to know your decision by the end of the week."

Realizing that Andy was sincere, and knowing his indecision might cost him one of his most valued employees if he continued to procrastinate, the manager told Andy that he could plan definitely to move in September.

Sometimes it is possible to make a critical statement in a noncritical way. "I think I could do my work more effectively if I received more feedback about what I'm doing," for example, or "I know I could do a better job if I weren't so afraid you'd lose your temper with me."

With some bosses, even this much would be going too far.

"I Don't Think That's an Adequate Offer"

One of the problems typically reported by women on the job involves negotiating salaries and raises. Even if they know men in the same or comparable positions are paid more, many women have trouble asking for what they know they are worth.

One of my patients, promoted to manager of the bank branch where she worked, was dismayed to discover later that she was being paid $10,000 less than the man she replaced. Though she's had several small raises since, her salary still doesn't match what he was earning when he left.

Clara has done so well that she's now been asked to take over another branch with twice the staff and twice the problems—but with no increase in salary.

"I told the vice president I really wanted the job, but I didn't want to take on the additional responsibility and put in the extra hours for no more money. And do you know what they did? They offered me a raise of $1,000. That's almost more insulting than no increase at all."

Her first impulse was to turn down the promotion or demand a $5,000 raise, but knowing her employer, she knew he would refuse. She didn't want to back herself into a corner she couldn't get out of, because she was bored with her present branch and welcomed the challenge of a new assignment. She handled the offer assertively and well.

"I don't feel this is an adequate offer," she said. "But I have decided to accept the position. However, I will definitely expect my new level of responsibility to be reflected in my next regular salary review."

If it is not, she plans to look for a higher salary at a competing bank.

"You'll Have to Get Here on Time . . ."

In spite of being extremely efficient, hard-working, innovative, and capable, Clara had a difficult time when she first reached the managerial level because she wasn't accustomed to directing subordinates.

She'd been close on a personal level to the tellers she worked with; they often told her their problems, and they socialized together. When new employees joined her staff, she immediately extended the same kind of friendship to them. It took her a while to realize that this approach was not working. She had to be the boss, which meant issuing orders and maintaining a comfortable distance between herself and those who worked for her.

One teller who was generally a very good worker was in the habit of arriving late for work every morning. Clara had protested, but not effectively, several times. When she finally said, firmly but pleasantly, "Unless you get here promptly every day I'll have to mention this on your next salary review," the girl quickly overcame her penchant for tardiness.

At first Clara felt that alluding to the salary review would be a threat. When she thought of it simply as a statement of fact—which it was—asserting herself this way became acceptable to her.

Like many other women managers who were promoted from secretarial or clerical jobs to positions of responsibility over others, Clara had to learn how to delegate work, to insist on reasonable standards of performance, and to say, "Be sure to complete this by Friday" without feeling guilty or overbearing.

Not a Superwoman to Her Secretary

"Few women are superwomen to their secretaries," a recent *Wall Street Journal* article reports. "As ambitious female managers toil their way toward the executive suite, tensions often develop with their secretaries—who, by and large, also are women."

Despite the fact that the secretary may not have made the same career commitment as her boss, she still may resent the fact that another woman is behind an executive's desk while she is still pounding a typewriter.

"Be aware of appearing *too* assertive," one woman advertising executive warns. Because some secretaries react negatively to a woman executive they see as "pushy," she approaches a secretary as "more of a partner instead of as a boss—as if [I were] in a task-force situation."

According to Janice Eddy, who runs affirmative-action workshops for large corporations, comments such as the following are frequently heard from male executives:

- "Women are too ambitious and want to get places too fast."
- "Women get too much attention."
- "People bend over backward to assure that women get promoted."

Men's resentment toward successful women is more subtle these days but it still exists, according to Beatrice Young, senior vice president of Harbridge House, a Boston consulting firm. "There was a time when being outright sexist and racist was OK. You were almost a hero. You would hear men say, 'I'll never work for a woman.' I don't think they feel any differently now, but they don't say it."

Much confusion exists about how successful women should be treated. A middle-aged executive commented, "I feel like if I extend my hand to a woman, she will feel I'm being too aggressive." He'd been taught that it was impolite to shake a woman's hand.

The Trouble with "Feminine" Speech

Men and women tend to have different styles of communication. When a woman "talks like a man," which may sometimes mean no more than being direct and to the point, she's often accused by both men and other women of being too aggressive.

Few women want to lose their femininity, but at the same time there are certain aspects of what is considered "feminine" communication that are absolutely not effective in the business world. Some habits to avoid are:

- Speaking too softly.
- Ending a sentence with a rising inflection.
- Tacking on an ending such as "That's all right, isn't it?"

- Putting yourself down with comments such as "This may be a dumb idea, but...."
- Replying to a compliment with a disclaimer such as "I was just lucky."
- Using "Um" or "Uh huh."
- Smiling supportively too often during a business meeting.
- Asking questions in a business conference to show interest, even if you don't want or need the information.
- Breaking eye contact inappropriately.

Men tend to interrupt more frequently, and women tend to let them get away with it. If someone interrupts you during a business conversation or meeting, simply continue talking as if you didn't hear the interruption. Be sure you do not speak so softly that you can be easily drowned out. On more formal occasions you can deal with an interruption by saying, "Please hold your questions until the end of my presentation."

If you are frequently interrupted by one of your colleagues, you may need to confront him or her directly by saying privately, "I'd really appreciate it if you would not interrupt me while I am talking."

The Old Office Romance

With more women working side by side with men at the corporate level, it appears that the office romance is becoming more of a fact of life than ever.

But romance in the office remains a much more serious problem for women than for men. I have yet to talk to a man who has suffered from an on-the-job romance. Yet it is a different story for women, and I have heard a number of them from my clients.

If you learn that someone else is having an office romance and it is affecting business (as it usually does), it ordinarily doesn't pay to assert yourself about it.

The *Wall Street Journal* reports the case of a 43-year-old West Coast woman hired by an entrepreneur as his chief operating officer. When she learned he was having an affair with one of her subordinates, in her twenties, she confronted her married boss. He admitted he was crazy about the young woman, and insisted that his feelings wouldn't get in the way of business. But after numerous conflicts resulting from the situation, the female executive resigned—feeling foolish.

According to another woman executive, speaking out about an office affair can be suicidal. "It's the old story about the bearer of bad tidings," she says. "You're calling someone else's professionalism into question—and you're the one who gets in trouble. If you push it, you have an enemy for life."

It's a Struggle to Juggle

Many doctors are finding that the conflicting demands of career and family are creating an increase in stress-related symptoms among working mothers. Fatigue, anxiety, depression, migraines, insomnia, and gastrointestinal disorders are turning up more and more frequently among women struggling to do everything.

Barbara J. Berg, author of *The Crisis of the Working Mother* (New York: Summit Books, 1986), feels that the stress results from the necessity of keeping roles separate. Early advice to ambitious women in the business world was to avoid all talk of home and family at the office: it wasn't professional, and would cause you to lose respect on the job.

But it isn't easy for a woman to keep such an important part of her life separate, and the psychological costs are high, Berg points out. It's difficult to make the transition from home to office even when everything is going smoothly.

"I've felt tremendous pressure ever since I started working part-time again," a young social worker, mother of a 2-year-old, told me recently.

When a child is sick or babysitting arrangements fall through, the strain is even greater.

A woman can't just sit calmly at work and forget that the babysitter is unreliable, that her child may be failing a test at school or is probably coming down with the flu. Yet, traditional double standards of professional conduct allow men, but not women, to talk about their family obligations at the office.

As one bank manager puts it: "Women must lead fragmented lives while men don't have the same restrictions placed on them. My husband can talk about his work with the man next door, and then go to the office and talk about our daughter's school play."

Berg suggests that if working mothers are to keep their health and sanity intact, they must consciously integrate, rather than segregate, their various roles.

"I was a woman divided into three parts," says a New York bank executive. "Mother, worker, wife. I didn't realize how segmented I felt until someone I'd telephoned asked who was calling and I had to think who I was at the moment. Now I make a conscious effort to discuss my children at work, and I ask my associates about theirs."

Can You Be Open about Family Responsibilities?

In some cases you can be assertive about your family responsibilities. In others you can't.

"My boss is not a family man and wasn't familiar with the necessities of child rearing," declares a sales executive. When she let her boss know about her 19-year-old son, for whom she had full responsibility following a legal separation from her husband, things improved and he was more flexible in his expectations.

Many corporations are becoming increasingly sensitive to family responsibilities. But many are not. It's a good idea to observe carefully how other female executives in your corporation have structured their roles before trying to arrange the privilege of leaving work early on occasion or curtailing a heavy travel schedule.

Women who still find it necessary to keep their family responsibilities out of the office may be able to avert some stress by advance planning that takes into account important events in their children's lives. Arrange your office calendar accordingly, and simply announce that you will be leaving early.

Dr. Sheila Akabas, director of the Center of Social Policy and Practice in the Workplace at Columbia University School of Social Work, advises women not to share information unless there is some advantage in doing so. A simple statement—"I have to leave early today"—is usually sufficient.

Or there may be alternative solutions. One woman I know who was frequently asked to attend late afternoon meetings began to tell her boss *before* the conference that she'd have to leave at a certain time. She'd offer to call him later in the evening or ask him to call her. There were no apologies, and no discussions of her family responsibilities—but she was assertive about her need to leave at a certain time.

Being effectively assertive at work always involves not only an awareness of your own needs and goals, but also a careful evaluation of your particular workplace. The results, in terms of stress reduction, are well worth the effort.

10
Improving Communication with Children

"My children are driving me crazy!"
"I'm at my wits' end!"
"My 2-year-old is in charge of the household!"

I hear complaints like these every week, if not every day. If you are a parent, I'm sure there have been times when you have either expressed or felt these same sentiments.

No matter how much we love our children, they are frequently a source of considerable stress. Improving communication is one way of reducing the stress. There's no way of eliminating it altogether because, being human, we're going to worry about our children at times and find some of their behaviors upsetting, if not infuriating.

"Josie is a very bright and determined little girl," one mother told me recently. "She's only 5, but she knows how to get everything she wants. Things are finally improving because I sat her down and said, 'Things have to change around here. You're the 5-year-old and I'm the mother. And from now on, *I'm* in charge.'"

That, with appropriate variations, is the message I think parents should be giving their out-of-control children from pre-school age through high school. Children have to be taught how to behave. They don't arrive in the world with built-in rules of behavior. They have to learn the difference between right and wrong and how to get along with others, assimilate the values of their society, learn socially acceptable ways of dressing and behaving, and, along with it, learn how to think for themselves and make their own decisions.

It certainly isn't easy to successfully communicate all of these messages, some of which may appear to be contradictory. And when some authorities recommend a permissive attitude, while others endorse strict discipline, it's difficult to know *what* to do. It's essential to have a clear understanding of your own values if you are to succeed in teaching them to somebody else.

Children, even teenage children, are actually more comfortable with parents who exercise reasonable discipline. I say "reasonable" because I feel parental rules and regulations should generally be limited to important matters. (I include acceptable manners in my definition of important.) You have the right to enforce the standards of behavior you think are appropriate, and you should do so. Your child needs a parent, not just another friend.

At the same time, if you are too authoritarian you'll discourage your children from decision making. According to Maurice Elias, an associate professor of psychology at Rutgers and co-director of a six-year research project designed to identify how parents and school systems can foster children's decision-making skills, children raised in authoritarian families fail to develop critical reasoning. In these families, parents retain strict control, and they are the only decision makers. Such an authoritarian style of parenting produces children who have a difficult time making decisions for themselves.

While children may seem easier to manage on a day to day basis because they learn to follow instructions, being overly authoritative is self-defeating in the long run. When they leave home, such children haven't developed any problem-solving skills.

Children who are skilled in decision making, according to these researchers, have higher self-esteem and are seen by teachers as better adjusted.

Be Positive and Be Specific

Children's self-esteem also depends on your letting them know—often—that they are very special people whom you love and value, and on your providing as much positive reinforcement as possible. Sarcasm and unwarranted criticism should be avoided at all times. Children of overly critical parents *never* grow up with good feelings about themselves. Try to praise accomplishment and effort every time it occurs, but avoid praising the whole person in such a way that you create an image nobody can live up to.

Adults often misunderstand each other's communications; children, with their more limited powers of abstraction, are even more likely to do so. Therefore, you should be very specific in your communications, so that your child knows exactly what you mean.

When a child does something that is unacceptable to you, try to keep cool. Losing your temper and screaming only reward misbehavior by drawing an inordinate amount of attention to it.

It's inevitable that occasionally you will say something you'll later regret. But bear in mind that remarks that make a child feel unwanted and unloved will be remembered long after the episode that provoked them has been forgotten.

Long, involved talks or lectures are seldom effective with young children. They'll just tune out. A brief explanation of why you've decided to withhold some privilege (with young children, imposing a time-out of five or ten minutes in a room alone with no toys is probably best) is sufficient. You have the right, as a parent, to simply say "no."

It's essential to be consistent. You can't be permissive one minute and strict the next and expect your child to grow up anything but confused.

Minor mishaps—spilling the milk, knocking over a can of paint, or breaking a glass—do not warrant anger or criticism, only constructive action.

Naturally, you'll be upset at times over conflicts and problems with your children. It's important to recognize feelings that your child is stirring up in you—and to recognize, as well, that your child is having feelings. That is, he or she is experiencing certain bodily sensations just as you are when you are upset, but he or she may not know how to describe or label the feeling.

For example, your child may say, "I don't like so and so," or "I hate so and so." If you respond, "You shouldn't talk that way," you'll just squelch the feelings. If you say instead, "It sounds like something has happened that made you angry," you'll be helping your child identify and express his or her feelings. That will avoid trouble for him or her, and you, later on in life.

It's important not to inhibit the expression of anger, even when it is directed at you. And you can—and should—let your child know when you are upset, uncomfortable, annoyed, or furious. But do not be insulting or attack his or her personality.

Your child needs ongoing help from you in learning to describe his or her feelings. Seeing you express yours will help your child to express his or hers.

What's Your Style of Responding?

Parents develop different styles of responding to children, some of which are more effective than others.

Advice-giving, such as "You ought to . . . ," "I'd just go ahead and do it," or "The right thing to do is . . . ," often isn't too helpful. (Of course, there are times when parents must give advice. That's one of their functions. But if you're too prompt or offer advice on every occasion your child will never learn to weigh alternatives and make decisions for himself or herself.)

And rushing in to be supportive and comforting ("Don't worry, lots of people have that happen"; "You'll feel better after you have a cookie and some milk") may have the effect of brushing the problem aside.

The best approach when your child confides an upsetting event or feeling is to try and draw him or her out without being judgmental. Some parents are naturally gifted at this, while others, if they work too hard at it, wind up sounding like an over-zealous therapist. I think it's best to keep your responses simple, letting your child know you understand what he or she is saying without probing or overinterpreting.

Your child will feel better when his or her feelings are acknowledged and he or she is spared a sermon on responsibility (e.g., "It's your own fault for leaving all this work until the last minute."). Frequently this is all that is needed to help a child move on to constructive action or a more positive outlook.

Being a good parent is a challenging, often difficult, and emotionally demanding occupation. But by working to improve your communication you will be minimizing the harmful effects of stress on you *and* your children.

11
Sexually Speaking

It's possible, of course, to be relatively happy and healthy without any sex at all. Sex is the one physical drive that can be suppressed for long periods of time without devastating consequences.

Yet almost everyone would like to have a satisfying sex life, and would feel better as a result. Sometimes, when no partner is available, masturbation can fill the need for a purely physical release.

Women who need to overcome guilt about sexuality in order to assert themselves sexually through masturbation, either as an end in itself or as a bridge toward a more fulfilling sexual relationship with their partners, may want to read *For Yourself: Fulfillment of Female Sexuality—A Guide to Orgasmic Response* (New York: New American Library, 1976) by Lonnie Garfirle Barbach, or *Becoming Orgasmic: A Sexual Growth Program for Women* (Englewood Cliffs, New Jersey: Prentice-Hall, 1976) by Julia Heiman, Leslie LoPiccolo, and Joseph LoPiccolo.

Becoming comfortable with your own body and your own sexuality is one important avenue toward sexual fulfillment. Another is learning to communicate openly with your partner about sex.

Many couples, even those in happy and mutually fulfilling relationships, are either unable to talk about sex at all or find it so anxiety-provoking that they prefer to avoid the topic.

Helen Singer Kaplan, head of the sex therapy program at New York Hospital's Payne-Whitney Clinic, declares that the lack of open communication about feelings, wishes, and responses is one of the most important obstacles to full sexual enjoyment.

It's impossible to satisfy your partner fully or to be sexually satisfied by your partner unless you can both express your likes and dislikes honestly. If you don't know how your partner feels about what you are doing—and he or she doesn't know how you feel—there is absolutely no way you can achieve a fully satisfying sexual relationship.

"I've Never Talked about This Before"

Even in these sexually liberated times, difficulties in communicating about sexual matters are extremely common. When patients first begin to talk about sex in the therapeutic situation, they often start off by saying, "It's hard for me to talk about this. I've never talked about it with anyone before."

I have heard this remark, almost in identical words, from teenagers, young marrieds in their twenties, and women and men in their fifties.

What surprises me is the number of people who have even been in therapy for marital problems, sometimes with more than one therapist and over a period of several years, who have never broached the topic of sex with their therapists. The therapists didn't broach it either.

Only yesterday a man came to see me about "a personal problem." He wanted to break away from a woman he'd been living with for several years, and return to his wife. He described his mistress as "boring."

Yet his one prior effort to break away from this young woman had resulted in a total psychosomatic upset: he couldn't eat, suffered constant headaches and insomnia, and after two weeks left home again and went back to his mistress.

"I must be addicted to her," he commented. "It was like a physiological withdrawal reaction." (A recovered alcoholic, he knew all about withdrawal.)

This man had seen two prior therapists without resolving his conflict. He had never brought up the issue of sex, and neither had the therapists. When I asked him directly about his sexual relationship with both women, he fumbled for words and said he'd never discussed this with anyone before. But he now realized sex must be part of his problem.

If therapists, who are supposed to be able to talk openly about such matters, are so reluctant to bring them up, is it any wonder that almost everybody else is reluctant too?

While guilt and anxiety about sex and talking about sex appear most prevalent among those who, like this particular patient, have experienced a strict Catholic upbringing and education, it is widespread among others as well. Since many parents never mention sex at all or do so with obvious embarrassment, it isn't surprising that children grow up thinking that sexual matters are not fit topics for discussion.

Familial and cultural conditioning, then, is one reason why communication about sex is so difficult. Another is the fear that expressing your own sexual needs and preferences will lead to rejection or will hurt your partner's feelings. Women, especially, often hesitate to make suggestions because they feel their partner doesn't want to be told how to make love.

"I can have an orgasm when I masturbate," some women tell me, "but my husband doesn't do it right."

When I ask if she's told him how she'd *like* him to do it, the answer is almost invariably "No"—or "Oh, I couldn't!"

Communication Can Be Nonverbal

In the beginning, when you are just learning to be open and honest about your sexual desires, you may find it easier to communicate nonverbally. Gently guiding your partner's hand so it touches you in the most pleasing way, or exerting a slight pressure on his hand so it will stay a little longer where it already is, can express your wishes in a subtle manner.

Sexual approaches can be nonverbal as well, and initiating sex with a look your partner recognizes or a lingering kiss seems more romantic than a verbal statement like, "Can we fool around tonight?" Believe it or not, this is how some people do it; and then they wonder why their partners aren't responsive. But when I suggested to the patient who described her husband's usual approach this way that perhaps his technique was at fault, she exclaimed, "Oh, no! It's *my* problem."

Women have been conditioned to believe, in most cases, that it *is* their problem. Even though they usually know from their own experimentation that it takes them much longer to reach a climax than it takes their husbands, they feel guilty about it.

They don't realize, and often their husbands don't either, that it is normal for the sexual response to build up more slowly in women. Ignorance of this basic difference in sexual timing and reluctance to discuss the matter absolutely ensures, in many cases, that the woman will remain permanently unsatisfied and that her husband will feel inadequate as a lover.

While sex therapists use a variety of techniques to help patients overcome specific sexual difficulties, a basic goal of almost all sex therapy is enabling the partners to communicate openly about their sexual likes and dislikes. You can begin to do this with your partner by saying, while you are making love, "That feels good," or "I like that."

When you want to make a suggestion, be careful to phrase it in a positive way: "It would feel even better if you would..." or "I'd like it if you would...."

If possible, avoid negative comments or criticism. These are damaging to the ego and to the relationship. Of course, if your partner is doing something you don't like, you need to tell him or her about it. But do so tactfully.

If there are marked differences in sexual preferences or desired frequency of intercourse, you must find a way of discussing these issues directly. There will have to be some give and take on both sides. Compromise isn't a matter of reaching a mathematical average where sexual matters are concerned.

There is literally no sexual problem that can be satisfactorily resolved without open communication.

If you are sexually frustrated, you must tell your partner. It's essential to disclose your true feelings clearly and candidly. Otherwise, your partner can only guess what you are thinking and feeling. And guessing isn't good enough.

PART 7
If You Become Ill

1
Who Are the Survivors?

Even if you have positive attitudes and supportive relationships and take reasonably good care of yourself, at some time in your life you may become seriously ill.

You may experience too many life changes in a short period of time; you may come in contact with an environmental or infectious agent your body is unable to combat due to stress or fatigue; or you may suffer an accident that leaves you mildly or even severely incapacitated.

If one of these events should befall you, positive emotions and supportive relationships can help you overcome it.

Changes in the immune system linking emotions to the body's susceptibility to disease also affect the individual's ability to recover from such diseases as cancer, flu, colds, and genital herpes.

In a study of 57 women with breast cancer at King's College Hospital in London, researchers found a significant correlation between emotional response three months after a mastectomy and their survival rates ten years later.

- Of the ten women who initially denied they had had cancer and rationalized the operation as a preventive measure, five were still alive ten years later.
- Of the ten who reacted with a fighting spirit—"I'm going to beat this thing"—seven were alive after ten years.
- Among the 32 "stoics," who showed no signs of distress, 24 were dead after ten years.
- Of the five who felt hopeless, believing there was nothing further they could do, four had died.

Lydia Temoshok, a psychologist at the University of California at San Francisco, reported in recent research that melanoma patients who expressed feelings of anger and distress had more positive immune responses than those who suppressed such feelings.

And episodes of genital herpes are related to feelings of depression, according to Margaret Kemeny, a psychologist at the University of California Medical Center. Subjects in her study were more likely to report outbreaks of herpes when they felt depressed, at which times their levels of T-cells, which are involved in controlling viruses, declined.

While the scientific explanations are only starting to be understood, the importance of attitudes in recovery from illness is not a new idea. It was recognized as early as 1870 that deep anxiety, the loss of hope, and disappointment were often followed by the growth and increase of cancer.

Judith Glassman, in researching *The Cancer Survivors* (New York: Dial Press, 1983), met scores of survivors as well as many cancer patients who later died. She found that the will to live was the most essential aspect of survival; without it, patients invariably died.

If a patient chooses not to recover from an illness, there is very little that anyone can do to alter its course.

O. Carl Simonton has found that patients who beat the statistics and live, despite diagnoses of incurable cancer, are those who make statements such as "I can't die until my son graduates from college" or "They need me too much at work" or "I won't die until I've solved the problem with my daughter."

Those who succeed in overcoming a life-threatening illness believe that they can exert some influence over its outcome. Their positive attitudes enable them to actively participate in the healing process.

If you are the patient, do not accept your condition stoically; fight.

"My own total involvement was a major factor in my recovery," writes Norman Cousins in *Anatomy of an Illness as Perceived by the Patient: Reflections on Healing and Regeneration* (New York: W. W. Norton, 1979). "People have asked what I thought when I was told by the specialists that my disease was progressive and incurable. The answer is simple. Since I didn't accept the verdict, I wasn't trapped in the cycle of fear, depression, and panic that frequently accompanies a supposedly incurable illness."

Many people actually don't care whether they live or die. They may say they do, but their actions say the opposite. Perhaps they feel they don't have a lot to live for. They're retired; their children have grown up; they're widowed or divorced; they're not able to get out and play golf or tennis any longer. They have little to provide a sense of meaningfulness and purpose in their lives.

If you are ill, you can survive—but you have to believe you can do it. And you have to *want* to do it.

"I Won't Let You Die!"

Close, supportive emotional ties are probably the most powerful incentives you can have to overcome your illness, whatever it is. And they can *help* you overcome it as well.

Patients interviewed by Glassman often declared that their will and strength were reinforced by a loving mate who refused to allow them to die. But rather than showering them with pity, they insisted that the patients focus on their own wish to recover.

Human love and family support can also be a powerful force in the recovery of heart patients. "Nowhere is the power of human contact more readily apparent than in the period of emotional crisis that follows the sudden occurrence of a heart attack," writes James Lynch in *The Broken Heart: The Medical Consequences of Loneliness* (New York: Basic Books, 1979).

As the Simonton Cancer Treatment Center in Fort Worth, Texas, it is a policy that all patients entering the program must be accompanied by a spouse or, if they are unmarried, widowed, or divorced, by a close family member. The reasons for this are twofold. First, the support of spouse and family can be an invaluable aid in helping patients modify their attitudes and carry out directions.

Second, spouses and family members often need as much support and guidance in coping with their feelings as patients do. Watching someone you love live through a life-threatening disease is a devastating and confusing experience.

In dealing with cancer patients and their families, Dr. Simonton stresses the need for open expression of feelings—fright, terror, anger, self-pity—on the part of both patient and family members.

"Grief is a normal response," he writes. "The family must try to accept it. Holding in feelings and maintaining composure in the face of death does not define bravery. . . . If you find yourself trying to change how others feel, stop yourself. It will lead to pain and blocked communication. Nothing can hurt a relationship more than for people to feel they cannot be themselves."

There's a difference between being supportive and babying the patient. Being supportive means communicating openly about fears and acknowledging the potential risks and pain involved. Babying is conveying a message such as "Now, you know you've got to take it. It won't hurt you. It's good for you. And that's all we're going to hear about that."

It is essential for family members to avoid taking the role of rescuer. To overcome illness, you need the love and support of your family. But you cannot leave your recovery to anyone else, no matter how caring and loving that person may be.

You must accept the responsibility for your own recovery.

2
You and Your Doctor

There is another relationship that is of major importance in your recovery. That is the relationship between you and your physician.

If you are ill, you are probably already under the care of a specialist, presumably one to whom you have been referred by your internist or general practitioner—and hopefully one in whom you have confidence and faith. If you do not feel comfortable or satisfied with the doctor who is treating you, you should find another as quickly as possible. Your physician, whether a specialist or a primary care physician, should be interested in *you* as well as in your illness.

Of course, it seldom pays to scurry from doctor to doctor in a frantic search for a miracle cure, like the chronic pain patient or the hypochondriac who refuses to accept medical reassurance that nothing is really wrong. It isn't unusual for people who have been diagnosed as having a fatal disease, most often cancer, to travel thousands of miles and invest thousands of dollars in pursuit of rescue.

This is not the same as seeking out the specialist who is best equipped to deal most skillfully and most effectively with your illness. You should look for the best care you can obtain, even if this means travelling to Minnesota or San Francisco or Phoenix, provided you have the financial means to do so.

It goes without saying that when elective surgery is recommended you should seek a second opinion. Many insurance companies now routinely require this; otherwise they may refuse to honor your claim.

What Does That Mean?

"My doctor said I have to have an angiogram. What does that mean?"
"My doctor says I have a fibroid. What does that mean?"
"My doctor recommended a mammogram. What is a mammogram?"

"My doctor wants me to have a stress EKG. What is that?"

"My doctor says I might have a subclinical thyroid problem. What does *that* mean?"

If you have never left a doctor's office wondering, "What does *that* mean?" you are in the minority.

Most people are so flustered when they receive a diagnosis they do not understand that they fail completely to ask the questions that will elicit the answers they need. This is especially true if they were already upset *before* visiting the doctor.

Women, especially, are likely to be intimidated by their physician—who probably maintains his position of authority by addressing the patient by her first name while she is expected to call him "Doctor." I have heard this complaint many times from women patients. Others, of course, are more comfortable when the status distinction is preserved.

Whether you regard your physician as an equal or as a guru to whom you willingly defer, you *must* learn to ask questions.

Many physicians—the good ones—make a sincere effort, without prompting, to explain their recommendations and their terminology. But if you do not understand, ask. If you still do not understand, ask again. If you have questions in advance of your appointment, bring a list of them along, because it is quite likely, under the stress of the examination or the discussion, that you will forget what you meant to say.

Your physician should be willing to take the time to answer your questions fully. Simply knowing what to expect before entering the hospital or undergoing an unfamiliar medical procedure can result in a tremendous reduction of anxiety.

This point was illustrated dramatically by a study of 97 patients after elective abdominal operations. Those who were visited the night before by their anesthetists, were told about the postoperative pain they would experience, and were shown how to relieve the pain by relaxing the muscles required only half the amount of postoperative narcotics as did the control patients. And they were ready for discharge an average of almost three days earlier than the controls.

Your Doctor and Your Family

In addition to technical competence and the willingness to answer your questions, it is essential that a physician who is treating you for a serious illness—or any illness for that matter—relate to you, and members of your family, as a human being who cares about you.

Many busy physicians, especially specialists dealing with life or death situations, appear too busy to be bothered with a patient's family. I know this from personal experience; my father was hospitalized several different times in four different hospitals in the two years before he died, at age 83, of congestive heart failure.

I spent enough time attempting to corner physicians making their rounds to realize just how frustrating and defeating such an endeavor can be. In three out of four hospitals, the physicians' attitudes toward my mother and myself bordered on outright rudeness, yet we were totally at their mercy.

Fortunately, all of my father's doctors gave the impression that they cared about *him*. They just didn't have the time to answer questions from his wife or daughter.

In his final illness at Barnes Hospital in St. Louis, however, he was under the care of an internist who had known the family for years and whose reassuring presence was a great help to all of us. (Two heart attacks earlier had necessitated emergency hospitalizations, under other physicians, nearer his home.)

But this relationship was not built up after he was stricken with a heart attack. It was a continuing relationship extending over many years among my father, my mother, and the physician.

This doctor cared. My father knew it, my mother knew it, and I knew it.

The Physician Holds the Lifeline

"During the past four years, I have had the opportunity to talk to hundreds of patients suffering from serious illness," writes Norman Cousins. "I doubt that it is just a coincidence that so many of the patients who seem to be getting the most out of their treatment are the ones who say they have been inspired by their physicians.

"There are qualities beyond pure medical competence that patients need and look for in their doctors," he continues. "They want reassurance. They want to be looked after and not just looked over. They want to be listened to. They want to feel that it makes a difference to the physician, a very big difference, whether they live or die. They want to feel that they are in the doctor's thoughts. In short, patients are a vast collection of emotional needs.

"The physician holds the lifeline," Cousins declares. "The physician's words and not just his prescriptions are attached to that lifeline."

Hippocrates recognized this long ago when he declared that some patients recover their health simply through their contentment with the goodness of the physician.

Practitioners of Hippocratic medicine realized that the potential for cure was within the patient, and that the function of the physician was to activate and support the patient's own capacity for self-restoration.

Although the ever-present threat of a malpractice action these days makes it essential for physicians to communicate hard facts in a way that cannot be misunderstood, this can be done while emphasizing the hope of recovery and the possibility that recovery can occur, regardless of the mathematical probabilities.

Many physicians have mastered the art of communicating without crippling. They tell their patients about others who have recovered from similar conditions. Whatever the actual prognosis, these doctors convey the truth without destroying the hope that is so essential for healing.

"He's a Goner"

A physician's words, carelessly or callously spoken, can remove that hope.

Recent research indicates that what patients hear under anesthesia can later act upon them like a post-hypnotic suggestion.

In one study, according to a *New York Times* article, patients under anesthesia were told during surgery that they would feel a need to touch their ears in a postoperative interview. Later, in the interview, the patients did tug at their ears, though none of them recalled hearing the suggestion.

It has been found that when it is suggested to patients during surgery that one hand will become warmer and the other cooler, the hands respond to the suggestion just as they would in a hypnotized subject.

These discoveries seem to indicate that traditional operating room banter may have to be toned down. Remarks such as "He's a goner" or "Holy Moses, this is a terrible bone graft" are hardly conducive to the patient's subsequent peace of mind.

Your Doctor Is Your Friend

When I was growing up in a small town in southeast Missouri, my family doctor (who was present at my birth and all subsequent important medical occasions of my life for many years) was also the father of one of my best friends. I saw him almost every day when I stopped by my friend's house on my way to school.

He removed my father's tonsils in his office, and came to call at our house when I came down with a childhood illness. If I was sick but not very sick, I went to see him in his office behind the drugstore where I usually stopped off with my friends to have a Coke or an ice cream soda after school. His wife played bridge with my mother, and my friend and I learned about sex from his medical books.

When I was ill and consulted Dr. LaRue, I didn't have to worry about whether he remembered me or not. He knew everything there was to know about me, my father, my mother, and my grandmother, and his house was almost as familiar to me as my own.

Though those days have long passed, I have been fortunate in finding an internist in Connecticut I like and trust, and whom I consider my friend as well as my physician. I can get in touch with him when I need to, and I know he is interested in me as well as in my ailments. I'm seldom sick, so I don't see him often, but it is comforting to know that he is there when I need him.

Others I've heard about have been less fortunate. Some move from doctor to doctor in an attempt to find one in whom they have confidence. Still others have been misdiagnosed and mistreated. Some have been subjected to the dehumanizing procedure of getting their medical services through an HMO (because their employer pays for it) where they may see a different doctor each time.

A woman who moved here two years ago from Cleveland told me recently that she still goes back to Cleveland to see her ophthalmologist, her gynecologist, and her dermatologist. She says there aren't any good doctors in Connecticut; the good ones are all in Cleveland.

And many people I talk to have no doctor at all. If they become ill, they will have to consult a doctor they have never seen before and may never see again.

How to Choose a Good Doctor

The time to locate a family doctor is before you become ill. Everyone needs to have medical checkups at regular intervals, though not necessarily annually, and everyone needs to have a doctor to call in an emergency. Ideally, the same doctor should care for all members of your family.

Many people choose a doctor with much less care than they would devote to selecting a new car or a new television set, operating perhaps on the premise that all doctors are equal.

But all doctors are *not* equal.

Most licensed physicians have acceptable credentials. That is, they graduated from an accredited medical school (all U.S. medical schools are accredited) and presumably received a thorough medical education. However, this tells you nothing about the extent to which they keep abreast of new medical developments, or their capacity for relating to you as one human being to another.

Dr. George LeMaitre, author of *How to Choose a Good Doctor* (Andover, Massachusetts: Andover Publishing Co., 1979), suggests that when looking for a new doctor you avoid those who are either very young or very old. Physicians over 60, he points out, are likely to retire, become ill, or die while you still need them. It is also quite possible, though there are striking exceptions, that their medical education is by now quite out of date.

You should choose a doctor who is Board Certified in either internal medicine or family practice (the local hospital or your reference librarian can give you this information). Your doctor should also have admitting privileges at a good nearby hospital.

Check with friends and acquaintances whose judgment you respect about their knowledge of the physicians you are considering. You need to know how accessible the doctors are when you need them, how long they keep you sitting in their waiting rooms, how thorough and reliable they are, their fee schedules, and whether or not they are easy to talk to.

In the final analysis, you are the one who must decide whether or not the doctor you have selected is the right one for you. Does he or she, as well as any office staff, treat you courteously and cooperatively? Does he or she answer your questions fully? Does he or she take a careful medical history and perform a careful examination? (A thorough evaluation of a new patient should take at least an hour.)

And, perhaps most important of all: do you feel comfortable trusting this person with your life? Does his or her attitude indicate an interest in you as an individual?

If not, find another doctor.

3
How to Find Psychological Help

If you have psychological symptoms, or somatic symptoms for which your doctor can find no physical explanation, or simply are aware of problems within yourself or within your marriage that you have been unable to solve on your own, you may want to consider seeking help from a psychiatrist, psychologist, or social worker.

Your relationship with your therapist can be a significant source of support in your life as well as helping you to resolve specific problems and to improve your relationships with yourself and with others.

But finding a good therapist is just as difficult as finding a good primary care physician (if not more so).

There are no licensing requirements for "therapists" and anyone can claim to be one. As a rule of thumb, it is generally unwise to become involved with anyone who identifies himself or herself primarily as a "therapist" or "psychotherapist."

Many such individuals are graduates of master's degree programs in counseling, psychology, or marriage and family counseling, or they may have been trained in Gestalt Therapy, Transactional Analysis, Rational-Emotive Therapy, Neuro-Linguistic Programming, or a variety of other specialized techniques.

The problem with such training programs is that they do not guarantee even a minimum level of competence. My recommendation is that you consult *only* a person who is a psychiatrist (M.D.), a licensed psychologist (Ph.D.), or a social worker (M.S.W.), unless you have a very strong reason for selecting a therapist who does not have one of these three recognized credentials. Most insurance coverage providing psychiatric benefits will pay only for the services of a psychiatrist or licensed psychologist.

Appropriate credentials do not make a good therapist, any more than they make a good physician. But they at least ensure a basic background of acceptable training.

Many people choose therapists even more casually than they choose physicians. Some of my patients are referred by physicians, school psychologists, clergymen, or former patients. Others call because they have read one of my books, have seen me on television, or have read a newspaper article about me.

In any given week, however, at least half of the calls I receive result directly from my listing in the Yellow Pages or from local newspaper advertising.

Some patients, especially phobics, choose me because I am the closest; some because I am a woman. Others choose me because I list certain specialties—phobias, shyness, assertiveness, hypnosis for smoking and other problem habits—for which they seek help.

There are so many schools of therapy that, for the uninitiated, making an informed choice among the psychiatrists, psychologists, and social workers who are available in your area may be extremely difficult.

Joel Kovel, in his book *A Complete Guide to Therapy: From Psychotherapy to Behavior Modification* (New York: Pantheon, 1977), lists 21 varieties and subvarieties of therapy, ranging from Freudian psychoanalysis at one end of the spectrum to behavior therapy at the other. And I can think of several varieties that he omitted.

Regardless of the school of therapy, the personality, competence, and warmth of the therapist are of paramount importance. This is because your relationship with the therapist is the most essential element of therapy. If the therapist is not genuinely interested in helping you overcome your problem and achieve personal growth so that you can develop your own potential as a unique individual, you should not be in therapy with that person.

Some sample comments I've heard from patients about prior therapists:

"I think he was just interested in the money, not in me. He sat there with his feet up and I don't think he was even listening half the time."

'She *knitted* while I was talking to her."

"I was so scared of him that I never said a word. I kept going every week for a year; I was afraid that if I stopped going, I'd get worse."

"When I tried to discontinue therapy, my counselor told me she thought it would be a terrible mistake. I assumed I must be very ill; I must be much worse off than I thought I was. I thought she must know better than me; after all, she was the therapist."

"All we did was talk about general things. He never asked me about my sex life or my marriage. I didn't bring it up, and neither did he."

If you are not making progress, or do not feel comfortable with your therapist, you are free to leave at any time. This is a matter you should judge for yourself; under no circumstances should you feel obliged to continue against your wishes.

On the other hand, you shouldn't necessarily expect to *enjoy* therapy sessions (though many people do). You may feel, like one of my patients, "that it's embarrassing to go in and bleed all over somebody else." In any case you are going to be uncovering some issues that are painful or difficult to talk about; but with a sensitive, empathetic therapist you will find these discussions enlightening and beneficial.

Kinds of Therapy

Among the therapies most widely available today are:

- Psychoanalysis, based on Freud's work and practiced by a steadily diminishing number of therapists, generally involves three to five sessions a week and may go on for years. It is a therapy for the very rich, who are more interested in an exploration of the unconscious than in making changes in their lives. It stresses insight and understanding, reached through free association, interpretation, and transference.
- Jungian analysis, which developed when Jung ceased to follow Freud's methods, emphasizes personal growth, dream interpretation, and exploration of the collective unconscious with its archetypes or universal symbols.
- Humanistic therapies, based on the work of Carl Rogers, aim for individual growth through the unconditional acceptance and positive regard of the therapist. It is entirely non-directive and is not suited to a rapid resolution of problems.
- Group therapy may consist of problem-oriented groups, composed of people who share the same problem (phobias, shyness, marital problems, drug addictions, etc.) or they may be heterogenous, and they may be open-ended, lasting indefinitely, or time-limited. They are most effective when social relationships are a problem, or when support from others experiencing the same difficulties would be of more value than the support of an individual therapist.
- Behavior therapy tends to be brief and problem-oriented. It has been especially effective with phobias, assertive difficulties, and other specific problem behaviors.
- Cognitive therapy, an offshoot of behavior therapy, deals with changing maladaptive thought patterns (as does Rational-

Emotive Therapy). Cognitive therapy has been found quite effective in the treatment of depression.
- Sex therapy, also a behavioral approach, deals directly with sexual issues and almost always involves treating the couple. Impotence, premature ejaculation, vaginismus (painful contraction of the vagina), and a lack of orgasmic response in women are among the sexual dysfunctions that frequently can be treated successfully in a relatively short time.
- Hypnotherapy may be used for the exploration of unconscious conflicts; for the recall of repressed memories; for the control of problem behaviors such as smoking, overeating, and nail biting; for the relief of phobias, anxieties, and insomnia; for the improvement of concentration; and for pain control.
- Marital and family therapy, as the terms imply, treat the couple or the family, not just the individual. Since so many physical and psychological problems grow out of family relationships, couple or family therapy is the treatment of choice for a much wider range of difficulties than has previously been thought.

Even in cases of severe clinical depression, interpersonal therapy is as effective as drug therapy, according to a recent major National Institute of Mental Health study of 250 clinically depressed patients. (Cognitive therapy also proved equally effective with less severely depressed patients.)

There is some evidence indicating that individual therapy may actually result in marital deterioration, since change in one part of a system inevitably results in changes in other parts as well.

In one study of 39 depressed married patients who insisted there were no marital problems, the spouses evidenced pathological reactions as the patients improved. Twenty-one reacted with depression and severe anxiety; four made unsuccessful suicide attempts; still others threatened divorce, reverted to alcohol dependency, or became openly hostile.

Husbands of female agoraphobics sometimes become anxious and depressed as their wives improve. Slow, steady improvement may allow husbands to adapt to marital changes without developing severe problems of their own, but they may be unable to tolerate a drastic change in the balance of power within the relationship.

Many patients seeking psychiatric treatment deny that marital problems exist; if such difficulties are acknowledged, they are frequently attributed to the psychiatric disorder (while in fact the reverse may be true). Often patients have undergone a wide range of individual treatments without experiencing any relief.

Nevertheless, a person with psychiatric problems may fear involving the spouse and may even be reluctant to ask him to meet the therapist under the guise of "helping me with my problem."

Sometimes a fear of direct confrontation of marital problems is behind this unwillingness; the patient is too dependent on the spouse to risk upsetting the balance in the relationship. In other cases a wish to preserve personal secrets, such as an extramarital relationship, may be the explanation.

In selecting a marital or family therapist, look for a psychiatrist, licensed psychologist, or social worker, who *in addition* is a member of the American Association of Marriage and Family Therapists. Many members of this association lack the academic credentials I recommend; they may be graduates of a master's program in counseling, in psychology, or in marital and family relations. However, there is no guarantee that such individuals have had sufficient training to recognize or effectively deal with psychopathology either individually or in a family system.

And, of course, there is the added problem that a marital therapist must be able to relate satisfactorily to both partners without giving the impression of "taking sides."

Whether you have been referred to a therapist or have made your selection from the Yellow Pages, there are certain questions you should ask when making an initial phone call. You should find out the therapist's basic approach (Freudian, behavioral, cognitive, etc.) and ask his or her credentials if you do not already know them. You should ask about the therapist's experience in dealing with the particular problem you have. And you should ask about his or her fees, the method of payment, and whether or not insurance coverage applies.

If the therapist does not have time to answer your questions courteously (within reason—do not expect a half hour's free consultation by telephone) or tries to pressure you into an immediate appointment if you are not ready to make one, look for another therapist.

And if for any reason you simply don't like the sound of the person's voice, continue your search.

During your initial appointment, if you make one, you will further evaluate the therapist. You should feel confident by the end of the hour that you like and can trust this person, and believe with a reasonable degree of certainty that he or she can help you with your problem.

Not every good therapist is good for everyone. Only you can tell which is the right one for you.

4
How to Find Help within Yourself

If you are willing to try something that may sound unacceptably fanciful on first consideration, you may be able to find a wonderfully helpful source of strength within yourself.

Many people find it possible to relate to an inner self who takes the form of a guide, healer, or adviser, enabling them to tap sources of intuitive knowledge and wisdom that otherwise would remain unavailable to the conscious mind.

"After I was hypnotized to stop smoking, I felt that my inner self was walking along with me to help me resist temptation," a patient told me recently. "I found it very easy not to smoke, because my inner self was there to help me."

You do not need to be hypnotized to find your inner self. You can do so on your own by following procedures that have been practiced for centuries.

Although Jungian psychoanalysis was the first major psychological school to suggest that patients establish communication with the spontaneous images produced by the unconscious during meditation, the notion of the healing dream—in which the savior or doctor-god appears—was common among many ancient peoples: the Greeks, Hebrews, Egyptians, Indians, Chinese, Japanese, and Muslims.

In ancient Greece, thousands of pilgrims visited the healing tomb at Epidaurus to pray for curing dreams in which the god Asclepius appeared. He may have appeared in a form similar to his statue, or as a boy, or sometimes even as an animal. Whatever his form, he reached out and touched the afflicted pilgrims and cured them, or told them what they must do to be cured.

As many as 400 temples in honor of the god Asclepius existed in the ancient world and were in active use for nearly 1,000 years. It is thought that the ancient practice of dream incubation may have been originally used primarily to cure sterility, and that later its purpose became more general: to obtain advice on problems or to be healed from a variety of afflictions.

To induce a desired dream, the ancient Greeks visited their dream induction temples and sanctuaries, places of great beauty and tranquility, where they would not be distracted from their purpose. Before falling asleep they clearly formulated their intended dreams, providing the unconscious with a powerful self-induced suggestion.

You can practice dream incubation by making a clear statement to yourself as you are falling asleep: "I want a dream in which a wise counselor will tell me what to do about..."; or "I want a dream in which my doctor will tell me how to feel better." Hypnotists often suggest to their patients that they will dream about specific topics; you can make these suggestions to yourself, as well.

But it is not necessary to be asleep and dreaming to experience curative encounters with your inner guide, who may be thought of as a counselor, spirit guide, imaginary friend, physician, god, or master.

You can summon your inner guide by allowing yourself to reach a deep and comfortable state of relaxation and letting your imagination carry you to a beautiful and tranquil sanctuary of your own. It may be either real or imaginary, but it must be a place you can visualize clearly and a place in which you feel completely relaxed and at peace.

Summoning Your Inner Guide

Close your eyes and relax deeply and think of yourself in that private inner sanctuary. Spend a few minutes there just relaxing and getting oriented. Then imagine that within your sanctuary you are standing on a path stretching off into the distance, and that you are starting to walk up the path. As you do, in the distance you begin to see a form moving toward you, radiating a clear, bright light.

As you come closer to each other the details of the form emerge, and you can see whether it is a man or woman. The age and features of the individual become apparent to you, and the closer you get, the more clearly the form comes into focus.

Greet this being, and ask his or her name. Accept whatever name comes to you first.

Your inner guide may take the form of a respected authority figure—a wise old man or woman, a doctor, a religious figure—with whom you are able to carry on an internal conversation, asking questions and receiving answers.

Or your guide could appear as an animal who is endowed with

special insights and wisdom. He or she may be whimsical, eccentric, unusual, dramatic, or exotic; naturally the guide will know everything about you, since he or she is a reflection of your inner self.

Unless he or she is completely unacceptable to you, welcome your guide in whatever form he or she first appears, and speak to him or her in an open and friendly way.

Dr. O. Carl Simonton, who recommends that his cancer patients use this technique, relates the case of one who consulted his "inner physician" concerning his fear of girls and sexuality; she recommended that he try to become more responsive to people in general as a first step. To his amazement, when he followed this advice his fear of people began to diminish.

Another, who frequently resisted psychological self-examination, found an inner guide named "Dr. Fritz" with whom she was able to discuss emotional issues she avoided facing with her real-life physician.

"Do not be discouraged if you do not make contact with your guide or receive information from it on your first attempt," cautions Dr. Simonton. "Because this is a part of yourself that you may not have paid attention to for years, reestablishing communication often takes time and patience."

Once you have discovered your inner guide, you should discuss anything with him or her that is on your mind—or anything your adviser would like to talk about.

Your adviser can provide suggestions about reducing stress and pain, offer support and protection, use his or her power to give you total pain relief for a few moments, and help you to discover the message behind your pain.

Naturally you can talk to your inner guide not only about illness, but about decisions you must make or about difficulties you are having in your relationships. And because his or her advice will be coming from an inner part of yourself that you may be ignoring at a conscious level, it will be good advice.

Maintain an ongoing relationship with this imaginary figure. Conversing with your inner guide is not a silly game, as you may feel it is initially, but a powerful way of utilizing your own unconscious thoughts and feelings.

Index

A

Abusive relationships, 93–97
Ackerman, Nathan, 15
ACTH, anger and, 158–59
Adams, Abigail, 103–4
Aerobic exercise, 116–17
Affection, benefits of, 131–33
Akabas, Sheila, 147, 205
Al-Anon, 21
Alarm reaction, in General Adaptation Syndrome, 4
Alateen, 21
Alcoholics Anonymous (AA), 19
Alcoholism, 19–21, 53
Alexithymia, 41
American Association of Marriage and Family Therapists, 231
Angeli, Marcia, 47
Anger, learning to control, 158–63. *See also* Temper
Angina, relaxation and, 113
Anorexia nervosa, 17
Anxiety. *See also* Stress
    hypnotherapy for, 230
    ordeal therapy for, 124
    as symptom, 51
Arterial disease, 159
Arthritic process, 34–35
Assertiveness, 178–82
    behavior therapy for, 229
    by expressing needs, 186–90
    nonassertiveness and, 178–81
    responding to criticism and, 198
    role playing for learning, 181–82
    by saying "no," 191–95
    by saying what you mean, 183–85
    of working women, 199–205
        family responsibilities and, 204–5
        feminine speech and, 203–4
        managerial responsibilities and, 204–5
        men's resentment and, 202
        salary negotiation and, 200–201
        secretary/female boss relationship and, 201–2
        sexual involvement and, 203–4
Asthma, 27, 113
Authoritarian families, 207
Autoimmune disease, 35
Azrin, Nathan, 73–74, 120–22

B

Baby talk, 55
Bailey, Covert, 118

Barbach, Lonnie Garfirle, 210
Baruch, Grace, 10-11
Battered wives, 93-97
Bed wetting, ordeal therapy and, 124
Behavior therapy, 229
Bell, Alexander Graham, 104
Benson, Herbert, 111-14
Berg, Barbara J., 204
Berkman, Lisa, 6
Bernard, Jesse, 16
Bicycling, as exercise, 118
Binge eating, 23-25. *See also* Bulimia
    ordeal therapy and, 124, 125
    record keeping for, 68
Blushing
    describing onset of, 61-62
    positive thinking for, 135
Bodily sensations, awareness of, 41
Boredom
    exercise and, 117-18
    marriage and, 79-82
Bowlby, John, 102
Brainstorming, for symptom recognition, 48
Breathing control
    for nervous habits, 120
    for stuttering, 121-22
Bridge technique
    for emotional awareness, 41, 43
    for symptom recognition, 48
Bruch, Hilde, 17-18
Bulimia, 50. *See also* Binge eating
    confession of, 168
    family and, 17-18

C

Cancer
    despair and, 31-33
    emotional response and recovery from, 217-18
    nonassertiveness and, 180
    patient's inner guide and, 234
    support systems and recovery from, 71-72, 219
Cannon, Walter, 47
Cassileth, Barrie, 47
Challenge, survival and, 9
Cholesterol
    exercise and, 115
    relaxation and, 113
    stress and, 28
Chronic pain syndrome, 36-37
Clenching reaction, for nail biting and hair pulling, 121
Cognitive therapy, 229-30
Colitis, 26, 90
Commitment, survival and, 9
Communication. *See also* Assertiveness
    with children, 206-9
    compliments in, 174-77
    in doctor/patient relationship, 223-24
    "feminine" style in business world and, 202-3
    happy talk, 174-77
    hypertension during, 29, 43, 172-73
    indirect vs. saying what you mean, 183-85
    listening and, 154-55
    needs and feelings expressed in, 186-90
    in sexual relationships, 210-13
    techniques for effective, healthy, 172-73
    Type A personality and, 172, 173
Competing reaction, for nervous habits, 120-22
Compliments, responding to, 174-76

Index

Confiding, as beneficial, 167-71
    in therapist, 170-71
    in women, 170
    in written confessions, 169-70
Control, survival involving, 9
Cousins, Norman, 47, 141-43, 145, 218, 223
Coyne, James, 73
Creative separation, 91-92
Criticism
    expressing, 196-97
    responding to, 198

D

Dating, saying "no" in, 191-93
Depression, 41
    cognitive therapy for, 230
    exercise and, 115
    genital herpes and, 218
    nonassertive behavior and, 180
    as symptom, 50-51
De Shazer, Steve, 127
Despair, cancer and, 31-33
Diabetes, relaxation and, 113
Discipline, with children, 207
Divorce. *See also* Marriage
    fear of closeness in relationship and, 82-83
    support systems and, 69-71
Doctor/patient relationship, 221-26
    choosing doctors, 225-26
    doctor as friend in, 224-25
    effective communication in, 223-24
    family/doctor relationship and, 222-23
    question asking and, 221-22
    second opinions and, 321
Dream incubation, 232-33
Dutton, Don, 94

E

Eating disorders. *See also* Binge eating; Bulimia
    anorexia nervosa, 17
    hypnotherapy for, 230
    obesity, 22-25, 63-64, 89-90, 116
Eczema, 27
Eddy, Janice, 202
Egotistic altruism, 151-53
Elias, Maurice, 207
Emotional awareness, 41-45
    of bodily sensations, 41
    bridge technique for, 41, 43
    expressing, 186-90
    memory visualization for, 43-44
    rating sheet for, 44-45
    relaxation for, 41-42
Erickson, Milton, 123-24, 125, 126
Exaggerated role-taking, for positive interactions, 138
Exercise
    benefits of, 115-18
    in ordeal therapy, 124
Exhaustion, in General Adaptation Syndrome, 4
Eye blinking, competing reactions overcoming, 122

F

Faith Factor, with relaxation, 114
Family. *See also* Marriage
    alcoholism and, 19-21
    anorexia nervosa and, 17
    bulimia and, 17-18
    problem behaviors and, 126-28
Family myth, behavior influenced by, 103-4
Family therapy, 15, 27, 230-31
Father/son relationship, parental modeling and, 100-101
Favors, saying "no" to, 193

Feelings. *See* Emotional awareness
Fields, Joan, 117
Flight or fight response, 26, 112
Flint, Barry, 47
Forgiving, for positive thinking, 138–40
Fox, Emmet, 139
Free-floating hostility, overcoming, 158–63
Freud, Sigmund, 15
Friedman, Meyer, 28, 156–57, 159, 160–61, 163
Friendships. *See also* Support system
    maintaining, 156–57
    men vs. women and, 156

G
Gantt, W. Horstly, 132
Gastrointestinal disorders
    colitis, 26, 90
    ulcers, 26, 92
General Adaptation Syndrome (GAS), 4
Glassman, Judith, 218, 219
Goals, for positive thinking, 136–38
Greenwood, Edward D., 115
Grief work, 168
Group therapy, 229
Guilt
    lying causing, 146–48
    psychological repercussions of, 149–50

H
Hair pulling, 59
    describing onset of, 62
    eliminating, 120, 121
Haley, Jay, 123–25
Hand tapping, competing reactions to overcome, 122
Happy talk, 174–77
Headache. *See* Migraine headaches

Head jerk, competing reaction to overcome, 121
Heart attack, 115
    stress and, 28–29
    support system and recovery from, 219
Heart disease. *See also* Heart attack; Type A personality
    anger and, 159
    listening and, 154–55
    relaxation and, 112–13
Heart rate
    exercise and, 116, 118
    human contact and, 132
Heiman, Julia, 210
Henderson, Marilyn, 91
Herpes, depression and, 218
Hindy, Carl, 102
Holmes, Thomas H., 3–4
Honesty, benefits of, 146–48
"Hook, The," for anger, 161–62
Housekeeping, problem, 55
Humanistic therapies, 229
Humor, sense of, 141–45
Hypertension
    communication and, 29, 43, 154–55, 172–73
    exercise and, 115
    relaxation and, 113
Hypnosis
    for nervous habits, 120
    for problem behaviors, 123
Hypnotherapy, 230, 233
Hypochondria, 37

I
Illness. *See also* Doctor/patient relationship; Eating disorders; Psychosomatic disorders; *specific illnesses*
    behavioral inhibition and, 169

loneliness and, 6–7
marriage and, 8–9
positive emotions and supportive relationships and recovery from, 217–20
relaxation and, 112–13
secondary gain from, 36–37
stress and, 3–4, 5–7
support system and, 71–72
Imitating, for positive interactions, 138
Incest, confession of, 168
Indirect communication, saying what you mean vs., 183–85
Inner guide, help from, 233–34
Inner self. *See* Self
Insomnia, overcoming
hypnotherapy for, 230
ordeal therapy for, 124, 125
record keeping for, 67
Isometric contraction, nervous tics overcome by, 121

J
Japanese, social support system of, 6
Jealousy, overcoming, 128
Jung, Carl, 104, 229, 232

K
Kandel, Denise, 10
Kaplan, Helen Singer, 210
Kemeny, Margaret, 218
Kovel, Joel, 228
Krieger, Dolores, 132
Kushner, Ellen, 117

L
Lateness, overcoming, 126–27
Laughter, benefits of, 141–45
Lazarus, Arnold, 138
LeMaitre, George, 226

LeShan, Lawrence, 31–32, 180
Lin, Nan, 170
Lip biting, competing reactions to overcome, 122
Listening, therapeutic aspects of, 154–55
Loneliness, illness and, 6–7
LoPiccolo, Joseph, 210
LoPiccolo, Leslie, 210
Lord, Diana, 72–73
Love relationship, parental modeling and, 101–3
Lying, avoidance of, 146–48
Lynch, James, 29, 132, 147, 154–55, 172, 219

M
McClelland, David, 170
McDougall, William, 141
McGoldrick, Monica, 104
Marital therapy, 230–31
Marriage. *See also* Family; Relationships
confiding in mate and, 120
creative separation saving, 91–92
dissatisfaction in, 77–82
alcoholism and, 19–21
boredom and, 79–82
nurturance lack and, 78–81
sex-role problems and, 16–17
women and, 15–16
exercise and, 117–18
happy, 8–9
health affected by, 88–97
colitis, 90
migraine headaches, 88–89
nervous breakdown, 93
obesity, 22–25, 89–90

Marriage *(continued)*
    physical abuse, 93–97
    questionnaire on, 96–97
    ulcers, 92
  as hopeless, 88–97
  marital therapy and, 230–31
  rating, 84–87
  sexual relationship in, 210–13
  shock theory of, 15–16
Masturbation, 210, 212
Meditation, anxiety relieved by, 111–14
Memory, visualization of and emotional awareness and, 43–44
Men
  marriage and, 16
  sex-role problems and, 16–17
Mental health, 8–11
Migraine headaches, 77
  avoiding aura of, 60
  marriage causing, 88–89
  record keeping for, 66
Modeling. *See* Parental modeling, influence of
Moody, Raymond A., Jr., 141
Moral code, guilt and, 149–50
Mother/daughter relationship, parental modeling and, 98–100
Mourning, process of, 168
Multiple sclerosis, 35
Musto, David F., 103–4

N
Nail biting
  describing onset of, 62
  eliminating, 120, 121
  as nervous habit, 59
Needed, necessity for feeling, 151–53
Needs, expressing, 186–90
Negative feelings. *See* Criticism
Negative thought, thought-stopping and, 136

Nervous habits, 57–59. *See also* Overcoming symptoms and problem behaviors
  eliminating, 119–22
    competing reaction for, 120–22
    hypnosis for, 120
    relaxation for, 120
    support system and, 73–74
  hair pulling as, 59, 62, 120, 121
  nail biting as, 59, 62, 120, 121
  stuttering as, 119, 120, 121–22, 135
  tics as, 57, 119, 121
  tongue sharpening as, 57–58
Network. *See* Support system
"No," saying, 191–95
Nonassertiveness, 178–81. *See also* Assertiveness
Nonverbal communication, about sex, 212–13
Norepinephrine, anger causing production of, 158–59
Nunn, R. Gregory, 73–74, 120–22
Nurturance, marriage and, 78–79

O
Obesity, 63–64
  exercise and, 116
  marriage causing, 22–25, 89–90
O'Neill, Eugene, 104
Ordeal therapy, problem behavior interrupted by, 124–25
Osteoporosis, 115
Overcoming symptoms and problem behaviors, 60–68
  descriptions for, 60–64
  stress record for, 65–68
  time reference of action noted for, 64–65
  viewing action in mirror for, 62–63

P

Pain
  chronic pain syndrome, 36–37
  hypnotherapy for, 230
  laughter overcoming, 142–43, 144
  relaxation for, 113
Painter, Susan Lee, 94, 95
Panic attack, onset of, 61
Parent/child relationships, communication in, 206–9
Parental modeling, influence of, 98–105
  family myth role and, 103–4
  in father/son relationship, 100–101
  in love relationship, 101–3
  in mother/daughter relationship, 98–100
  questionnaire on, 105
Paul, Norman, 91
Pennebaker, James, 167, 168, 169
Personal worth, 151–53
Phobias, 42
  behavior therapy for, 229
  hypnotherapy for, 230
Physical abuse, in marriage, 93–97
Physical contact, benefits from, 131–33
Polygraph, 146
Positive thinking, 134–40
  change for, 135–36
  communication expressing, 174–77
  forgiving for, 138–40
  imitating for, 138
  intolerance for negative communication with, 134–35
  specific goals defined for, 136–38
  thought-stopping for negative thoughts in, 136
  visualization for, 136, 137–38

Problem behaviors. *See also* Nervous habits; Overcoming symptoms and problem behaviors
  behavior therapy for, 229
  doing something different to eliminate, 126–28
  in family system, 126–28
  hypnotherapy for, 230
  identifying, 52–56
  interrupting, 123–25
    hypnosis for, 123
    motivation for, 123
    ordeal therapy for, 124–25
Psychiatrist, 227
Psychoanalysis, 229
Psychologist, 227
Psychosomatic disorders, 3. *See also* Symptoms recognition
  asthma as, 27, 113
  awareness of feelings and, 41
  of gastrointestinal tract, 26, 90, 92
  heart disease as, 28–29
  hypertension as, 29–30
  migraine headaches as, 30
  of skin, 27
Pulse, exercise and, 116, 118

R

Racano, Alfredo, 117
Rahe, Richard H., 3–4
Rape, confession of, 168
Record keeping, of symptoms and problem behaviors, 65–68
Rejection, positive thinking to reverse, 135
Relationships. *See also* Marriage
  closeness in, 82–83
  laughter in, 144–45
  maintaining contact with, 156–57
  rating, 84–87

Relationships. *(continued)*
    saying "no" in, 191–95
    support needs in, 77
Relaxation
    anxiety relieved by, 111–14
    for emotional awareness, 41–42
    for nervous habits, 120
    for visualization, 137–38
Resentments, letting go, 138–40
Resistance, in General Adaptation Syndrome, 4
Rheumatoid arthritis, 34–35
Rogers, Carl R., 109, 229
Role playing, assertiveness learned by, 181–82
Roles, mental health related to, 10–11
Rosenman, Ray, 28
Rubin, Lillian, 72

S
Sabotage, weight problems and sexual relationships and, 24–25
Sacks, Oliver, 30
Sager, Clifford, 91
Salary negotiation, assertiveness regarding, 200–201
San Francisco Recurrent Coronary Prevention Project, 160
Schweitzer, Albert, 141–42
Secondary gain, in illness, 36–37
Second opinion, for elective surgery, 221
Self
    becoming, 109–10
    help from within, 232–34
Selye, Hans, 3, 4, 151
Separation, creative, 91–92
Sex-role problem, in marriage, 16–17
Sex therapy, 210–13, 230

Sexual relationships
    office romance and, 203–4
    open communication about, 210–13
    saying "no" to, 191–93
    weight problems and, 23–25
Shaking hands, positive thinking to reverse, 135
Shaver, Phillip, 101–2
Shock theory, of marriage, 16
Shoulder jerking, competing reaction to overcome, 121
Sifneos, Peter, 41
Simonton, O. Carl, 32–33, 37, 180, 218, 234
Singer, Jerome I., 47, 72–73
Skin, stress response of, 27
Sleep, as problem, 54–55. *See also* Insomnia, overcoming
Smoking, 64
    hypnotherapy for, 230
    as problem, 53–54
Social Readjustment Rating Scale, 4
Social worker, 227
Soft aerobics, 118
Spouse, as confidante, 170
Stein, Richard, 118
Sternberg, Robert, 16
Stress. *See also* Anxiety
    body's reaction to, 4
    exercise relieving, 115–18
    flight or fight response, 26, 112
    illness and, 3–4, 5–7
    meditation for, 111–14
Stress record, 65–68
Stuttering, eliminating, 120
    with competing reactions, 121–22
    with positive thinking, 135
Superego, guilt and, 149–50

Index

Support system, 69–76
    of divorcee, 69–71
    effective, 73
    of ill patient, 71–72, 212–20
    negative, 73–74
    nervous habits and, 173–74
    protective value of, 5–7
    rating sheet for, 74–76
    of widow, 69–70
Sydenham, Thomas, 141
Syme, Leonard, 6
Symptoms recognition, 46–51. *See also* Overcoming symptoms and problem behaviors
    brainstorming for, 48
    bridge technique for, 48
    depression and, 50–51
    emotional traumas occurring along with, 49–51
    resistance to, 46–48

T

Talking. *See* Communication
Tannen, Deborah, 183
Tardiness, overcoming, 126–27
Teenagers, saying "no" to sexual involvement by, 192
Teeth grinding, competing reaction to overcome, 122
Temoshok, Lydia, 217–18
Temper, 64–65, 127
    overcoming, 127, 158–63
        ordeal therapy for, 125
    as problem, 52–53
Tensing, for nervous tics, 121
Therapeutic touch, 132–33
Therapist. *See also* Therapy
    choosing, 227–29, 231
    as confidante, 170–71
Therapy, 227, 229–31
    behavior therapy, 229
    cognitive therapy, 229–30

    group therapy, 229
    humanistic therapies, 229
    hypnotherapy, 230, 233
    Jungian analysis, 229
    marital and family therapy, 230–31
    psychoanalysis, 229
    sex therapy, 230
Thoits, Peggy, 10
Thought-stopping, in positive thinking, 136
Thumbsucking, ordeal therapy to overcome, 125
Tics, as nervous habit, 57, 119, 121
Tongue sharpening, as nervous habit, 57–58
Touching, benefits of, 131–33
Transcendental Meditation, 111, 113
Traumatic bonding, 94–95
Truth, benefits of, 146–48
Type A personality, 28, 30
    anger control and, 158–63
    communication and, 172, 173
    identifying, 163
Type B personality, 159

U

Ulcers, 26, 92

V

Viederman, Milton, 9
Visualization, for positive thinking, 136–38
Volunteer activity, 151–53

W

Walking, as exercise, 116–17, 118
Weight problems. *See* Eating disorders; Obesity
Weir, Tamara, 9
Widow, support system of, 69–70

Willoughby, Raymond R., 16
Wilson, Woodrow, 158
Women
    as confidantes, 170
    employment (*see also* Assertiveness)
        marital dissatisfaction and, 16–17
        marital satisfaction and, 10–11
    marital dissatisfaction and, 15–16
        sex-role problems and, 16–17
    roles of, and mental health, 10–11
    saying "no" by, 191–95
Work, gratification of, 151–53. *See also* Assertiveness
Wortman, Camille, 71
Written confessions, benefits of, 169–70

Y

Young, Beatrice, 202